Dialectical Encounters
Contemporary Turkish Muslim Thought in Dialogue

Taraneh R. Wilkinson

EDINBURGH
University Press

Edinburgh University Press is one of the leading university presses in the UK. We publish academic books and journals in our selected subject areas across the humanities and social sciences, combining cutting-edge scholarship with high editorial and production values to produce academic works of lasting importance. For more information visit our website: edinburghuniversitypress.com

© Taraneh R. Wilkinson, 2019, 2020

Edinburgh University Press Ltd
The Tun—Holyrood Road
12 (2f) Jackson's Entry
Edinburgh EH8 8PJ

First published in hardback by Edinburgh University Press 2019

Typeset in 11/15 Adobe Garamond by
Westchester Publishing Services

A CIP record for this book is available from the British Library

ISBN 978 1 4744 4153 7 (hardback)
ISBN 978 1 4744 4154 4 (paperback)
ISBN 978 1 4744 4155 1 (webready PDF)
ISBN 978 1 4744 4156 8 (epub)

The right of Taraneh R. Wilkinson to be identified as author of this work has been asserted in accordance with the Copyright, Designs and Patents Act 1988 and the Copyright and Related Rights Regulations 2003 (SI No. 2498).

Contents

List of Figures   v
Acknowledgments   vii
Note on Conventions   ix

I Introduction

1 Introduction: Turkish Muslim "Theology" and Religion in Turkey   3

2 Roots and Authorities: Resituating Revisionist and Ankara Paradigms in Light of Other Authorities   27

II The Individual and Authority in Dialectical Continuity

3 Alpyağıl's Case for Canon   65

4 Inclusions and the Role of the Individual   93

III A Theological Anthropology of Empowerment

5 Düzgün's Case for a Religion of Freedom   127

6 Human Agency, Responsibility, and *Tawḥīd*   162

IV Conclusions

7 From Dialectics to Direct Address: Turkish
   Theologians on Atheism and Other Religions   187
8 Conclusion: Reflections on Turkish Islam, Modernity,
   and Dialogue   227

Bibliography   247
Index   267

Figures

1.1	Theology Faculty Journals	11
1.2	The Marmara University Theology Faculty	12
1.3	Disciplinary Structure of a Turkish Theology Faculty	13
1.4	Abbreviations for Alpyağıl's Works	20
1.5	Abbreviations for Düzgün's Works	21
4.1	Cover of *Difference and Commentary*	98
4.2	Key Milestones in Islam's Narrative of Modernity	101

Acknowledgments

I express my heartfelt gratitude to family, friends, and colleagues. Without your support, encouragement, and guidance this work would not have been possible. I am especially grateful to every Turkish theologian who took time out of his or her busy schedule to share with me a measure of hospitality, knowledge, and insight. Many thanks to Recep Alpyağıl and İz Yayıncılık for allowing me to reprint the cover of Fark ve Yorum (figure 4.1).

While there are more names than I can list here, I want to name some of those of family, friends, and guides whose support and companionship has helped me along this path: Steve Wilkinson, Barbara Phillips, Carl Wilkinson, Vern and Grace Wilkinson, Sarah Greenbaum, Julia L. Lamm, Gerard Mannion, Daniel A. Madigan, Theresa Sanders, Leo Lefebure, George Archer, Bill Rogers, Tasi Perkins, Rachel Friedman, Diego Sarrio Cucarella, Jason Welle, Rosabel Ansari, Michael Ben Sims, Abdallah Soufan, Halla Attallah, Christina Tang, Abdulnasır Süt, Hasan Kaplan, Asma Khoshmehr, Yalda, Toğrul, Joel and Tanya Rasmussen, Josh Mugler, Brian Flanagan, Carol Day, Matthew Anderson, Pamela Klasova, Luc Silie, Alexander Massad, Amanda Hopson, Caroline Smith, Matthew Balensuela, Carla Edwards, Gabriel Crouch, François Coulont-Henderson, Cleveland Johnson, Ray Kim, Caroline Stine, Darren Marshalsea, Annemarie McCartney, Lauren O'Day, Maider, Moira and Bill Copeland, Jessica Abhat, Ryu and Harumi Susato, Rebecca

Johnson, Andrew Lim, Rouya Seghaier, Jiana Sabeh, Danny A. Ramadan, Alyson Wharton-Durgaryan, and Katherine Wharton.

Serafettin Pektaş has offered invaluable feedback and drawn my attention to important resources. I thank him as well as Philip Dorroll, Felix Körner, Sinan Ciddi, Joshua Ralston for their expertise and time taken to help me with this project.

FSCIRE has served as my academic home while finalizing this manuscript. I cannot count myself lucky enough for the scholarly companionship I have found there.

Finally, I express my heartfelt gratitude to Muhammad Ridwaan for his invaluable help in preparing this manuscript for publication and to the capable editors at Edinburgh University Press. Any remaining errors are my own.

Note on Conventions

For Arabic transliterations, I follow the *Encyclopedia of the Qur'ān*, ed. Jane D. McAuliffe. In contrast to classical Islamic sources, Modern Arabic names are not transliterated in this way and instead follow common English spellings. Common Arabic words like "hadith" and "sharia" (with the exception of "Qur'ān") also follow common English spellings, but italicized Arabic words are transliterated in the same manner as classical Islamic sources.

As for Turkish script, the Turkish alphabet is rendered as is. It is phonetic and contains the additional letters c, ç, ğ, ı, ş, ö, and ü. The c is pronounced like the "j" in *judge*. The ç is pronounced like the "ch" in *cheese*. The ğ has no English equivalent and is largely silent. The ı is darker and further back in the throat than the "i" in *pick*; it contrasts with the i, which is like the "ea" in *flea*. The ş is pronounced like the "sh" in *shape*. And the ö and ü are similar to the German letters of the same appearance.

The Turkish academic printing situation can be more ephemeral compared to European or North American academic publishing rhythms. Where appropriate, reprinting information is cited for Turkish works. Central works discussed list both original publication date and a reprinting date (if available), and in the case of some works I specify the number of reprintings to better indicate their popularity. Also, even with a printed copy in hand, sometimes full publishing details are not available.

I generally follow the M. A. S. Abdel Haleem English interpretation of the Qur'ān and indicate when I modify this translation.

Dates are given in Common Era.

For brevity, the *Encyclopedia of Islam*, Second Edition, edited by P. Bearman, Th. Bianquis, C. E. Bosworth, E. van Donzel, and W. P. Heinrichs is cited as *EI2*. I also make use of the *Turkish Encyclopedia of Islam*, or *İslâm Ansiklopedisi* (Türkiye Diyanet Vakfı), and do not abbreviate its name when citing.

INTRODUCTION

1

Introduction: Turkish Muslim "Theology" and Religion in Turkey

When many people think of Islam today, they think of sources in Arabic, despite the fact that the mother tongue of most Muslims is a language other than Arabic. When the word "theology" is uttered, the immediate connotation is *Christian* theology. Yet, in this inquiry I direct the reader's attention to contemporary *Turkish Muslim theology*, or the academic realm of Turkish *ilahiyat* faculties.

Turkish *ilahiyat* faculties as they are known today arose shortly after the founding of the modern Turkish Republic. They are state-funded institutions of higher education and offer spaces for Muslims in Turkey to pursue the academic study of religion alongside their religious conviction. Although these institutions are state funded, this does not necessarily mean that their function can be reduced to politics. Instead of approaching these faculties through a political lens or from the question of secularism, I make a case for the complexity and irreducible theological value of Turkish *ilahiyat* faculties, focusing especially on their engagement with Western and Christian sources. I look at the intellectual output of these faculties across several topics, often heavily associated with modernity, which also serve as central topics of discussion in contemporary European and Anglophone Christian theology: authority, atheism, skepticism, and religious pluralism. Since these subjects are common areas of discourse in the Western academy, my hope is also to engage those readers more familiar with Christian theology than with Islam.

Literature on religion in Turkey has tended to fall into dualistic schemas—modernity vs. tradition, religion vs. secularism, or Western vs. Islamic sources. What if these dualities are insufficient and at times misleading when it comes to understanding the complex dynamics of Turkish academic theology? The present analysis proposes a more complex schema. Drawing on the work of Felix Körner and Philip C. Dorroll, this schema is meant to resist reductive interpretations of Turkish theology that might frame Turkish theological projects in terms of static binaries. Körner argues that Turkish theology faculties are places particularly open to a modern engagement with the Qur'ān and he identifies the influence of hermeneutical philosopher Hans-Georg Gadamer along with the influence of Muslim scholar Fazlur Rahman on contemporary Turkish debates concerning historicity and interpretation of scripture. Dorroll looks at the early history of Turkish theology faculties and identifies a Turkish interpretation of a classical Islamic theological school as central to Turkish theology's self-understanding as well as open to reform and to modern values. Dorroll refers to this Turkish interpretation as "The Ankara Paradigm" and looks at its continuing influence into the twenty-first century. The influences of Gadamer, Rahman, and strong elements of the Ankara Paradigm apply to many of the figures studied here; however, I push back against the implied dualities lingering in the analyses of Körner and Dorroll. For while both scholars look at the theological arguments present in Turkish theology faculties, their analyses both imply modern values are a positive standard and do not use Turkish theological efforts to dialectically challenge and redefine this standard. In my reading, Turkish theological endeavors have the resources to dialectically challenge and move beyond the dualities through which religion in Turkey is so often defined.

State-funded Turkish theological faculties and their affiliated organizations distinguish themselves from other religious voices and authorities in Turkey today through a unique and intentional double dialogue—one with European and Anglophone scholarship and one with classical, and sometimes modern, Arab Islamic authorities. Otherwise stated, Turkish theology is characterized by a dialectical threefold schema of engagement.

In short, scholarship on religion in Turkey still operates within frameworks of binaries, such as tradition vs. modernity or the religious vs. the secular; but Turkish theology does not neatly fit into binaries. Analysis of Turkish theology should therefore not be reduced to such binaries and should instead engage Turkish theology for its theological value. To better engage this theological value, I propose a threefold schema in which Turkish theology involves a dialectical engagement of Turkish/Ottoman, Arabic, and Western sources. This threefold schema is dialectical, complex, creative, and—while primarily internal—it carries implications beyond Turkish theology. Ömer Mahir Alper, a Turkish theologian and philosopher, remarked over two decades ago that:

> The conceptions of Islamic philosophy in Turkey, as is the case with many serious intellectual issues, have been basically determined by the perspectives of the three trends of thought called Islamism, Turkism, and Westernism, the origins of which can be found in the 19th century Ottoman Empire.[1]

Unlike Alper's paradigm, which assigned each label to a specific scholar, my schema is dialectical, and all three elements can be found in a given scholar.[2] In other words, instead of labeling a Turkish theologian as an Islamist, a Turkist, or a Westernist, I examine the work of Turkish theologians as constructive combinations of these dialectical aspects of Turkish intellectual heritage.

To best illustrate this complexity, along with the pervasiveness of this schema, I focus on questions of authority, and then tackle Turkish responses to doubt and other religions. The range of examples is intended to demonstrate the pervasive nature of this threefold schema. As stressed above, the purpose of the threefold schema is to encourage non-reductive theological evaluations of Turkish theology, and with this aim in mind I have fleshed out each set of examples with sustained theological engagement. I target a range of arguments to highlight in concrete detail the importance of not reducing Turkish theology to overly simple binaries. Naturally, to appreciate Turkish theology for its complexity and its potential theological contributions, schemas alone do not suffice. I therefore illustrate my proposed dialectical threefold schema with the concrete particulars of engagements, as the aim is not to reduce Turkish theology to the proposed threefold schema but rather to use this schema to better engage Turkish *theological* contributions.

A multifaceted analysis offers both a breadth of context as well as the opportunity for moments of theological depth. Examples from Turkish theological discussions on authority, doubt, and other religions all serve to illustrate the complex dynamics present in Turkish academic theology, particularly vis-à-vis their use and appraisal of Western and Christian sources. By examining several related topics, I resist reducing the discussion to a question of whether or how well Turkish theology has grasped or applied Western or Christian scholarship relevant to any one topic of discussion. It is problematic and, at best, superficial to reduce an intellectual appraisal of Turkish theology to a question of whether or not the institution as a whole is sufficiently modern or has satisfactorily grappled with a particular concept. To appreciate Turkish academic theology *qua* theology it is useful, perhaps necessary, to look in detail across a broader spectrum of topics, since theological nuance, creativity, and insight—even in Christian settings—often lies in the details and annals of individual argument. As a scholar once remarked, "Theology is an abstraction in a way theologians are not . . ."[3] Engaging Turkish theology *qua* theology entails engaging individual arguments and individual theologians alongside the broader context in which this theology is produced.

Before laying out the subsequent chapters of this analysis, I will address two related questions: what are Turkish *ilahiyat* faculties and why is it defensible to refer to them as theology faculties? Below is a brief history of the *ilahiyat* faculties and an explanation of the word *"ilahiyat."*

Theology Faculties in Turkey: An Introduction

> In classical Islam, the literal meanings of the three terms for theology are as follows: (1) *kalām*, 'words', 'speech', 'discourse'; (2) *uṣūl al-fiqh*, 'the roots of law'; and (3) *uṣūl ad-dīn*, 'the roots of religion'. [. . .] Thus, in Islam, there is no term equivalent to 'theology' as the 'science of God' . . .
>
> —George Makdisi[4]

> The idea of a higher religious academy has its roots in the philosophy of the Ottoman era.
>
> —Mehmet Paçacı and Yasin Aktay[5]

The current political and ideological climate in modern Turkey has roots in initial reforms and movements harking back to the nineteenth century. Beginning with the Tanzimat Period (1839–76) and the First Constitutional Era (1876–8), the then Ottoman Empire was already attempting to reshape itself along more Western models on many fronts. However, with Sultan

Abdülhamid II's suspension of parliament in 1878, lasting transformation was postponed until the outbreak of the Young Turk Era (1908–18), followed by the termination of the Ottoman state in the aftermath of World War I. With a Turkish victory over the encroaching Western powers, a new republic was established and the caliphate officially abolished (1923 and 1924, respectively). At this moment in Turkish history, there arose a new emphasis on Turkish and Muslim identity as constitutive of a national framework.[6] In less than a decade, the new nation of Turkey underwent a massive and far-reaching transformation: all major religious educational institutions were banned by the Unification of Education Law in 1924, religious orders were similarly banned the following year (this included dervish lodges, small mosques, and Sufi orders), the Roman calendar was adopted, and in 1928 the Latin alphabet along with the European metric system were placed in effect. This last change in alphabet and measurements was done in tandem with a wider language reform tailored to remove Persian and Arabic influence from modern Turkish in favor of Turkic recoveries and European borrowings. By 1929 Arabic and Persian were no longer taught in elementary or secondary education, and the imam schools and the faculty of divinity in Istanbul, which had been established in 1924, were closed in 1933.[7] By the 1930s, a significant shift towards a secular emphasis on national identity was underway.[8]

Despite this dramatic shift to a Western secular ideal, the question of Muslim identity was destined to resurface with the establishment of the multiparty system in 1946.[9] The tensions between secular and religious models for statehood only grew more pronounced as the century progressed. As a result, state involvement in religion came to represent a key feature of Turkish politics. This did not entail an abolition of Muslim identity, but rather a refashioning of Muslim identity under Turkish nationalistic auspices. Kemerli sums up the situation:

> The view that Turkish secularism is hostile to religion and eliminated it from the public sphere has also been disputed. Rather than disestablishing religion, secular nationalization in Turkey brought it under strict state control. The institutional locus of this control has been the *Diyanet İşleri Başkanlığı* (Directorate of Religious Affairs), which was established after the abolition of the caliphate in 1924 and the state's appropriation of the properties of pious

foundations . . . rather than unmitigated hostility, Turkish secularism entails a pragmatic approach to religion that involves selective promotion and frequent accommodation.[10]

After the end of the early Kemalist period, Turkey had several moments of rapprochement with "less secular" trends. However, until recently, military coups have discouraged the Turkish state system from tilting too strongly away from what were seen as Kemalist secular ideals. The first successful Turkish *ilahiyat* faculty opened in Ankara in 1949. In the mid-twentieth century, faculties of theology, closely associated with state views on religion, were known for lax practice; prayer was not offered regularly and not all staff fasted.[11] By the 1980s there were only ten higher education institutions of Islam in Turkey, and in 1982 all of these institutions were converted to *ilahiyat* faculties.[12] The 1990s saw growth and increased dynamism in Turkish theology; there were twenty-four faculties, and 1997 saw a peak in enrollment and perceived importance, with a decline following 1997.[13]

The trajectory of Turkish theology faculties has changed again under the current ruling party in Turkey, the AKP. The AKP (*Adalet ve Kalkınma Partisi*), Justice and Development Party, is an offshoot of the earlier Welfare Party (Islamicist *Refah Partisi*) and has been in power since 2002. It offers its own casting of Turkish Muslim identity, which has its share of both popular approval and criticism. Far from banning the secular military, it has aggressively tamed it through ongoing scandals such as the infamous Ergenekon conspiracy.[14] Despite recent electoral setbacks in the summer of 2015 and the attempted coup in July of 2016, the AK Party remains the dominant face in the Turkish political landscape. Presently, funding for the current Directorate of Religious Affairs (now *Diyanet Vakfı*)[15] as well as research libraries like that of İSAM[16] in Istanbul remains tied to AKP politics and policies. Along with a new relation to the military and a new casting of the state's role in religion there has come an increased interest in the continuity between the Turkish state and its Ottoman past. That is, under the AK Party, revisiting Ottoman heritage has grown more popular; the party has actively stressed Muslim identity in the form of continuity with the Ottoman past.[17] When the AK Party came to power in the early 2000s, there were two dozen faculties, and by the close of 2015 there were at least eighty-six opened, only forty-six of which actually accommodated students.[18] Judging from this recent surge in numbers, it is clear that, as state-funded institutions, the current government has invested heavily in the project of theology faculties.[19] Moreover, a new type of faculty is being opened—called an "*İslami İlimler Fakültesi*" or a "Faculty of Islamic Sciences."[20] With these developments in mind, state-driven change seems to be an ongoing but not exclusive factor in the landscape of Turkish theology faculties.

The first instance of a government-regulated institution devoted to the study of *ilahiyat* can be traced back to 1900 and beyond, in the late Ottoman Empire and in connection with what is now known as the University of Istanbul.[21] In the earliest years of the Turkish Republic, the first faculty devoted to *ilahiyat* operated from 1924–33 but closed due to poor matriculation.[22] The present generation of *ilahiyat* faculties began with the opening of the Ankara University *Ilahiyat* Faculty in 1949, intended to be a beacon among other scientific institutions.[23] The People's Party moved to establish the first Islamic Theological Faculty in Ankara in 1948,[24] leading to its formal opening in 1949. This new institution took root in a new intellectual space cleared by the abolishment of the traditional Islamic educational system in 1924, left fallow for nearly a quarter of a century.[25] The faculty emerged from the wider bounds of Atatürk's vision, often characterized as a renewer and modernizer of Islam. As Körner writes, "[Atatürk] seems to have been able to distinguish between Islam as a sclerotic blockage against modernization, and Islam as a tradition able to evolve."[26] For Körner, the founding of these new theological faculties represented a step in the direction of genuine innovation, a break with the past, with only a minor measure of continuity with earlier Ottoman efforts at educational reform. By contrast, Turkish theologian Mehmet Paçacı and sociologist Yasin Aktay have stressed Turkish theology's continuity with Ottoman past, claiming that "idea of a higher religious academy has its roots in the philosophy of the Ottoman era."[27] Aktay and Paçacı stress the irony that even Westernization and modernization are part of the Turkish Republic's inheritance from its "Ottoman predecessors."[28] Stressing greater continuity between Turkish theologies of the modern republic and higher education in the Ottoman Empire, Paçacı and Aktay note the earlier presence of a Turkish Faculty of Theology of Istanbul University abolished in 1933 as evidence of some historical continuity.[29] Körner, for his part, does note the existence of a previous Ottoman faculty of theology, founded in 1847, but dismisses it with the implication that the time was not yet ripe.[30]

Paçacı and Aktay's account of the birth of Turkish theology faculties stresses continuity between Ottoman and Turkish identity, whereas Körner's account emphasizes the rupture. Yet, what do Turkish faculties of theology officially make of themselves? The official website of the first and still a foremost theology faculty functioning in Turkey, the Theology Faculty of Ankara University, notes that the inception of a modern theology faculty came into being with the idea of founding a "modern" university. This was marked by the decision made in 1846 to open a *"Dar'ül Fünûn,"* or faculty of sciences (i.e., university) in Istanbul. The project continued along with major setbacks, until the faculty was shut down in 1871.[31] However, in the 1900s a new faculty of sciences was opened in Istanbul—an institution which eventually offered religious and philosophical courses. Further, with the start of the Republican Era, a movement was made in 1924 to open a theology faculty in affiliation with the university in Istanbul. From 1924 to 1933, the first state theology faculty offered courses in history of religions, Islamic history, history of Islamic philosophy, metaphysics, sociology of religion, psychology of religion, history of Turkish religion, history of Islamic sects, history of *kalām*, history of Islamic jurisprudence, history of Sufism, Arabic, ethics, and the history of philosophy. Even when the theology faculty was not kept open after 1933, courses on religion were taught in the literature department within the Institute of Islamic Sciences—history of *kalām*, history of Sufism, Iranian literature, history of Islamic sects, and history of religions. A mere sixteen years after the closure of the first faculty, the present-day faculty of theology in Ankara was opened. Although Ankara marks the first of now many theology faculties across Turkey, it certainly did not appear out of the blue.

Throughout I will refer to these *ilahiyat* faculties as theology faculties. Similar to a college or school within a university, these faculties boast a broad range of studies, from traditional Islamic sciences, sociological disciplines, to history of religions, and the study of non-Muslim faiths. The Ankara University Theology Faculty (figure 1.1), the Marmara University Theology Faculty (figure 1.2), and the Istanbul University Theology Faculty, for instance, all host about twenty distinct subdepartments nested under three main departmental

Figure 1.1 Theology Faculty Journals. (Source: photo taken by the author in the Ankara University Theology Faculty, December 2, 2015.)

divisions (figure 1.3).[32] The three main departmental divisions (Turkish singular: *bölüm*) are the Department of Fundamental Islamic Sciences (*Temel İslâm Bilimleri Bölümü*), the Department of Philosophical and Religious Sciences (*Felsefe ve Din Bilimleri Bölümü*), and the Department of Islamic History and Islamic Arts (*İslam Tarihi ve Sanatları Bölümü*). Standard subdepartments within a theology faculty include the study of Qur'ān commentaries (*tefsir*), study of hadith (*hadis*), Islamic law (*İslam hukuku*), Islamic theology (*kelam*), Sufism (*tasavvuf*), logic (*mantık*), history of philosophy (*felsefe tarihi*), Islamic philosophy (*İslam felsefesi*), philosophy of religion (*din felsefesi*), sociology of religion (*din sosyolojisi*), psychology of religion (*din psikolojisi*), history of religions (*dinler tarihi*), history of Islam (*İslam tarihi*), and even the history of Turkish Islamic arts (*Türk İslam sanatları tarihi*). Islamic law and Islamic theology are both part of the Department of Fundamental Islamic Sciences

Figure 1.2 The Marmara University Theology Faculty. (Source: photo taken by the author November 20, 2015. During the author's visit to the Marmara Theology Faculty scholars Rahim Acar, Bilal Baş, and İsmail Taşpınar graciously offered their welcome, time, and advice on this project.)

(*Temel İslâm Bilimleri Bölümü*), whereas history of religions and Islamic philosophy fall under the Department of Philosophical and Religious Sciences (*Felsefe ve Din Bilimleri Bölümü*).

Set apart on its own self-contained campus, a Turkish theology faculty is meant to be broad in disciplinary scope, incorporating traditional Islamic sciences along with sociology, history, and philosophy. Much in the same way as Euro-American theology is increasingly challenged to scientifically engage other academic disciplines without sacrificing confessional identity, Turkish theology faculties are set up to engage topics within and outside the repertoire of traditional Islamic sciences. It is also in light of this disciplinary diversity that I have selected several topics through which to engage Turkish theological contributions, since valuable theological insight might be gleaned from various corners of the Turkish theology faculty.

The Turkish *İlahiyat* Faculty

Department of Fundamental Islamic Sciences (*Temel İslâm Bilimleri Bölümü*)	Department of Philosophical and Religious Sciences (*Felsefe ve Din Bilimleri Bölümü*)	Department of Islamic History and Islamic Arts (*İslam Tarihi ve Sanatları Bölümü*)
• Qur'ān Commentaries (*Tefsir*)	• Islamic Philosophy (*İslam Felsefesi*)	• Islamic History (*İslam Tarihi*)
• Hadith (*Hadis*)	• Philosophy of Religion (*Din Felsefesi*)	• Literature of Turkish Islam (*Türk İslam Edebiyatı*)
• Islamic Law (*İslam Hukuku*)	• History of Religions (*Dinler Tarihi*)	• Turkish Religious Music (*Türk Din Musikisi*)
• Kalām (*Kelam*)	• Sociology of Religion (*Din Sosyolojisi*)	
• Sufism (*Tasavvuf*)	• Psychology of Religion (*Din Psikolojisi*)	

Figure 1.3 Disciplinary Structure of a Turkish Theology Faculty. For a complete list of subdisciplines see, for instance, Istanbul University Theology Faculty's listing: <http://ilahiyat.istanbul.edu.tr/tr/akademikkadro> (last accessed September 11, 2018).

İlâhiyât fakülteleri, or Turkish theology faculties, are influenced by Western philosophy and Western study of religion as well as in active engagement with it.[33] Although the term *ilâhiyât* appears in classical theology, the Arabic word has never designated "theology" in the sense of the whole academic discipline—it had been used to mean metaphysics, to label questions about God, and to refer to rational theology, but never as the title for a faculty.[34] In modern Turkish, *ilâhiyât* is also used to refer to religious or mystical love poems.[35] In modern Farsi, essentially the same term designates "theology"—a word also used to designate theological faculties in Iran.[36] When referring to theology faculties the spelling of *ilâhiyât* is commonly simplified to *ilahiyat*.

I use the term "theology" to refer both to the faculty itself and to some of the intellectual output produced by these faculties. While it is true that the term "theology" is not an unproblematic label, it is nonetheless used by some academics in Turkish. Another word used in these faculties to translate *"ilahiyat"* is "divinity," which also carries some Christian connotations.[37] The word *ilahiyat* originally comes from Arabic, and one of its earliest known uses was by the medieval philosopher Ibn Sīnā (d. 1037) to refer to the metaphysics portion of his magnum opus, *al-Shifā'*.[38] According to the *Turkish Encyclopedia of Islam* (*İslâm Ansiklopedisi*), the term *"ilâhiyyât"* refers to beliefs and doctrines concerning God's essence and attributes, the first of three main categories of Sunni belief.[39] *İlahiyat* does not, however, designate a theology faculty in modern Arabic, and its use in the Turkish context arose visibly at the turn of the twentieth century, amid ongoing discussion on how to use or coin Arabic terms in modern Turkish.[40] The modern *ilahiyat* faculty functions more as a college with multiple departments than as theology or religion departments do in Europe and North America. As mentioned above, the range of subjects taught includes traditional Islamic sciences, sociological approaches to religion, theological approaches to religion, and more. When I refer to these faculties as theology faculties, I follow some Turkish usage and scholarly precedent and I do not mean a theology department exactly as one might be found at a Christian institution of higher learning.[41] In a second sense, I employ the term "theology" in a more relational signification, suggesting that Christian theologians might be able to recognize and appreciate that Turkish theologians share with them common issues, interests, challenges relative to other academic disciplines that do not explicitly cultivate confessional values alongside academic rigor.[42]

Although I will use the word "theologian" for both Muslims and Christians, Turkish theologians can still distinguish themselves from their Christian counterparts by calling themselves *"ilahiyatçı"* rather than *"teolog"*—the Turkish word for a Christian theologian. So, to clarify, I am a *"teolog"* speaking about the ideas and intellectual projects of *"ilahiyatçı"* scholars.[43] That is, having started my intellectual formation in Christian philosophical and theological traditions, I have taken up the study of Islamic religious thought, especially as it has developed in Turkish "theology" or "divinity" faculties in the past two decades. Having a Christian theological background has been exceedingly helpful in this effort to understand Turkish academic theology, since many Turkish theologians do Muslim theology in heavy engagement with Christian theological and philosophical sources. In fact, it is almost impossible to appreciate the intellectual output of some Turkish theologians without also being fairly versed in Western philosophy and religious thought. Nonetheless, this does not make knowledge of Christian theology sufficient for appreciating Turkish Muslim theology.

Turkish theology is also marked by domestic dynamics, an increasing sense of Ottoman heritage, sustained efforts to speak to Muslim communities outside Turkey as well as to academic milieus around the world. This often results in a subtle play of intersecting contexts, including contexts outside the sphere of theology. This admixture can be confusing, even daunting to an outsider. Political concerns and climates affect Turkish theology along with other religious and intellectual concerns; the line between theology and politics is not always easy to draw. At times, this complexity endemic to Turkish theology can default into clichés, name dropping, or superficial intellectual bricolage. Yet, Turkish theology is also fertile ground for synthesis and for a remarkable breadth of perspective across academies, both domestic and foreign. Within any given academic milieu, the questions deemed worth asking are often assumed and are only challenged as the academic field itself evolves. Turkish theologians are in the challenging situation of having to juggle the academic standards and assumptions of multiple milieus—academic theology at home, non-academic religious discourse in Turkey, religious studies and theology abroad (often on Western terms), and even Persian or Arab trends in the academic study of religion. With different academic milieus also come different ideas of what it means to bear authority. Instead of reducing or confining the subject of religious discourse in Turkey to debates on politics or secularism, as much previous literature has done, a closer look at Turkish academic Muslim theology is needed.

Many Turkish academic theologians use Arab-Islamic sources to mediate their own authority vis-à-vis the Western construct of modernity, effectively redefining modernity and its terms. In other words, through engaging European and Anglophone theologies, these Turkish theologians are reclaiming the concept and perceived tenets of "modernity" with Arab-Islamic sources. In this process of reclamation, Turkish theologians have dialogued extensively with Western Christian theological and philosophical resources. Some might even accuse these theologians of overly grounding their discourses not in Arab-Islamic sources but in Western terms and discussions. My own analysis intentionally focuses on Turkish engagements with Western sources. I frame this Turkish theological engagement as an intentional and critical dialogue, able to recast and reformulate terms of the discussion, such as modernity, authenticity, authority, and interreligious dialogue. Turkish theologians and others affiliated with Turkish academic theology have been forging their own double dialogue with Western authoritative traditions and non-Turkish Muslim authoritative traditions, while at the same time affirming the viability, insights, and even continuity of Turkish/Ottoman Muslim intellectual authority. In other words, Turkish theology is characterized by a dialectical threefold schema of authoritative intellectual traditions. This complex and multifaceted internal dialogue of traditions offers insights for those interested in theology and thought within and outside Turkey.

Much prior scholarship exists examining religion in Turkey, but this scholarship generally takes a political or sociological vantage. Apart from the work of Felix Körner and Philip C. Dorroll, little work has been done to explicitly examine Turkish theological voices for their theological value. Even Körner's work limits itself to questions of scriptural hermeneutics. Nevertheless, he has rightly signaled an untapped and lively discussion in state-funded Turkish theological faculties, a vein which, despite the international activities of many Turkish theologians and scholars, remains largely inaccessible to those who do not speak Turkish.

State-funded Turkish theology faculties are spaces that mediate academic/scientific, religious, and individual authorities. Western authority, Ottoman authority, Arab and Islamic authority, and modern Turkish authority all play various roles. Lines are not always clearly drawn, and there is not always consensus on what counts as an authoritative voice or what counts as an authoritative appropriation of a tradition. Individual voices, along with legacies of entire traditions, flow together into theological discourses seeking to reach Turkish Muslims in a modern age of science, pluralism, and globalization.

To speak of authority in the context of Turkish Muslim theology is especially tricky. Theology faculties are not only spaces for diverse types of authorities but are also spaces of contested authorities. One camp of contestation, tracing back to the early days of Kemalism, is the historical divide between those labeled "modernist" theologians and their critics. And while it would be tempting to divide theological output along political lines or into camps of traditional vs. modern, my treatment resists both possible approaches. First, what sorts of discourse qualify as traditional forms of Islamic authority is itself a contested subject. Second, who qualifies as a modernist and what being a modernist entails also defy clean consensus. Furthermore, to reduce theological output to political projects or a paradigm of tradition vs. modernity is reductive and at times misleading. This is especially true since debates on tradition vs. modernity, or even the religious vs. the secular, are—from both ends of the conversation—a very modern phenomenon.

Today state-funded Turkish theological faculties and their affiliated organizations distinguish themselves from other religious voices and authorities in Turkey through a unique and intentional double dialogue—one with European and Anglophone scholarship and one with classical (and sometimes modern) Arab-Islamic authorities. As a double dialogue, there are at least three partners in conversation: the West, the Arab and wider Islamic world, and Turkey (along with its Ottoman past). Turkey stands in the middle and develops its own self-understanding as it continues to dialogue with its interlocutors. This work offers an analysis of some of the significant theological aspects of said dialogue and further endeavors to encourage Anglophone scholars more familiar with Christianity than Islam to take greater interest in an exchange of which they are often, wittingly or not, already a part.

The bulk of my analysis draws on printed publications and online Turkish theological journals.[44] In addition to the printed word, I have enjoyed the intellectual, moral, and spiritual support of various Turkish academic theologians as well as the generous hospitality of both the Marmara University Theology Faculty in Istanbul and the Ankara University Theology Faculty in Ankara—two important faculties, which I visited in late 2015.

What Lies Ahead

This book is divided into four parts. The rest of part one of this book continues with chapter two, entitled ***Roots and Authorities: Resituating Revisionist and Ankara Paradigms in Light of Other Authorities***. This chapter explains how an understanding of Turkish theology as Muslim theology in dialectical tension with multiple traditions can develop and challenge previous literature on Turkish theology. Specifically, it takes up the work of two scholars of Turkish theology faculties: Felix Körner and Philip C. Dorroll. Körner wrote on revisionist Qur'ān hermeneutics in Turkish theology faculties at the turn of the twentieth and twenty-first centuries. Körner argued that Turkish theology was in a unique position to undertake a truly modern Muslim approach to the Qur'ān. Much has changed since Körner wrote on

Turkish theology; however, I criticize him on a conceptual point: the standard that constitutes a truly "modern" approach is still brought in from outside the Turkish discussion, reinforcing the old Islam vs. modernity binary. By contrast, Dorroll comes much closer to breaking out of binaries in his treatment of Turkish theology. In his work on the Ankara Paradigm, which focuses on Turkish theology during the mid-twentieth century, he argues for a seminal vein in Turkish theology that considers itself modern by tradition. Nevertheless, his discussions, even if critical, are still framed within a religious vs. secular binary. For my part, by treating Turkish theology as both subject and source of conceptual frameworks, I emphasize the dialectical aspect of Turkish theology in its interactions with Turkish identity, the classical Arabic tradition, and Western intellectual tradition, thereby highlighting theological moments of engagement that resist reduction to binary frameworks.

Part two takes up the question of individual authority and dialectical continuity in the work of Recep Alpyağıl. Chapter three, entitled ***Alpyağıl's Case for Canon***, introduces the reader to the figure and work of Istanbul theologian and philosopher of religion Recep Alpyağıl. I lay out his case for an inclusive canon of philosophy of religion and why Alpyağıl thinks it is needed in the context of an authentically Turkish and Muslim study of philosophy of religion. In his case for an inclusive canon, Alpyağıl turns to the example of French philosopher of religion Paul Ricoeur and his discussion of intertextuality. By teasing out the parallels between Ricoeur's legacy in philosophy of religion and Alpyağıl's use of Ricoeur's example for a Turkish paradigm, I argue for the dialectical and complex nature of Alpyağıl's proposed path forward: that an authentically Turkish and Muslim philosophy of religion is intertextual and inclusive. Chapter four, entitled ***Inclusions and the Role of the Individual***, continues the discussion of Alpyağıl's work. While the previous chapter discussed the question of what constitutes an authentically Turkish Muslim canon of philosophical theology and why it is integral to the Turkish context, this chapter investigates Alpyağıl's idea as to what this canon might look like in practice, how it relates to religious hermeneutics, and the role of the individual Muslim in navigating and drawing meaning from such a canon. For Alpyağıl, the individual stands in "hypoleptic" continuity with her past, best represented as a spiral that reaches back to the past and simultaneously moves forward into the future. I argue that Alpyağıl's vision of the believing individual in continuity with past and with future is a prime example of how Turkish theology can dialectically make use of multiple intellectual traditions to resist being reduced to simplified binaries.

Part three takes up a different Turkish theologian and a different disciplinary angle, delving more directly into questions of the individual's relationship to religion. Chapter five, ***Düzgün's Case for a Religion of Freedom***, takes up the work of Ankara theologian and *kalām* scholar Şaban Ali Düzgün. I treat his Muslim understanding of *fiṭra*, or primal human nature, and how he uses this Muslim concept to redefine what it means to be primitive. From his understanding of primal human nature, I construct his theological anthropology—one defined by both Enlightenment values and classical Islamic understandings of the God–world relation. I argue that his dialectical use of Islamic and "Western" concepts not only allows him to cast authentic Islam as compatible with Western values of individual freedom, but also allows him to actively defend individual agency and worth in the face of double standards, be they religious or secular, and in the face of Western individualism gone to the extreme. Chapter six, ***Human Agency, Responsibility, and Tawḥīd***, further explores Düzgün's take on human agency, moving from an abstract sense of communal responsibility towards more concrete and constructive Muslim responses to the trauma of Western colonialism. By highlighting his understanding of human agency, I explore Düzgün's theological and conceptual toolbox, showing how he draws confidently on Enlightenment and classical Islamic resources to produce a holistic vision of the individual in positive relationship with God. Specifically, I show how Düzgün finesses conceptions of human knowledge and affirms human plurality, a plurality facilitated by divine unity that does not stand in antagonistic relationship to individual agency. For Düzgün, *tawḥīd*, or God's utter oneness, stands in positive and open relation to an empowered individual piously conscious of her responsibility to society and to those around her.

The fourth and final part widens the lens of discussion to include a greater range of Turkish theologians. Chapter seven, ***From Dialectics to Direct Address: Turkish Theologians on Atheism and Other Religions***, while still featuring discussions drawn from the work of Alpyağıl and Düzgün, also offers a survey of Turkish theologians' general responses to Christianity, atheism, and religious pluralism. I argue that in the Turkish theological context, these three issues mutually implicate one another, with some exception. In addition to treating the work of Alpyağıl and Düzgün, this chapter also engages the work of other Turkish scholars, including Mahmut Aydın, Adnan Aslan, Mehmet Bayrakdar, and the late Yaşar Nuri Öztürk. The final chapter, *Conclusion: Reflections on Turkish Islam, Modernity, and Dialogue*, draws together the host of dialectical elements encountered in the work of Alpyağıl, Düzgün, and those Turkish theologians touched upon in the previous chapter's survey. In reaffirming the dialectical aspects of Turkish theology, that is, its complex relationship to multiple intellectual traditions, I turn the discussion outward towards the implications these dialectical encounters have for

Recep Alpyağıl

WK: *Wittgenstein ve Kierkegaard'dan Hareketle Din Felsefesi Yapmak* (2002, 2013)	*Doing Philosophy of Religion with Wittgenstein and Kierkegaard as Points of Departure*
KTHH: *Kimin Tarihi, Hangi Hermenötik? – Kur'anı Anlama Yolunda Felsefi Denemeler I* (2003, 2013)	*Whose History, Which Hermeneutic? Philosophical Essays on the Way to Understanding the Qur'ān I*
DCDD: *Derrida'dan Caputo'ya Dekonstrüksiyon ve Din* (2007, 2010)	*Deconstruction and Religion from Derrida to Caputo*
FY: *Fark ve Yorum – Kur'anı Anlama Yolunda Felsefi Denemeler II* (2009, 2014)	*Difference and Commentary: Philosophical Essays on the Way to Understanding the Qur'ān II*
TO: *Türkiye'de Otantik Felsefe Yapabilmenin İmkanı ve Din Felsefesi* (2010, 2014)	*The Possibility of Creating an Authentic Philosophy in Turkey and Philosophy of Religion: An Investigation into the Example of Paul Ricoeur*

Figure 1.4 Abbreviations for Alpyağıl's Works.

conceptualizing modernity's relationship to Islam and towards the implications Turkish theology might have for continued Muslim–Christian encounters at the academic level.

Abbreviations for Works by Alpyağıl and Düzgün

For the sake of brevity in citing, I have used abbreviations to designate the most quoted works of the two thinkers who feature in this section. The following tables (figures 1.4 and 1.5) delimit each scholar, the assigned abbreviations, the titles in Turkish as well as English translation, along with publication

Şaban Ali Düzgün

DBT: *Din, Birey ve Toplum* (1997; ?; 2014)	*Religion, Individual, and Society*
ST: *Sosyal Teoloji: İnsanın Yeryüzü Serüveni* (1999; ?; 2012)	*Social Theology: Humanity's Global Adventure*
ATT: *Allah, Tabiat ve Tarih: Teolijide Yöntem Sorunu ve Teolojinin Metaparadigmatik Temelleri* (2005; 2012)	*God, Nature and History: The Question of Method in Theology and Theology's Metaparadigmatic Foundations*
VB: *Varlık ve Bilgi Aydınlanmanın Keşif Araçları* (2008)	*Being and Knowledge: The Ways of Revealing Enlightenment*
CDDD: *Çağdaş Dünyada Din ve Dindarlar* (2012; 2014)	*Religion and Religious [People] in the Contemporary World*
SYEI: *Sarp Yokuşun Eteğinde İnsan* (2016)	*Humans Surrounded by a Precipitous Slope*

Figure 1.5 Abbreviations for Düzgün's Works.

dates. Because the works are in Turkish, I have used abbreviations which reflect the Turkish title rather than my English translations of the titles. Since the discussion of these two authors will continue into the final chapters of this work, the abbreviations will be used throughout.[45]

Notes

1. Ömer Mahir Alper, "The Conceptions of Islamic Philosophy in Turkey," in Sinasi Gunduz and Cafer S. Yaran (eds), *Change and Essence: Dialectical Relations Between Change and Continuity in Turkish Intellectual Tradition* (Washington, DC: The Council for Research in Values and Philosophy, 2005), p. 123.
2. Alper's paradigm fits better with Turkish thought of the early and mid-twentieth century.
3. Boyd Blundell, *Paul Ricoeur Between Theology and Philosophy* (Bloomington, IN: Indiana University Press, 2010), p. 171.
4. George Makdisi, *Ibn 'Aqil: Religion and Culture in Classical Islam* (Edinburgh: Edinburgh University Press, 1997), p. 75.
5. Mehmet Paçacı and Yasin Aktay, "75 Years of Higher Religious Education in Modern Turkey," in Ibrahim Abu-Rabi' (ed.), *The Blackwell Companion to Contemporary Islamic Thought* (Oxford: Blackwell, 2006), p. 123.
6. Ayşe Saktanber, *Living Islam: Women, Religion & the Politicization of Culture in Turkey* (New York and London: I. B. Tauris, 2002), p. 131.
7. Mustafa Köylü, "Religious Education in Modern Turkey," in Gunduz and Yaran, *Change and Essence*, p. 49.
8. Saktanber, *Living Islam*, p. 143.
9. Saktanber, *Living Islam*, pp. 149–51.
10. Pınar Kemerli, "Religious Militarism and Conscientious Objection in Turkey," *International Journal of Middle East Studies* 47 (2015): p. 283.
11. Köylü, "Religious Education in Modern Turkey," p. 54. Köylü goes as far as to say the faculties were considered, in their earlier days, antithetical to the cultivation of true religious feeling.
12. Köylü, "Religious Education in Modern Turkey," p. 55.
13. Köylü, "Religious Education in Modern Turkey," pp. 55, 59–60. While not treated extensively here, the 1990s were a very active period for Turkish theology.
14. Kemerli, "Religious Militarism and Conscientious Objection in Turkey," p. 290. She writes, ". . . dominant Islamist groups in contemporary Turkey—including the AKP and Gülen—endorse rather than challenge the militarist-nationalist

interpretation of Islam that has been utilized by the state in support of Turkish militarism since the foundation of the republic." The Ergenekon affair refers to the indictment, long trial process, and imprisonment of members affiliated with the Turkish military on the grounds that they were plotting against the current AKP government. The government's response in the aftermath of the July 2016 coup has brought further changes to the relation of ruling political party and Turkish military.

15. For their official website, see: <https://www.tdv.org/> (last accessed September 9, 2018). Established in 1924, this government institution formalizes Friday sermons and manages the training of religious officials.

16. İSAM is an abbreviation for *İslam Araştırmaları Merkezi* (The Center for Islamic Studies) and is affiliated with the 29 Mayıs University. For more information, see: <https://www.29mayis.edu.tr/hakkinda-44.html> (last accessed September 9, 2018). Their center is equipped with a large research library. In the summer of 2013 the author visited this library as a guest researcher with the help and hospitality of Turkish colleague and theologian Abdulnasır Süt. Felix Körner wrote that the center, "a non-university scholarly institution [. . .] founded in 1993, is a branch of the Türk Diyanet Vakfı and seems to have unlimited financial resources." Felix Körner, *Revisionist Koran Hermeneutics in Contemporary Turkish University Theology: Rethinking Islam* (Würzburg: Ergon Verlag, 2005), p. 56.

17. See, for instance, Malik Mufti, "The AK Party's Islamic Realist Political Vision: Theory and Practice," *Politics and Governance* 2 (2014): pp. 28–42. Mufti notes that it has become common to apply the term "Neo-Ottoman" to the political and religious identity promulgated by the AK Party.

18. By 2013, according to an announcement of Raşit Küçük—head of the High Council for Religious Affairs at the time—there were already eighty-six faculties. See "Türkiye'de kaç ilahiyat fakültesi var?" ["How many Theology Faculties are there in Turkey?"], published Nov 5, 2013, <http://www.haber7.com/guncel/haber/1024883-turkiyede-kac-ilahiyat-fakultesi-var> (last accessed November 3, 2016). It seems that between 2013 and 2015 the number of theology faculties did not notably increase. However, Mevlüt Uyanık (see n20) notes, a new type of faculty (Faculty of Islamic Sciences) was launched 2012–13. Turkish theologians have described these new faculties as something like "seminaries."

19. This growth in numbers has often meant the faculties are thinly spread.

20. On these new faculties, see, for instance, Mevlüt Uyanık's online article "Türkiyedeki İlahiyat Fakülteleri" ["Theology Faculties in Turkey"] on Eilahiyat.com:

<http://eilahiyat.com/index.php/arsivl/kategoriler/ilahiyatci-yazarlar/191-mevlut-uyanik/2839-turkiyedeki-ilahiyat-fakulteleri> (last accessed November 3, 2016).

21. Howard Reed, "The Faculty of Divinity at Ankara I," *Muslim World* 46 (1956): p. 296. Reed refers to the Ottoman institution as a "Faculty of Theology," but the current Istanbul University Faculty of Theology refers to it primarily as a department or branch (*şube*) and only parenthetically as a faculty (*fakülte*), which is larger and more independent, like a college or school within a university. See the official history page of the Istanbul University Theology Faculty: <http://ilahiyat.istanbul.edu.tr/?p=6056> (last accessed February 19, 2017).
22. H. Ahmed Sevgi, "İlâhiyât Fakültesi," in *İslâm Ansiklopedisi* (Türkiye Diyanet Vakfı), <http://www.islamansiklopedisi.info/> (last accessed February 20, 2017).
23. Fazlur Rahman, *Islam and Modernity* (Chicago: University of Chicago Press, 1982), p. 92. In this work, Rahman treats the early history of Turkish theology faculties in context of larger Muslim projects of education and responses to modernity.
24. Körner, *Revisionist Koran Hermeneutics*, p. 50.
25. Mustafa Köylü puts the actual religious education gap between 1932 and 1949, in his "Religious Education in Modern Turkey," p. 52.
26. Körner, *Revisionist Koran Hermeneutics*, p. 53.
27. Mehmet Paçacı and Yasin Aktay, "75 Years of Higher Religious Education in Modern Turkey," in *Muslim World* 89:3–4 (1999): p. 389. The same quote reappears without change in the 2006 version of the article.
28. Paçacı and Aktay, "75 Years of Higher Religious Education in Modern Turkey" (2006), p. 122. This is a slightly updated version of the 1999 article.
29. Paçacı and Aktay, "75 Years of Higher Religious Education" (1999), p. 390.
30. Körner, "Turkish Theology Meets European Philosophy: Emilio Betti, Hans-Georg Gadamer and Paul Ricœur in Muslim Thinking," *Revista Portuguesa Filosofia* 62 (2006): p. 806.
31. See the Ankara Divinity (i.e., Theology) Faculty official webpage under "*tarihçe*" (history): <http://www.divinity.ankara.edu.tr/> (last accessed October 19, 2015). All subsequent data in this section on courses offered, institutions opened and closed, and dates are taken from this page.
32. The general structure of subdisciplines in these faculties is uniform across Turkey. An additional fourth department for religious education is usually included as well. The standard subdepartments within a faculty have changed somewhat over the years.

33. Felix Körner gives an explanation of the word *"ilāhiyāt"* as used in the Turkish context, "'*İlāhiyāt*' appears in many classical works of theology. But in Arabic it has never meant 'theology' as the whole academic discipline." He further explains that the word could be used to mean metaphysics, to designate questions concerning God as such, to mean rational theology (in paired distinction with *sam'īyāt*, or the positive religious knowledge which is not accessible through reason alone but must be heard through tradition). *Revisionist Koran Hermeneutics*, p. 55.
34. Körner, *Revisionist Koran Hermeneutics*, p. 55.
35. See, for instance, the work of Sufi master Ken'an Refâî, *Ilahiyat-ı Kenan*, ed. Yusuf Ömürlü and Dinçer Dalkılıç (Istanbul, 1988). See also Ken'ân Rifâî's *İlâhiyât-ı Kenan* (Istanbul: Eğitim, Kültür ve Sağlık Vakfı Neşriyat, 2013). Ken'an Refâî (1867–1950) was an Ottoman/Turkish Sufi master of the Rifā'ī Order.
36. The word for theology in Farsi/Persian is الهیات. See, for instance, the Theology Faculty of Tehran University: <http://ftis.ut.ac.ir/> (last accessed September 11, 2018).
37. The Ankara Faculty, for example, uses the term divinity, whereas the Istanbul Faculty uses the word theology on their English language webpage. Compare Ankara University's *Ilahiyat* Faculty site <http://divinity.en.ankara.edu.tr/> with Istanbul University's *Ilahiyat* Faculty site <http://ilahiyat.istanbul.edu.tr/en/> (both last accessed February 19, 2017). Even Ankara's Turkish language page web address includes the word "divinity": <http://divinity.en.ankara.edu.tr/> (last accessed September 11, 2018).
38. See Avicenna, *The Metaphysics of The Healing: A Parallel English–Arabic Text*, trans. M. E. Marmura (Provo, UT: Brigham Young University Press, 2005). Rosabel P. Ansari brought this particular usage to my attention.
39. Yusuf Şevki Yavuz, "Usûl-i Selâse," in *İslâm Ansiklopedisi* (Türkiye Diyanet Vakfı), <http://www.islamansiklopedisi.info/> (last accessed February 20, 2017).
40. For first-hand accounts of major Turkish intellectuals' disagreements over the proper use of Arabic terms in Turkish academic discourse from the early to mid-twentieth century, see İsmail Kara, *Din ile Modernleşme Arasında: Çağdaş Türk Düşüncesinin Meseleleri* [*Between Religion and Modernization: Issues of Contemporary Turkish Thought*] (Istanbul: Dergâh Yayınları, 2003).
41. See Körner, *Revisionist Koran Hermeneutics*.
42. The analogy between Christian theology and Turkish theology has limits. Turkish theologians will generally not be interested in Mariology or Trinitarian theology outside of a subdepartment of the history of religions; whereas scholars in

a Turkish department of philosophy of religion are likely to share more concerns with Christian thinkers, such as how to read scripture, how to integrate science with a religious worldview, or what language means for theology.

43. Sometimes Turkish theologians also refer to Christian theology as *ilahiyat* and to a Christian theologian as an *ilahiyatçı*. For instance, Şinasi Gündüz does so in his *Küresel Sorunlar ve Din* (Ankara: Ankara Okulu Yayınları, 2010), p. 81.

44. A brief methodological note: my choice of concepts and figures to engage was largely guided by the concepts and figures I found Turkish theologians engaging—particularly so for Euro-American scholars, with the exceptions of Thomas Bauer, Shahab Ahmed, and Oddbjørn Leirvik.

45. Frequently cited works ordered by date of original publication. Neither of the lists exhaust either author's publications. For a more complete list of each author's publications, see bibliography. Full citations will be given as the works appear in subsequent chapters.

2

Roots and Authorities: Resituating Revisionist and Ankara Paradigms in Light of Other Authorities

> Our nation can neither abandon its sacred religion, nor dispense with the necessities of modern life. Reason requires not to sacrifice one of these inclinations to the benefit of the other, but rather to try to reconcile them.
>
> —Ziya Gökalp (1916)[1]

Scholarship on Islam in contemporary Turkey, with relatively few exceptions, underemphasizes or passes over the complex relationship of Islamic scholarship in Turkey to multiple authoritative traditions. These authoritative traditions include classical Islamic sources, increasingly Ottoman sources, contemporary Islamic thought outside of Turkey, as well as Western philosophical and theological discourses.[2] In the case of Turkish theology faculties, I have suggested to characterize these various engagements in terms of a dialectical threefold schema or a double dialogue, a characterization which emphasizes the complex interplay between Turkish, Arab-Islamic,[3] and Western sources and authorities. The threefold dialectical schema is one of complex interactions, where dynamic complexity provides impetus for new, creative theological contributions.[4] The threefold schema is meant primarily as a heuristic for navigating and evaluating Turkish theology in non-reductive fashion. Further, the constructive dialogues and theological conversations that arise as Turkish theologians navigate these different courses of authority are neither stuck in past nor do they jettison tradition, being neither bluntly modernist nor outright reactionary.

In Anglophone and European scholarship, the two scholars who do tackle some of the theological complexity of Turkish theology faculties are Felix Körner and Philip C. Dorroll. While I am indebted to both, I also criticize both for tending to praise "modernist" (Dorroll) or "revisionist" (Körner) theologians in terms of their compatibility with modernity. I differ from them in that I problematize the concept of modernity, asking in turn how Turkish theologians problematize and redefine modernity. As such, my treatment avoids the label "modernist," even if Turkish theologians at times use the word. While there are real divisions among Turkish theologians, I do not view "non-modernist" or "non-revisionist" theologians as standing outside the complex negotiation of authorities occurring in Turkish theological discussions.

This chapter will engage the work of Felix Körner and Philip C. Dorroll, delineate my own position in relation to their work on theology, and delve more deeply into the authoritative traditions which inform Turkish theology.

Scholarship on Religion in Turkey

> Islam matters to Turkey in a way few outsiders appreciate.
>
> —M. Hakan Yavuz[5]

The modern Republic of Turkey was founded in 1923 after the collapse of the Ottoman Empire in the wake of World War I. In addition to being a home to numerous non-Muslim religious minorities, Turkey is also a country of intra-Muslim religious diversity. The majority of scholarly attention has focused on the Islam of Sunni groups which are often cast in ideological tension with the secular state, such as the Gülen and Nurcu movements, or on the Islam of minorities such as the Kurdish Alevis. There exists a rich variety of Islamic identities and groups in Turkey, and Turkish state-funded theology faculties have received relatively less attention in secondary literature on religion in Turkey.

Much of the literature on Turkey treats Islam only to bring it within a framework of politics and sociological analysis. While notable exceptions exist on the religious thought and contributions of Said Nursi and Fethullah Gülen, even those discussions tend towards the political.[6] And though newer works do challenge the older, more established narrative of the secular Republic vs. the traditional Ottoman Empire, these same works remain heavily focused on the categories of secularism and religious identity that earlier generations of scholarship felt little need to challenge. Although the secularization hypothesis is no longer unquestioned canon in debates on modernity and religion, most literature on Turkey and religion remains within a framework that emphasizes the political dimensions of religion. Such an emphasis on secularization, politics, and religion fails to appreciate or engage the variety of theological options and engagements available.[7] Further, broader scholarship has increasingly challenged the underlying assumption that secularization represents an inevitable outcome of modernization.[8] And while it may not be practically possible to get around the impact of secularism when dealing with religion and modernity; nevertheless, it should be stressed that, in Turkey, secularization did not come into existence with the birth of the Republic; some of its origins are indeed Ottoman.[9] Thus, while secularism and secularization are important for understanding religion in Turkey, secularization is not a monolith that emerged *ex nihilo* with the rise of the Republic.

Markus Dressler urges for scholarship to move beyond what he calls Turkey's "monodimensional modernist narrative."[10] For Dressler, the problem with lingering in categories like secularism and modernity is that it tends to flatten out discussions of religion and state into a "monolinear narrative."[11] In short, "the master narrative of the Turkish modernization experience needs to be broadened."[12] It is paramount not to get caught in a strict dichotomy of religious vs. secular when speaking of Turkish history and the role of religion in Turkish identity. Although there is danger of losing perspective by overemphasizing rupture and secularism or, conversely, by overstressing religion and continuity, there may exist less polarized avenues of schematizing religion in Turkey. Dressler, for instance, speaks of the "asecular" dimensions of religion— religious trends and voices that, though marginalized, were not caught up in the religio-secular paradigm.[13] What if the focus were shifted to religious voices not wholly subject to the religio-secular dichotomy, or better still, to voices that actively challenge this dichotomy's reductive framing of their confessional contribution? These could be religious voices that respond self-reflexively to the religio-secular dichotomy, challenging its binary reductionism. I contend there are such voices among Turkish theologians.

Philip C. Dorroll and Felix Körner have both taken up the study of Turkish theology faculties. Apart from the contributions of these scholars, little work has been done to explicitly examine Turkish academic theological voices for their theological value in the Euro-American academies. Dorroll argues that progressive Turkish theological views on the compatibility of reform and religion are self-understood to be authentic expressions of Turkish Islam rather than political ideologies. Dorroll's work rightly challenges reducing progressive trends in Turkish theology to political agendas, but his scholarship on Turkish theology still operates within discussions of secularism. Körner also rightly points to the value of Turkish theology for its contributions to wider theological discussions outside of Turkey, yet he does so by stressing Turkish theology's modern qualities. Körner has, nevertheless, rightly signaled an untapped and lively discussion in state-funded Turkish theological faculties, a vein which despite the international activities of many Turkish theologians and scholars remains largely inaccessible to those who do not speak Turkish.

Körner on Hermeneutics in Turkish Theology Faculties

> Turkey is, as will be seen, a great blank on the Western map of Muslim exegesis.
> —Felix Körner[14]

Felix Körner, SJ, at the Pontifical Gregorian University in Rome, has done extensive work on the subject culminating in two books relevant to our current discussion: *Revisionist Koran Hermeneutics in Contemporary Turkish University Theology* (2005) and *Alter Text - neuer Kontext: Koranhermeneutik in der Türkei heute* (2006), the latter being primarily a collection of translations from Turkish scholars into German. He is currently the leading European scholar on the subject of Turkish theology faculties.[15]

Körner emphatically points to the Turkish faculties of theology as both *terra incognita* for Western scholarship and as a potentially fruitful field for theological cross-pollination and growth. In his enumeration of criteria suitable for his projected desideratum of "revisionist Koran hermeneutics," he argues that the uniqueness of Turkish theology faculties provides an academic landscape that is nearly *sui generis* in its embodied synthesis of Western philosophical methodology and its Muslim heritage.[16] This synthesis represents opportunity; especially in the arena of Muslim quranic exegesis, he argues it offers a chance to get beyond the dichotomy of viewing sacred text either merely as a product of history or as an entity entirely untouched by the historical continuum.[17]

The unique intellectual currents at play in these theology faculties draw Körner's scholarly attention. Here he sees the mark of secularism and Western thought combined with genuine theological and traditional engagement—an environment strikingly analogous to Western universities' theology and religious studies departments yet nevertheless wonderfully distinct from its Western counterparts. Turkey serves as an opportunity for the development of a revisionist Qur'ān hermeneutics from "within." This means quranic scholarship might well look to Turkey for novel responses to current sticking points in Muslim scholarly interpretations of the Qur'ān;[18] for example, the issue of how human agency and historicity apply to the Qur'ān as revelation sent from God.[19] Importantly, in the scholarly toolbox of Turkish scholars active in these theology faculties Körner finds the pervasive influence of the renowned philosopher of interpretation Hans-Georg Gadamer (1900–2002), famous for his philosophical hermeneutics.[20] Körner identifies also Pakistani Muslim scholar Fazlur Rahman (1919–88), along with his views on historicity, as another figure of major influence. Turkish theologians are themselves aware that Gadamer and Rahman have strongly influenced Turkish hermeneutics. Yasin Aktay has remarked that Rahman's soft historicism "has dominated the common Turkish theological paradigm."[21] And Körner's enthusiasm for the modern possibilities of Turkish theology finds precedent in Rahman's earlier comments on Turkey's religious education reform:

> Turkey is fortunate in having to make a fresh start because it has the opportunity to interpret the medieval intellectual heritage and give it new shape—which [. . .] is a basic desideratum in all current attempts to integrate the modern and the traditional.[22]

In more recent history of Turkish theology, Felix Körner has identified a group of Ankara theologians who in the 1990s took it upon themselves to coordinate and edit a series of books under the title of "the Ankara School" (*Ankara Okulu*). Many of the Turkish works cited here hail from this now relatively well-established publishing series. By Körner's estimation, these scholars in particular showed a noteworthy interest in engagement with Christian theology. Körner recounts:

> Some of the younger academic staff constitute what they call "a tradition." They see themselves as—creatively—continuing trains of thoughts of their own Ankara teachers such as Hüseyin Atay, who has recently gained some fame

outside Turkey, and especially Mehmed Said Hatiboğlu. Several academic teachers, now in their forties, have in the course of their studies spent some time at European or North American universities. These thinkers form a team, not homogenous but with an ambition to publish their ideas jointly. They are editing a series of books titled "Publications of the Ankara School," thus presenting themselves as a movement of thought. The series contains translations of books—prominently by Fazlur Rahman—into Turkish and collections of articles as well as original contributions; and its publication policy betrays a particular interest in Christian theology. In English, members of the "school" characterize their own "tradition" as "Islamic modernism."[23]

While much of the landscape of Turkish theology faculties has changed since the 1990s, many of these self-ascribed "Islamic modernists" are still active, though the labels they use for themselves may have changed. While never a rigid school, there is even less homogeneity now than there was twenty years ago.

Körner's interest in Turkish theology faculties remains relatively limited to questions of hermeneutics and sacred text. Beyond this, even his interest in hermeneutical questions leans heavily towards discussions that engage modern standards of historicity, referring to internal debates on how Turkish theologians should make sense of the historical and divine when interpreting the Qur'ān and the hadith tradition. Yet, focusing solely on questions of hermeneutics, while important, is only one facet of Turkish theology and it may obscure the wider currents of engagement with European and North American philosophical or religious trends.

Dorroll on the Ankara Paradigm

Philip C. Dorroll has studied the intellectual roots of some of the most common assumptions in Turkish theology. One of his most helpful insights is his identification of what he calls the "Ankara Paradigm" and its fundamental assumptions.[24] According to Dorroll, the Ankara Paradigm has some of its roots in late Ottoman thought, and while associated with Kemalist views on the religious and the secular, the paradigm does not fundamentally assume that modernity and tradition are at odds. Further, Dorroll argues for three fundamental commitments of the Ankara Paradigm: "a broad notion of religious humanism, a commitment to religious reform, and the elaboration of a specifically *Turkish* Islamic heritage."[25] Essential to this paradigm is the recognition that religion has social value and expression, or in other words sociology is valuable within the study of religion. Dorroll notes both how Émile Durkheim (1858–1917) functions as a formative model and influence for the Ankara Paradigm and how, theologically speaking, there is an especial focus on the value of the individual.[26] While there is currently no *unified* school that consciously aligns with the original Ankara Paradigm, these assumptions and attitudes still prevail in much of the Turkish theological world.

Philip C. Dorroll has also explored the scope and impact of the Māturīdī school in Turkish theology of the mid-twentieth century. This too is a mark of the "Ankara Paradigm" and is characterized by a humanist and modernist reading of Māturīdī theology and Ḥanafī jurisprudence.[27] This paradigm, though viewed by its critics as an extension of Kemalism and therefore not authentically Muslim, uses a humanist reading of classical Islamic sources long associated with Turkish and Ottoman Islam in a way that, distinct from Kemalism, does *not* assume a fundamental antagonism between the secular and religious. In short, to be modern and Muslim is not only an authentically Turkish way of being Muslim, it is also a true and valid expression of universal Islam. Dorroll explains:

> The Ankara Paradigm's essential argument, especially as it has been elaborated by contemporary Turkish Islamic modernists, may be phrased in this way: religion exists to bring fulfillment to human beings. It therefore must be understood with respect to its impact on human individuals and the societies in which they live. [. . .] Turkish Islamic modernism and reformism therefore reflects the essence of true Islam.[28]

Dorroll further argues that the use of pre-modern Islamic thinkers, in particular al-Māturīdī, to support modern assumptions shows that, for some Turkish theologians, modernity and tradition do not form a dichotomy. Although I am less inclined to start from the assumption that modernity and tradition stand as a dichotomy to be disproved, my own analysis builds on this basic argument. In other words, by arguing for the complexity of authority and identity in Turkish theological discourse, I support the general claim that a significant number of Turkish theologians do not see modernity as incompatible with tradition.²⁹ Nor do I dispute Dorroll when he writes in the context of Turkish theology:

> Religious "tradition" is the necessary ground of the religious believer's construction of her own sense of agency or participation in a particular religious community. Tradition is not simply the static "other" of modernity. Nor does it have to be identified with conservatism . . . ³⁰

Further, while I avoid the framework of the religious vs. the secular, I nevertheless agree with Dorroll when he writes:

> Reformist or modernist Islamic thought does not create something arbitrary with respect to "traditional" discursive frameworks, opposed to the authenticity of (conservative) tradition. Rather, it redraws the boundaries between certain key concepts in pre-existing discursive frameworks, in this case between the religious and the secular.³¹

That is to say, in Turkish theology faculties, perceived divisions between "modernist" and "traditional" do not map out neatly onto a dichotomy of the religious vs. the secular. Whether "traditional" or "modernist," there is always some negotiation of past and present. The question becomes *what* constitutes authentic expression of tradition and, by extension, Islam. Dorroll writes:

> The analysis of reformist Islamic thought in Turkey shows that the bases of "modernist Islam" are not dissimilar from its conservative counterpart, and that it involves a similar process of negotiation between the secular and the religious mediated through understandings of "tradition." The analysis of the history of modernist Islam in Turkey thus demonstrates that the debate between modernist and conservative Islamic thinkers in the modern era is not a question of whether or not to follow authentic Islamic tradition. It is instead a debate over what actually constitutes Islamic tradition, with each ideological side defining "tradition" through specific configurations of the boundary between the religious and the secular.³²

In the present analysis, I prefer not to use the label "modernist," because it may do more to obfuscate than to clarify in terms of classifying various contemporary Turkish theologians.³³ Nonetheless, I agree with Dorroll that the debate of the mid-twentieth century and now is one, not of tradition vs. modernity, but of whose interpretation of tradition counts as authentic Islam. And instead of dividing the camps of discussion into modern, on the one hand, and traditional readings of classical Islamic sources, on the other, I will focus on those readings that engage multiple canons of authority—namely, Turkish academic theology, classical Islam, and Anglophone/European Christian intellectual output.

For Dorroll, a "humanistic religious philosophy" is a hallmark of the Ankara Paradigm.[34] Dorroll argues that the Ankara Paradigm's appropriation of al-Māturīdī represents an especially humanist reading of Islam still present in the views of Turkish theologians today. In this reading, the value of the individual stands front and center. As an example, he looks at the work of Hanifi Özcan.[35] Specifically, Dorroll uses the example of Hanifi Özcan's reading of al-Māturīdī to show that the basic assumptions of the Ankara Paradigm are still held by many Turkish theologians today.

"Neo-Ḥanafism" and Humanism

The religious humanism of the Ankara Paradigm puts the individual at the center and stresses religious freedom. Dorroll asserts that the strong positive valuation of religious freedom stems from a "neo-Ḥanafī" theological trend, of which theologian Hanifi Özcan is a prime example.[36] Dorroll characterizes this neo-Ḥanafī trend as a modern, "individual-centered" view of religion, and "fundamentally humanist."[37] Moreover, this Islamic humanism is marked by a specific understanding of *tawḥīd*, or the affirmation of God's unity. The connection between a humanist understanding of Islam and *tawḥīd* lies in the determination of what is essential to religion and what belongs to changing human circumstance, where "even if religion's origins are divine, its institutional structures are human."[38] The matter becomes distinguishing between the parts of religion that are contingent and the parts of religion that are eternal. For Özcan, the key to determining which parts are eternal is *tawḥīd*: as Dorroll explains, "this eternal content [for Özcan] is the reality of the Oneness of God, the ultimate principle of monotheism *(tawḥīd* in Arabic, *tevhid* in Turkish)."[39] *Tawḥīd* functions like the foot of the compass that remains steady in the center as time and circumstance lead the outside foot to draw circles of different size. Divine unity is the central piece, the capstone of religion. While *şeriat* (*sharīʿa* or "sharia") is "the complex of Islamic belief and practice," it is *dīn* (religion) which "signifies what is eternally true in Islam, namely, *tawḥīd*."[40]

Dorroll treats Özcan on the eternal characteristic of religion and the contingent, adaptive aspects of sharia but Dorroll does not, at least to my knowledge, treat this in light of Fazlur Rahman's influence on Turkish theology faculties. Importantly, Fazlur Rahman's discussion of historical contingency and religion's eternal truths in the context of Qur'ān hermeneutics has played a widespread role in Turkish discussions of the essence vs. the contingent facets of true religion.

As noted by Felix Körner and Turkish theologians themselves, Fazlur Rahman's views on quranic hermeneutics have made significant impact on Turkish discussions of what counts as essential and what can be relegated to specific historical context.[41] For instance, influential Turkish theologian Mehmet S. Aydın provides a summary appraisal of Fazlur Rahman, strongly praising Rahman for not only understanding the importance of Islamic "modernism" but also for paving the way for it at both the abstract and lived level.[42] M. S. Aydın further notes that Islamic modernism falls into a long tradition of Islamic "revival" (*iḥyāʾ*) stretching back to al-Ghazālī (d. 1111) and including Ibn Taymiyya (d. 1328).[43] With so many historical precedents, he holds it would be a great mistake to view Islamic modernism as a Western product.[44] Further, he picks up on Rahman's stern criticism of Ashʿarī theology and on its overemphasis of divine agency over human agency[45]—a criticism echoed in other Turkish theologians who ostensibly ground their theology in Māturīdī sources. M. S. Aydın also explains how Rahman's hermeneutical approach to the Qur'ān involved the importation of two hermeneutical approaches—that of the Italian scholar Emilio Betti (1890–1968) and the German thinker Hans-Georg Gadamer, one emphasizing the possibility of objectivity, the other emphasizing the inescapable reality of historical context.[46] Finally, he defends Fazlur Rahman as a thinker who was not opposed to tradition, but rather steeped in it.[47] Drawing this back to the legacy of al-Māturīdī, I suggest that the Turkish *Wirkungsgeschichte*, or effective history, of Maturidism and other classical sources may at least in part elide with some more modern discussions, such as Fazlur Rahman's work on Qur'ān hermeneutics.

Al-Māturīdī, Abū Ḥanīfa, Islamic Humanism, and the Ankara Paradigm

Broadly speaking, Turkish Ottoman history favors Ḥanafī jurisprudence; and since Ḥanafī jurisprudence often goes hand in hand with Māturīdī theology, al-Māturīdī's history in Turkey touches on deep historical roots.[48] According to Bruckmayr, "the history of Ottoman *kalām* scholarship displays an ongoing and constant engagement with Māturīdī texts throughout the Ottoman period."[49] Today, Turkish theologians often refer to al-Māturīdī's major *kalām* work *Kitāb al-Tawḥīd* (*The Book of Unity*) and, significantly, al-Māturīdī's lengthy *tafsīr* work (Qur'ān commentary) *Ta'wīlāt al-Qur'ān*, which is currently being translated into Turkish.[50] Some relatively recent works on al-Māturīdī include a volume of collected essays entitled *Māturīdī's World of Thought*, edited by Şaban Ali Düzgün;[51] Hanifi Özcan's *The Problem of Knowledge in Māturīdī*[52] as well as his *Religious Pluralism in Māturīdī*; another collected volume *Imam Māturīdī and Māturidism*, edited by Sönmez Kutlu;[53] Hülya Alper's *The Relation of Reason and Revelation in Imam Māturīdī*;[54] and Harun Işık's *Human Freedom in Māturīdī*.[55] In addition, Abū'l-Mu'īn al-Nasafī (d. 1114), author of the largest comprehensive work of Māturīdī theology, stands out among the names who hail from the Māturīdiyya school of theology. Şaban Ali Düzgün has devoted a work specifically to this figure entitled *The God–World Relation according to Nasafī and Islamic Philosophers*.[56]

Turkish theologian Yusuf Ziya Yörükân (1887–1954), influential for his contribution to Turkish religious pedagogy, not only stressed reason and freedom of conscious but also highlighted the humanist values of Ḥanafī tradition.[57] In particular, he stressed the Ḥanafī sensitivity to diverse cultures and its role in the formation of an explicitly "Turkish Islam," known especially for its tolerance of diversity and social adaptability.[58] This too Dorroll identifies as part of the Ankara Paradigm, describing Turkish understanding of Ḥanafī jurisprudence as "notable for its respect for individual human reason and the human search for knowledge" and as the "humanist core of Islamic teaching and a spirit of religious interpretation found deep within Turkish culture itself."[59] By stressing the individual's capacity for creativity, reasoning, and reflection, the Turkish understanding of Ḥanafism stresses the individual's role in interpretation.[60] In other words, this means an Islamic championing of individual interpretive authority.⁶¹ This championing of individual interpretative authority will arise in the following treatments of Recep Alpyağıl and Şaban Ali Düzgün, though I do not use the labels "modernist" or "Ankara Paradigm" to engage their work.

Beyond Māturīdī and Ḥanafī Roots

When it comes to the Arab-Islamic tradition's influence on Turkish theology, four to five major figures and schools from classical Islam immediately come to the fore: al-Māturīdī and the Māturīdiyya tradition, Ḥanafī jurisprudence, Ibn Sīnā (Avicenna), Muḥammad al-Ghazālī (along with some Shāfiʿī jurisprudence), and Ibn ʿArabī/the Akbāriyya tradition.⁶² As we saw in Dorroll's analysis, Māturīdī and Ḥanafī influence have an especial historical significance for Turkish theology. Other authorative sources in Turkey can be found in the Ottoman legacy of al-Ghazālī or of Ibn ʿArabī. Ottoman madrasahs developed the mystical ideas of al-Ghazālī, Ibn ʿArabī and al-Suhrawardī (d. 1234),⁶³ and the thought of Ibn ʿArabī carried widespread significance both in Seljuk as well as Ottoman periods.

Historian Halil Inalcık identifies a long-standing division between Ottoman *'ulemā'* who tolerated and subscribed to some mystical views and associated practices and "fanatics" who condemned such views and practices.⁶⁴ Inalcık also notes the existence of trends of strict traditionalism and Ḥanbalī adherents in the Ottoman Empire—such tides stand against an elite Ottoman like Kâtip Çelebi (d. 1657), who defended mystics, Ibn ʿArabî, and a view of Islam as tolerant and open to change.⁶⁵ Other Ottoman intellectuals who developed Akbāriyya thought include Dâvûd El Kayserî, Kutbeddîn of Iznik and Yazıcızâde Mehmed of Gallipoli, Bâlî of Sofya (d. 1533), and Abdullâh of Bosnia (d. 1660).⁶⁶ Of these figures, Dâvûd El Kayserî has received theological attention in recent Turkish theological publications.⁶⁷

Traditions integral to Turkish theology are traceable to Ibn Sīnā, al-Ghazālī, and Ibn ʿArabī, not only Māturīdī theology and Ḥanafī jurisprudence. While Māturīdism's ties to Turkish past are often stressed by Turkish theologians, it is equally important to understand that Ashʿarism has played a significant role in Ottoman thought and, as such, is part of contemporary Turkish theological heritage. In fact, Ottoman curricula from the sixteenth to nineteenth centuries show fewer Māturīdī works than Ashʿarī works.⁶⁸

Al-Ghazālī (d. 1111), trained in the Ashʿarī school of theology, also holds significance for Turkish theology, and interest in his legacy can be seen in the number of recent publications—some in the commemoration of the 900th year since his death. *On the 900th Anniversary of Ghazālī's Death: 7–9 October, 2011, Istanbul* is a collection of works on al-Ghazālī by a host of Turkish scholars;[69] though the articles are in Turkish, the work also contains article abstracts in both Arabic and English. *Ghazālī Talks* (2012)[70] is another compilation of essays on al-Ghazālī written by Turkish scholars; it includes the work of İlhan Kutluer, Fehrullah Terkan, among others. There is also İbrahim Çapak's *Ghazālī's Conception of Logic* (2011).[71] *Ghazālī and Causality* (2012)[72] is a compilation and translation into Turkish of non-Turkish scholarly contributions on the long-debated question of al-Ghazālī's stance on divine agency in the natural world. Also, there are works such as *Ghazālī: His Philosophy and Influence on Islamic Modernism* (2012)[73] and *Knowledge and Method in Ghazālī's Philosophy* (2011).[74] Frank Griffel's seminal *Al-Ghazālī's Philosophical Theology* (2009) was even translated into Turkish by İbrahim Halil Üçer.[75]

In addition to al-Ghazālī, his philosophical predecessor Ibn Sīnā also has an important place in contemporary Turkish theology. Two heftier recent works on Ibn Sīnā are İlhan Kutluer's *Necessary Being in Ibn Sīnā's Ontology* (2013)[76] and Ömer Türker's *İbn Sînâ Felsefesinde Metafizik Bilginin İmkânı Sorunu* (2010).[77]

Finally, a work that falls in the tradition of both Avicenna and Ibn ʿArabī is Ömer Mahir Alper's *Being and Humanity: The Reconstruction of an Idea in the Context of Kemalpaşazâde* (2010).[78] Kemalpaşazâde (d. 1534), as Ö. M. Alper points out, stands in the traditions of Shāfiʿī jurisprudence, Māturīdī theology, as well as Avicennan and Akbāriyya philosophy.[79]

Late Ottoman Heritage—A Reclamation of Surprising Dimensions

Turkish theological faculties are not merely new and unique products of a modernist rupture with an Ottoman past. Rather, Turkish theology faculties are products of the "modern" Republic in continuity with an Ottoman past— both in a historical sense, as well as in a constructed sense.[80] That numerous academic theologians in Turkey today engage with scientific materialism, atheism, skepticism, and Euro-American philosophy is not altogether foreign to the late Ottoman intellectual landscape. Moreover, Turkish theologians continue to reclaim their Ottoman and especially late Ottoman heritage as part of their theological identities. As Silverstein aptly remarked, a "new generation of Islamic scholars and historians in Turkey are reconceptualizing the Turkish present's relationship to the Ottoman and early republican past."[81] Turkish theologians are part of this project of reconceptualization.

Mid- to late nineteenth-century Ottoman intellectuals were no strangers to materialism, skepticism, or even outright atheism. Yet, instead of a portrait of late Ottoman intellectuals grappling with Western intellectual challenges on questions of religion, the dominant narrative up until recently was of a decadent, decidedly unmodern religious past from which the "modern" project of a secular Turkish Republic haply emerged. Examples of dated and dismissive dichotomy abound, including tales of how Mustafa Kemal Atatürk "set out to break the loyalty of the Turks . . . to outmoded Islamic institutions and habits, and he sought to replace that loyalty with nationalistic zeal and energy."[82] Rupture is emphasized; the secular state's ties to its Ottoman intellectual heritage are minimized. This sort of black and white narrative underplays the variety of Ottoman reflections on science, European ideas, political/legal reform, and religion.[83]

It is well known that Ottomans of the nineteenth century instigated major modernizing reforms.[84] These started with education reforms under Mahmud II (r. 1808–39) and were followed by the famous Tanzimat Period (1839–76).[85] Less well-known is the fact that Ottoman intellectuals imported European materialism into discussions among the educated elite—many of whom prepared the underlying ideology that facilitated the birth of the Turkish nation-state. The Ottoman intellectual heritage was ignored and downplayed, and instead of investigating "the multifaceted and vibrant atmosphere of late Ottoman society," Turkish historians focused on "its authoritarian and despotic character," creating an artificial contrast to the "enlightened" and modern thought of the Turkish Republic.[86] Yet, this image of late Ottoman intellectual society has been changing, both in English and in Turkish scholarship. More recent approaches see late Ottoman society as "a social order where a wide variety of ideas and streams of thought competed, where a great diversity of publications flourished, and where educational institutions of good standing developed fairly rapidly."[87] Scholars, like Zürcher, argue for a portrait of significant continuity even amid rupture between Ottoman and Turkish identity. While the identity of "Turkishness" had developed under the influence of European Orientalism and other Turkic debates outside the Empire, for the Ottoman Turkish intellectual, Turkish identity was one piece in a multifaceted sense of self, which included Ottoman and Muslim identity.[88]

Some of the most surprising examples of late Ottoman intellectual diversity exhibit a profound interaction with European materialism, skepticism, and scientific pursuit. For instance, figures like Beşir Fu'ad (1852–87), Abdullah Cevdet (1869–1932), and Baha Tevfik (1884–1914) all contributed to Ottoman discussions on European materialism.[89] In the central parts of the Ottoman Empire of the late 1880s, the spread of German materialist Büchner's thought rendered the relationship between religion and science an intense object of dispute.[90] For example, with the translation of Büchner into Arabic in 1884, many intellectuals were divided into opposing camps over the question of evolutionary theory.[91]

Debates on materialism and Darwin were far from the beginning. Three decades earlier, Scotsman Charles MacFarlane on his mid-century visit to the Ottoman Royal Medical Academy was shocked to see cadavers and autopsies, and even more shocked when he asked the medical students about the religious implications of autopsies, one of whom responded in French: "It's not at Galata Saray that one must come and seek religion."[92]

Not only did some late Ottoman intellectuals move away from religion, but some actively promulgated the spread of scientific and scientistic ways of thinking.[93] Abdullah Cevdet, a medical student in the latter half of the nineteenth century, provides an intriguing example of conversion from religion to science—from a conservative religious education as a youth to an atheist within six months of starting his medical studies at the Galata Saray Royal Medical Academy. The conversion is visible from his poetry. Abdullah Cevdet moved from penning poems in praise of the Prophet to laments about the delusional nature of religion.[94] Yet, despite his rejection of a religious worldview, his belief in science and his effort to translate European materialist thinkers remained grounded in aspects of Islamic tradition. Embracing what he perceived to be a sacred duty, he effectively Islamicized his materialism through his "desire to follow the Prophetic hadith requiring all Muslims to attain 'wisdom and truth'."[95]

Materialist thinkers represent only one section of late Ottoman intellectuals. Even so, their presence in the Ottoman Empire implies questions of science vs. religion, skepticism, materialism, and atheism are not new topics of engagement for Turkish intellectuals, since these are already part of Ottoman heritage. Further, active engagement with European intellectual trends is a hallmark of both Ottoman and modern Turkish thought. Turkish theologians partake in and actively shape this shared heritage.

What Does Modernity Have to Do with it?

Anymore, it is hard to escape mention of "modernity" in either theological or sociological discussions. As Brian Silverstein writes in *Islam and Modernity in Turkey*, "The term 'modernity' has taken on a fetish status, is often deployed as a sign of trendiness, and is in danger of referring to just about anything and therefore, of course, nothing."[96] In broader discussions outside the Turkish context, "modernity is often read through its least impressive, most trivializing offshoots."[97] Scholarship on Turkey is no more immune to this trivializing danger than other disciplines. The term modernity has become so popular in academic works on Turkey and religion that one might wonder if looking at religion in Turkey can offer any new depth of perspective. In my view, the category is potentially useful, but only if the idea of modernity is taken critically and developed in dialogue with the actual phenomena it is meant to explain. To this end, rather than an explanatory category, in the context of Turkish theology, I find "modernity" is more helpful as a dialectical category. That is, various Turkish theologians have their own idea of what modernity entails, and it is more helpful to bring their definitions into the discussion, rather than simply take external definitions of modernity and rigidly apply them to Turkish discussions.[98] The result is an ongoing dialectic, or back and forth, on what it means to respond to and take part in modernity.

Modernity in various contexts connotes technology, the supremacy of rationality over traditional authorities, capitalist economies, nation-states, democratic forms of government, a questionable West–other dynamic, secularism, globalization, homogenization, devaluing of local rhythms, and disenchantment. For many, the question of modernity calls to mind the question of religion's place in modernity; in other words, "religion is not merely one topic among many for people who see themselves as modern; it is a—indeed arguably *the*—key site at which definitions of modernity have been formulated." For Brian Silverstein, Turkey is precisely one more "case in point" of religion's role in defining modernity.[99]

In this study, theological engagements with thinkers associated with the Enlightenment (in particular Baruch Spinoza, Blaise Pascal, René Descartes, Immanuel Kant, etc.), European Romanticism, nineteenth-century materialism, and modern hermeneutics (Friedrich Schleiermacher, Hans-Georg Gadamer, E.D. Hirsch Jr., etc.), or the scientific worldview, qualify as engagements *with* and responses *to* modernity. Also, theological discussions which assume or critically engage the vocabulary of modernity—science, skepticism, atheism, pluralism, globalization, etc.—should be counted as both responses *to* and products *of* modernity. While my initial designations rely heavily on Euro-American intellectual heritage to locate and identify dialogue with modernity, this nearly inevitable "Western" bias is not the final word but only a starting point open to development. For, the importance of engaging Turkish voices on modernity lies largely in the opportunity to rethink the category of modernity through a different set of perspectives and assumptions, ultimately rerouting starting points of reference.

Modernity functions as much as a positive standard of judgment as it does a label of condemnation. As a positive standard, the term modernity stresses individual freedom—legal, social, ethical, aesthetic, and so on. The modern subject's right and curse is the freedom to self-actualize, to subscribe to any range of subjective truths, and to live out any number of values. The modern moral outlook is that "we ourselves are the sources and creators of the values by which we live."[100] In the words of sociologist Anthony Giddens, ". . . modernity is vastly more dynamic than any previous type of social order."[101] However, modernity can also be polarizing, paralyzing, reductive, and intolerant of ambiguity.

From a philosophical angle, Charles Taylor provides a monumental account of the narrative of modernity. In his widely read *Sources of the Self*,[102] Taylor portrays modernity and the secular age as the troubled child of a destabilizing marriage of Enlightenment reason and the Romantic turn to individual feeling. For Taylor, the two horns of modernity are the "disengaged-instrumental" and the "Romantic-expressive"—the respective embodiments of Enlightenment and Romantic values.[103] With the disenchantment of the modern world, in order to escape a mechanically deterministic reality, people turned inward and celebrated the inner world of feeling, yet this inner world grew more and more divorced from public realities and calls to greater shared meaning. Taylor boldly declares, "We are now in an age in which a publicly accessible cosmic order of meanings is an impossibility."[104] As a result, instead of providing a bulwark against the dizzying advent of an industrial and technological era, this inner turn ultimately instigated a decentering of the self. However, the dizzying cornucopia of goods available to the decentered modern is not bad in and of itself—nor is any one good to be discarded if in an extreme form it proves detrimental. On this point, Taylor urges for the need to recognize "the multiplicity of goods" and the "conflicts and dilemmas they give rise to."[105] Taylor identifies the dangers of modernity's singlemindedness—either in raising one good above all others (like freedom[106]) or in abandoning a good which in radicalized form brings harm (like benevolence[107]), both of which reflect a deeply polarized understanding of how to apply values. But what theorists like Taylor do not single out as a facet of modernity is its signature intolerance of ambiguity—a clear corollary of Enlightenment values that uphold universal perspectives; God's-eye views; and the homogeneity of human reason across time, individuals, and cultures.

Ambiguity: The Canary in the Mineshaft

Scholar of Islam Thomas Bauer takes up the question of ambiguity, challenging the fundamental assumption still held by many theorists of modernity and religion—that literalism in sacred texts stands in fundamental opposition to modernity.[108] For Bauer, the "literal" interpretation is modern precisely in its rejection of polyvalence and ambiguity. This means that reactionary and fundamentalist readings are just as modern as their less "traditional" counterparts. By contrast, Habermas has described religious fundamentalism as an opponent of modernity: "This mindset, whether we encounter it in Islamic, Christian, Jewish, or Hindu form, clashes with fundamental convictions of modernity."[109] Against this common view of fundamentalism and literalism as anti-modern, Bauer carefully argues that fundamentalist interpretations of Islam are far removed from traditional Islam, in that the epistemological assumptions that drive their arguments are decidedly modern.

Bauer is not alone on this point. Turkish scholar of the Gülen Movement M. Hakan Yavuz writes:

> both Islamism and secularism are aspects of the same phenomenon (i.e., modernity). Even though they are historically not simultaneous, since secularism preceded and spawned its modern Islamist reaction, they eventually became intertwined through mutual interaction and conditioning each other.[110]

José Casanova, too, defines modern religions as "religions that are not only traditional survivals of residues from a pre-modern past but rather specifically products of modernity."[111] He further stresses the role non-Christian religions can play in forging their own understanding of secularism and modernity.[112]

How is intolerance of ambiguity a hallmark of modernity? Bauer casts modernization as a process of rationalization whereby ambiguity is not tolerated and he thereby resists viewing modernization as an inexorable development in universal human history.[113] Bauer explains:

> The process of bureaucratization and mechanization presses for unified standards and sees each ambiguity as disruption, and the efforts of computer science are pitted against the recognition of the inevitability of ambiguity in order to refine its strategies of disambiguation as far as possible. In the Classical Islamic world ambiguity was accepted as an unavoidable component of existence, [a component] which has good and bad sides, and hence can and must be observed and bounded, but not totally wiped out; whereas in Western Modernity, a small ambiguity-friendly intellectual discourse coexists alongside a powerful main current inimical to ambiguity. Precisely this component of modernization has led to considerable devastation in the Islamic world.[114]

For Bauer, the problem of modernity is not a question of traditional vs. modern, but a subtle play about what kinds of knowledge and thinking are truly valuable. In this light, he claims that pitting the Middle Ages against modernity is a false opposition; the real tension stands between "the modern desire for clarity" and "the post-modern potential of the Islamic post-formative tradition."[115]

Measuring Islamic intellectual trends by the standards of postmodernism is arguably no less reductive than trying to fit an Islamic understanding within the bounds of a popularized "modernist" framework. Yet, if we can set aside the category of postmodernism and modernity for a moment, it may be worthwhile to dwell on the significance of how reigning cultural and intellectual standards play subtle roles in delimiting what counts as knowledge and what counts as a defensible contribution to scholarly dialogue. In Bauer's study, he notes that, by the nineteenth century, the West was unable to understand the classical quranic commentators' tendency to put multiple interpretations side by side without explanation, framing this not as a lack in the commentaries but as a lack of Western culture to actively value "the possibility of parallel truths."[116]

In Bauer's reading of history, intellectual appreciation for certain ways of thinking and processing information was lost when the Islamic world imported European epistemological values and assumptions. Once Islamic discourse was put on the offensive by European critiques, the Islamic response to (in this case: Western) modernity's enmity towards ambiguity ended in rupture—that is, by adopting the same criteria for knowledge as the European critics of Islam, the earlier tolerance and sometimes celebration of ambiguity was not only no longer understood, but even seen by many Muslim intellectuals as a liability and an indication of decadence and decline.[117] Such a portrait is corroborated by Wael Hallaq's retelling of the history of Islamic law—one that stresses the rupture of an entire system of (in this case: legal) knowledge by forcing it to fit within Western legal frameworks.[118]

Bauer sees the historicization of the sacred text, whether from a Muslim or non-Muslim perspective as extremely reductive. It offers an apparent but deceptive way out, since looking for a kernel amid historical context is very much what a modern resistance to ambiguity fosters.[119] In his view, this modern approach converts rich, ambiguous, and multifaceted Islamic intellectual heritage into set doctrines which must be made rational, unambiguous, and defended at all costs. This process of historicization is incidentally what characterizes Fazlur Rahman's widely known method for reading the Qur'ān: the historical husk of the quranic milieu must be shucked off to arrive at a transcendent kernel that must then be repackaged to suit today's needs and context. Further, Rahman's take on quranic historicity and his understanding of Gadamer are very much at play in Turkish theological debates on sacred text.[120]

In the traditional reading of the Qur'ān, as Bauer argues, there is a positive value to ambiguity even in the variant readings of the Qur'ān—an ambiguity which, more often than not, scandalizes modern Islamic readings.[121] After all, with its variant readings, its elliptical and concise style, a veritable sea of interpretations, the Qur'ān is the ambiguous text *par excellence*.[122] Yet, in the pre-modern Islamic tradition, such a label vindicated rather than challenged the sacred status of the Qur'ān. It is, by contrast, today's readings, which operate under a modern assumption that ambiguity is not a value or a quality of richness, but unscientific, representing an intellectual liability or fault.[123]

Conclusion

Discussions of modernity cannot be divorced from the theological baggage that has produced, accompanied, and challenged reigning attitudes concerning modernity.[124] Theology—as much as philosophy, political theory, or technology—has an important, defining role in how modernity comes to be defined, perhaps even a role in challenging the very dichotomies ingrained in the modern mind.

Turkish theologians are active in addressing and redefining discussions of modernity, as just a cursory listing of recent Turkish titles suggests: Recep Alpyağıl's *From Derrida to Caputo: Deconstruction and Religion*; Şaban Ali Düzgün's *Religion and Believers in the Contemporary World*; İlhami Güler's *Theology of Resistance* or *New Approaches to Religion*; Şinasi Gündüz's *Global Problems and Religion*; Yaşar Nuri Öztürk's *Deism: Belief that Recognizes Nothing Sacred except God, Reason, and Morals*; Burhanettin Tatar's *Philosophical Hermeneutics and Authorial Intention: Gadamer vs. Hirsch*; and Zeki Özcan's *Theological Hermeneutics*—to name a few.[125]

There are also other academic writers who have joined in on this discussion—some outside the academy proper and affiliated with the Gülen Movement (Ali Bulaç, *Religion and Modernism*[126]), as well as other voices that overlap with theological discussions in Turkish sociology, literature, and philosophy departments (Caner Taslaman, *Modern Science, Philosophy and God*; Tülin Bumin, *Disputed Modernity: Descartes and Spinoza*).[127] There are also scholars trained in Turkish theology faculties, who have done graduate work in Europe or North America and return to find their place in philosophy, sociology or literature departments.[128]

It may be fruitful to draw from a hermeneutic of ambiguity-tolerance/intolerance in judging how much Turkish theologians are at once responding to modernity and also themselves a product of modernity. This hermeneutic of tolerating ambiguity may be especially helpful in coming to terms with the complexity of Turkish theology's roots and combined authoritative traditions. Turkish theology faculties are products of modernity in disputed continuity with their past, and because of this dynamic relationship they offer a rich resource for reconsidering the role of religion in modernity. Not only that, but Turkish theology faculties are a crucial component to understanding the complex web of religious currents in Turkey. Thus, engaging their theological output could not only add to the understanding of religion's role in Turkey but also challenge old perspectives on what it means to be religious and modern.

Notes

1. Markus Dressler, "Rereading Ziya Gökalp: Secularism and the Reform of the Islamic State in the Late Young Turk Period," *International Journal of Middle East Studies* 47 (2015): p. 519. Dressler cites from the original: Ziya Gökalp, "İttihad ve Terakki Kongresi [1]," *İslam Mecmuası* 3 (1916): p. 976.
2. Since the scholars that I treat use the word "Western" and "West" to characterize various intellectual and religious traditions with European and Anglophone ties and roots, I use this term throughout the section and elsewhere. When it is not unwieldy, I use the designation "European and Anglophone" and "Euro-American" to include Europe and English-speaking scholarship outside of Europe, like North America. These second designations I use in my own analysis, but I prefer to default to "Western" and "West," when the terms accurately reflect the views and designation of the scholars in question.
3. I lump references to Persian sources with the Arab-Islamic leg of the schema, since it is not independent enough to be considered a fourth relation. For this reason, I alternately refer to the Arab-Islamic point on this triad simply as broader Islamic identity. On another point, the double dialogue is, arguably, not entirely unique to the Turkish theology faculties. Given the international emphasis of the Gülen Movement, including its publications in Arabic and English, one could claim that the movement has also developed its own double dialogue—however, the Gülen Movement is known to be less centralized and is active in places like South Africa and Central Asia. It is also less strictly

devoted to the development of new theological ideas and approaches, being more oriented toward education, *hizmet* (service), and providing models for pious Islamic living.

4. In the neighboring context of Iranian Islamic political thought, Siavash Saffari also argues for the *creativity* of "neo-Shariatis" and their ability to get beyond old binaries of East and West. See his *Beyond Shariati: Modernity, Cosmopolitanism, and Islam in Iranian Political Thought* (Cambridge: Cambridge University Press, 2017). I am not the only one to make a case for intellectual creativity of a group of Islamic intellectuals in order to move past an old binary, but I stress the theological rather than the political dimensions.

5. M. Hakan Yavuz, *Toward an Islamic Enlightenment: The Gülen Movement* (Oxford: Oxford University Press, 2013), p. 51.

6. Pim Valkenberg's *Renewing Islam by Service: A Christian View of Fethullah Gülen and the Hizmet Movement* (2015) is one recent exception. Other scholars who write on Gülen with greater theological emphasis are Zeki Saritoprak, Thomas Michel, M. Hakan Yavuz, and Sydney Griffith. Also, Şükran Vahide, Colin Turner, and Hasan Horkuc treat Said Nursi with theological weight.

7. Tahir Abbas recognizes that the scholarly focus on politics often excludes theological elements, and, in his recent work, he tries to include theological dimensions in his social analysis of religion in Turkey. See Abbas, *Contemporary Turkey in Conflict: Ethnicity, Islam and Politics* (Edinburgh: Edinburgh University Press, 2017).

8. See, for instance, Charles Taylor's *A Secular Age* (Cambridge, MA: Belknap Press of Harvard University Press, 2007).

9. Nilüfer Göle, "The Civilizational, Spatial, and Sexual Powers of the Secular," in Michael Warner et al. (eds), *Varieties of Secularism in a Secular Age* (Cambridge, MA: Harvard University Press, 2010), pp. 253–4 fn.

10. Dressler, "Rereading Ziya Gökalp," p. 525.

11. Dressler, "Rereading Ziya Gökalp," p. 525.

12. Dressler, "Rereading Ziya Gökalp," p. 526.

13. Dressler, "Rereading Ziya Gökalp," p. 526. Jeremy F. Walton has recently identified two polar "fantasies" of absolute secularism and non-political Islam and looks at civil religious organizations. See Jeremy F. Walton, *Muslim Civil Society and the Politics of Religious Freedom in Turkey* (Oxford: Oxford University Press, 2017). While not without application, I think this sort of polarization can oversimplify the on-the-ground realities of theology faculties, in which reflections on the ideals of pure, non-political Islam and on secular currents

take place in a complex and changing environment, amid a host of other considerations.
14. Körner, *Revisionist Koran Hermeneutics*, p. 19.
15. See his faculty webpage: <http://www.sankt-georgen.de/lehrende/koerner.html> (last accessed September 11, 2018).
16. Körner, *Revisionist Koran Hermeneutics*, p. 47. Elsewhere, Körner also makes this case in his article "Turkish Theology Meets European Philosophy."
17. Körner, *Revisionist Koran Hermeneutics*, p. 40.
18. In describing the optimal grounds for advances in Qur'ān hermeneutics, Körner details, "Another criterion would be to look for places which to offer (a.) good conditions for a reception of new philosophical approaches, perhaps from Western traditions of thought, into Muslims' theology (b.) a fertile ground for new ideas to grow, and (c.) a climate conducive to a comparably open scholarly discourse. When scanning the map with this gauge, *Turkey* proves to be the primary destination of our expedition." *Revisionist Koran Hermeneutics*, p. 47.
19. On this point Körner cites his mentor Rotraud Wielandt, "Wielandt assesses the development of Muslim Koran interpretation as stuck in a dilemma. Either the Koran is seen as a fully human product and thus at the mercy of historical critique; or it is totally from God . . ." *Revisionist Koran Hermeneutics*, p. 40.
20. In chapter three, discussion will touch on a few direct references to Gadamer by a Turkish theologian (Alpyağıl) in an evaluative schema.
21. Yasin Aktay, "The Historicist Dispute in Turkish-Islamic Theology," in Gunduz and Yaran, *Change and Essence*, p. 77.
22. Fazlur Rahman, *Islam and Modernity: Transformation of an Intellectual Tradition* (Chicago: University of Chicago Press, 1982), p. 139.
23. Körner, *Revisionist Koran Hermeneutics*, p. 60.
24. The Ankara Paradigm identified by Dorroll and the Ankara School identified by Körner certainly share elements. The major difference is that Dorroll locates the genesis of the Ankara Paradigm in the mid-twentieth century and ties it to Ottoman roots, whereas Körner speaks of the Ankara School as a movement in the 1990s and concentrates on the question of scriptural hermeneutics.
25. Philip C. Dorroll, "The Turkish Understanding of Religion: Rethinking Tradition and Modernity in Contemporary Turkish Islamic Thought," *Journal of the American Academy of Religion* 82:4 (2014): p. 1040.
26. Dorroll, "The Turkish Understanding of Religion," p. 1041.
27. Two works by Dorroll on this are his PhD thesis and an article: Philip C. Dorroll, "Modern by Tradition: Abu Mansur al-Maturidi and the New Turkish

Theology" (doctoral dissertation, Emory University, 2013); Dorroll, "The Turkish Understanding of Religion," pp. 1033–69.
28. Dorroll, "The Turkish Understanding of Religion," p. 1058.
29. Dorroll refers to "liberal" Turkish theologians, but I would like to avoid use of this word due to its many and often polarizing connotations. I do not wish to highlight the imagined and embodied polarities of modern vs. tradition by labeling Turkish theologians who are not stuck in such polarities as "liberal." Generally, I do not evaluate theologians based on political alignment, and while "liberal" can mean something outside of politics, I prefer to focus directly on the claims and assumptions made by the theologians engaged here.
30. Dorroll, "The Turkish Understanding of Religion," p. 1034. Here he draws on Saba Mahmood. cf. Saba Mahmood, *Politics of Piety: The Islamic Revival and the Feminist Subject* (Princeton, NJ: Princeton University Press, 2005).
31. Dorroll, "The Turkish Understanding of Religion," p. 1036.
32. Dorroll, "The Turkish Understanding of Religion," p. 1036.
33. For one, the idea that conservatism as we understand it today is anti-modern is not an assumption I wish to critically take on. Secondly, Turkish theologians themselves may self-identify differently at different times and have varying opinions as to which of their peers qualify or do not qualify as modernist, depending on whether the term is conceived as a term of approval or of disapproval. Even if used as a term of disapproval or to place distance between one scholarly project and another, this is arguably less a question of modernity and more a question of perceived priorities—for instance, does this scholar value the literal authority of hadith traditions more than international discourse on human rights? Examples of how this plays out in engaged debate can be found in M. Hayri Kırbaşoğlu's *İslam Düşüncesinde Sünnet: Eleştirel Bir Yaklaşım* [*The Sunna in Islamic Thought: A Critical Approach*], 15th printing (Ankara: Ankara Okulu Yayınları, 2015), originally published in 1996, as well as İlhami Güler's *Sabit Din Dinamik Şeriat* [*Unchanging Religion, Dynamic Sharia*] (Ankara: Ankara Okulu Yayınları, 1999). Further, M. S. Aydın explained in 1990 that to a Muslim modernist, returning to the Sunna is not necessarily about returning precisely to the Prophet's example, but at least to the historical example of the first generations more broadly. See Mehmet S. Aydın, "Fazlur Rahman ve İslâm Modernizmi" ["Fazlur Rahman and Islamic Modernism"], *İslamî Araştırmalar* 4:4 (1990): p. 275. Cited as "Fazlur Rahman and Islamic Modernism."
34. Dorroll, "The Turkish Understanding of Religion," p. 1047.

35. See chapter seven for a brief treatment of this figure in the discussion of religious pluralism in Turkish theology.
36. Dorroll, "The Turkish Understanding of Religion," p. 1046.
37. Dorroll, "The Turkish Understanding of Religion," p. 1047. On this Dorroll cites Hanifi Özcan, "Modern Çağda Dinin Birey ve Toplum için Anlamı" ["The Meaning of Religion for Society and Individual in the Modern Age"], *Akademik Araştırmalar Dergisi* 32 (2007). At a later point in the discussion, Dorroll again stresses the "individual-centered" aspect of Turkish religion for Özcan. He explains, "Özcan argues that the 'Turkish understanding of religion' is properly characterized as 'realist' and 'individual-centered [*fert-merkezli*].'" Dorroll, "The Turkish Understanding of Religion," p. 1057.
38. Dorroll, "The Turkish Understanding of Religion," p. 1047.
39. Dorroll, "The Turkish Understanding of Religion," p. 1047. And Özcan's *Mâtürîdî'de Dînî Çoğulculuk* [*Religious Pluralism in Māturīdī*] (Istanbul: Marmara Üniversitesi İlâhiyat Fakültesi Vakfı Yayınları, 1999): pp. 33, 77. Even M. S. Aydın points to the value of *tawḥīd* in continually reforming and purifying Islam, praising past revival movements for appealing to this concept and criticizing them for not applying the concept holistically. Mehmet S. Aydın, "Fazlur Rahman and Islamic Modernism," p. 275.
40. Dorroll, "The Turkish Understanding of Religion," p. 1055. Also, Özcan, *Religious Pluralism in Māturīdī*, p. 47.
41. In particular, Felix Körner analyzes the work of Turkish theologian Adil Çiftçi on Fazlur Rahman along with Rahman's influence on other authors, including Mehmet Paçacı. See Körner, *Revisionist Koran Hermeneutics*. Though not treated here, Adil Çiftçi is the author of *Fazlur Rahman ile İslam'ı Yeniden Düşünmek* [*Rethinking Islam with Fazlur Rahman*] (Ankara: Ankara Okulu, 2000). To note, Rahman's *Revival and Reform in Islam* (2000) was translated into Turkish by Fehrullah Terkan (2006) and Rahman's *Major Themes of the Qur'an* (1980) by Alparslan Açıkgenç (1996). Other Turkish translators of Fazlur Rahman include Mehmet Aydın, M. Hayri Kırbaşoğlu, Salih Akdemir, A. Bülent Baloğlu, and Adil Çiftci. The majority of Rahman's major works seem to have been translated in the mid- to late 1990s. Translations into Turkish include: Fazlur Rahman's *İslam* [*Islam*], trans. Mehmet Aydın and Mehmet Dağ (Ankara: Ankara Okulu); *Ana Konularıyla Kur'an* [*Major Themes of the Qur'an*], trans. Alparslan Açıkgenç (Ankara: Ankara Okulu); *İslam ve Çağdaşlık* [*Islam and Modernity*], trans. M. Hayri Kırbaşoğlu (Ankara: Ankara Okulu); *Tarih Boyunca İslami Metodoloji Sorunu* [*Islamic Methodology in History*], trans.

Salih Akdemir (Ankara: Ankara Okulu Yayınları, 1997); *İslam'da İhya ve Reform* [*Revival and Reform in Islam*], trans. Fehrullah Terkan (Ankara: Ankara Okulu Yayınları, 2006). Works like F. Rahman's *Islam* and *Major Themes of the Qur'an* have been available in translation so long that the original printing dates are no longer listed on the most recent printings. The 1980s saw some of the first Turkish translations of Fazlur Rahman's works.

42. Mehmet S. Aydın, "Fazlur Rahman and Islamic Modernism," p. 273.
43. Aydın, "Fazlur Rahman and Islamic Modernism," p. 274.
44. Aydın, "Fazlur Rahman and Islamic Modernism," pp. 274, 283.
45. Aydın, "Fazlur Rahman and Islamic Modernism," p. 279.
46. Aydın, "Fazlur Rahman and Islamic Modernism," p. 280. Though his name comes up less frequently in article and book titles, Emilio Betti is still a significant influence for some Turkish theologians. Gadamer, however, appears more conspicuously in discussions.
47. Aydın, "Fazlur Rahman and Islamic Modernism," p. 282.
48. Wilfred Madelung explains the connection between the earlier Seljuk Turks, Ḥanafī law, and Māturīdī theology: "As a result of the Turkish expansion, eastern Ḥanafism and Māturīdī theological doctrine were spread throughout western Persia, ʿIrāḳ, Anatolia, Syria and Egypt. Numerous Transoxanian and other eastern Ḥanafī scholars migrated to these regions and taught there from the late 5th/11th to the 8th/14th century. Māturīdī doctrine thus gradually came to prevail among the Ḥanafī communities everywhere." W. Madelung, "Māturīdiyya," *EI2*, <http://dx.doi.org.proxy.library.georgetown.edu/10.1163/1573-3912_islam_SIM_5046> (last accessed September 15, 2016). A more recent perspective on this historical relationship can be found in Philipp Bruckmayr, "The Spread and Persistence of Māturīdī Kalām and Underlying Dynamics," *Iran and the Caucasus* 13 (2009): pp. 59–92.
49. Bruckmayr, "The Spread and Persistence of Māturīdī Kalām," p. 66.
50. Al-Māturīdī's *tafsīr* work was even labeled "book of the year" in 2008, and its translation to Turkish began late 2014, according to Turkish news site Milliyet, <http://www.milliyet.com.tr/yilin-kitabi-secilen-te-vilatu-l-kur-istanbul-yerelhaber-474862/> (last accessed December 11, 2016). It is possible that the *tafsīr*'s popularity is either a more recent phenomenon or that its influence is only slated to increase. Its present Turkish translation (ongoing as of late 2016) is the work of Bekir Topaloğlu, Kemal Sandıkçı, Yusuf Şevki Yavuz, Yunus Vehbi Yavuz, along with the help of dozens of other scholars. Four volumes are currently available in print. Eighteen total volumes are projected.

51. Şaban Ali Düzgün (ed.), *Mâtürîdî'nin Düşünce Dünyası* (Ankara: Filiz Matbaacılık, 2011 and 2014).
52. Hanifi Özcan, *Mâtürîdî'de Bilgi Problemi* (Istanbul: Marmara Üniversitesi İlâhiyat Fakültesi Vakfı Yayınları, 1993) and *Mâtürîdî'de Dînî Çoğulculuk* (Istanbul: Marmara Üniversitesi İlâhiyat Fakültesi Vakfı Yayınları, 1999; 2013), respectively.
53. Sönmez Kutlu (ed.), *İmam Mâturîdî ve Maturidilik*, 3rd expanded edn (Ankara: Otto Yayınları, 2011; original publication 2003). This includes translations of non-Turkish scholarship.
54. Hülya Alper, *İmam Mâtürîdî'de Akıl-Vahiy İlişkisi* (Istanbul: İz Yayıncılık, 2008).
55. Harun Işık, *Maturidi'de İnsan Özgürlüğü* (Ankara: Araştırma Yayınları, 2013).
56. Şaban Ali Düzgün, *Nesefî ve İslâm Filozoflarına Göre Allah-Alem İlişkisi* (Ankara: Akçağ, 1998).
57. For a treatment of Ḥanafism in relation to Ottoman history see Guy Burak, *The Second Formation of Islamic Law: The Hanafi School in the Early Modern Ottoman Empire* (New York: Cambridge University Press, 2015). Burak argues that not only did Ottomans favor Ḥanafī jurisprudence but that they developed a very specific reading of Ḥanafī jurisprudence. This specific Ḥanafī branch favored under the Ottomans, Burak argues, was part of a larger trend in the region towards dynastic influence on Islamic jurisprudence. Per Burak, Kemâlpaşazâde's *Risāla fī ṭabaqāt al-mujtahidīn*, one of the earliest Ottoman histories of the Ḥanafī school including biographies of its jurists, attributed lower individual authority to later generations, where the lowest level of individual authority was apportioned to the Ottoman generation it was written in (pp. 72–3). As such, historically speaking, the role of individual authority in terms of use of reason and greater flexibility was perhaps not always consciously associated with the Ottoman Ḥanafī tradition.
58. Dorroll, "The Turkish Understanding of Religion," p. 1044.
59. Dorroll, "The Turkish Understanding of Religion," p. 1050.
60. Dorroll, "The Turkish Understanding of Religion," p. 1051.
61. Dorroll, "The Turkish Understanding of Religion," p. 1059.
62. Al-Ghazālī and Avicennan thought were also an integral part of Ottoman discussions. For instance, the Ottoman scholar Hocazade (1434–88) famously wrote a gloss of al-Ghazālī's *Tahāfut al-falāsifa*, one of two scholars commissioned by Mehmet II (The Conqueror) to revisit al-Ghazālī's criticism of speculative philosophy—the other, less successful, author commissioned being 'Alā'

al-Dīn al-Ṭūsī. See İbrahim Kalın, "Hocazade (Muslihiddin Mustafa)," in Oliver Leaman (ed.), *The Biographical Encyclopedia of Islamic Philosophy* (London: Bloomsbury, 2006; 2015), pp. 151–2. Ibn ʿArabī's thought also became "Turkified" (I use this term artificially) through the works of Ṣadr al-Dīn Qūnawī (d. 1274) and later of Dâvûd El Kayserî (following the common Turkish spelling). El-Rouayheb numbers Dâvûd El Kayserî (Dāʾūd Qayṣarī) among the Persianate commentators (though Kayseri is currently a city in modern Turkey) and firmly in the Qūnawī tradition, which espouses a monistic reading of Ibn ʿArabī. El-Rouayheb, *Islamic Intellectual History in the Seventeenth Century: Scholarly Currents in the Ottoman Empire and the Maghreb* (New York: Cambridge University Press, 2015), pp. 244, 281. To note, in May of 2015 Uludağ University hosted an international scholarly symposium on Dâvûd El Kayserî; on this see the Kültür News report, <http://www.haber7.com/kultur/haber/1359895-uluslararasi-davud-el-kayseri-sempozyumu> (last accessed December 12, 2016).

63. Halil Inalcik, *The Ottoman Empire: The Classical Age 1300–1600* (1973; repr. London: Phoenix Press, 2000), p. 183. My citations refer to the 2000 printing.
64. Inalcik, *The Ottoman Empire*, p. 182. He writes, "In Ottoman society there was always a class of fanatical ulema who regarded the intellectual sciences, mysticism, music, dancing and poetry as impious; against these was a class which defended them as coming within the scope of religion. The fanatics were usually the popular şeyhs and ulema who preached and taught in the mosques, while the ulema in higher medreses or in government service formed the second group." It may be fruitful to ask in what ways modern Turkish academic theologians are a continuance of the second group.
65. Inalcik, *The Ottoman Empire*, p. 185. Elsewhere, Inalcik elaborates on the Ottoman elite's relationship to mysticism: "From earliest times mysticism was a main element in the thought of the Ottoman intellectual elite and was not confined to the popular beliefs of the tarîkats. This tradition goes back to the Seljuk period. The Seljuk sultans welcomed in their lands the famous scholars and mystics from Turkestan and Iran, fleeing before the Mongol invasion. Thus the Seljuk cities such as Konya, Kayseri, Aksaray or Sivas became the most brilliant centers of mystical thought in the Islamic world. [. . .] Like al-Suhrawardî, Ibn al-ʿArabî was personally invited to the Seljuk lands and honoured by the sultan. By interpreting and disseminating his works his stepson, Sadr al-Dîn of Konya (d. 1273), played a major part in establishing Ibn al-ʿArabî as a dominant influence in Turkish thought. Mystical belief thus became a

well established tradition among the sunnî ulema" (p. 199). Molla Fenari or Mehmed al-Fanarî is also included among those influenced by Ibn 'Arabī (p. 200).

66. Inalcik, *The Ottoman Empire*, p. 200.
67. Mehmet Bayrakdar has translated some of Dâvûd El Kayserî's work and Sema Özdemir has published a study on Dâvûd El Kayserî. See Dâvûd El-Kayserî, *Ledünnî İlim ve Hakiki Sevgi* [*Otherworldly Knowledge and Divine Love*], trans. Mehmet Bayrakdar (Istanbul: Kurtuba Kitap, 2011) and Sema Özdemir, *Dâvûd Kayserî'de Varlık Bilgi ve İnsan* [*Being, Knowledge and Humanity in Dâvûd El Kayserî*] (Istanbul: Nefes Yayınevi, 2014).
68. Bruckmayr, "The Spread and Persistence of Māturīdi Kalām," p. 69.
69. *900. Vefat Yılında İmâm Gazzâlî: 7–9 Ekim 2011, İstanbul* (Istanbul: Marmara Üniversitesi İlâhiyat Fakültesi Vakfı Yayınları, 2012).
70. M. Cüneyt Kaya (ed.), *Gazzâlî Konuşmaları* (Istanbul: Küre Yayınları, 2012; 2013).
71. İbrahim Çapak, *Gazâlî'nin Mantık Anlayışı* (Ankara: Elis Yayınları, 2011).
72. Yaşar Türkmen (ed.), *Gazâlî ve Nedensellik* (Ankara: Elis Yayınları, 2012). This volume includes articles from notable Ghazālī scholars, such as Binyamin Abrahamov, Michael M. Marmura, and Majid Fakhry.
73. Hasan Aydın, *Gazzâlî: Felsefesi ve İslam Modernizmine Etkileri* (Istanbul: Bilim ve Gelecek Kitaplığı, 2012)—a revised doctoral thesis originally published in 2006.
74. Mehmet Vural, *Gazzâlî Felsefesinde Bilgi ve Yöntem* (Ankara: Ankara Okulu Yayınları, 2011).
75. Frank Griffel, *Gazâlî'nin Felsefî Kelâmı*, trans. İbrahim Halil Üçer, 2nd printing (Istanbul: Klasik Yayınları, 2015).
76. İlhan Kutluer, *İbn Sina Ontolojisinde Zorunlu Varlık* (Istanbul: İz Yayıncılık, 2013).
77. Ömer Türker, *İbn Sînâ Felsefesinde Metafizik Bilginin İmkânı Sorunu* (Istanbul: İSAM Yayınları, 2010).
78. Ömer Mahir Alper, *Varlık ve İnsan: Kemalpaşazâde Bağlamında Bir Tasavvurun Yeniden İnşası* (Istanbul: Klasik, 2010).
79. Ö. M. Alper, *Varlık ve İnsan*, p. 8. Bruckmayr, by contrast, underplays Kemalpaşazâde's Māturīdī ties and emphasizes the Ash'arī influence in his thought: "Some of the influential Ottoman scholars, such as Kamālpāshāzāde indeed, appear to have been, in many aspects, more impressed by later Ash'ari scholars (*muta'akhkhirūn*), especially, al-Rāzī (Badeen 2008: 19), and thinkers

such as al-Ṭūsī, with their more philosophy-laden *kalām* than by the thought of the Māturīdiyya." Bruckmayr, "The Spread and Persistence of Māturīdi Kalām," p. 69.

80. Turkish scholars are increasingly looking to ground the modern Turkish theological identity in Ottoman past. Take, for instance, the *Osmanlı Araştırmaları/ Journal of Ottoman Studies* jointly published by İSAM and 29 Mayıs University.
81. Brian Silverstein, *Islam and Modernity in Turkey* (New York: Palgrave Macmillan, 2011), p. 13.
82. Nicholas S. Ludington, "Turkish Islam and the Secular State," *The Muslim World Today* (1984): p. 6.
83. A recent work by Stefano Taglia significantly helps to cover this English-language scholarship gap of Ottoman intellectual engagement. See his *Intellectuals and Reform in the Ottoman Empire: The Young Turks on the Challenges of Modernity* (New York: Routledge, 2015).
84. In a widely read work by Selim Deringil, *The Well-Protected Domains*, it is consistently argued that the Ottoman state in the nineteenth century played its part in a movement towards modernization. Selim Deringil, *The Well-Protected Domains: Ideology and the Legitimation of Power in the Ottoman Empire 1876–1909* (New York: I. B. Tauris, 1999; 2011).
85. Despite relatively constant contact with Europe, an increased attention to Western European civilization coincided with a recognition of the military threat of Russia. One Turkish historian's account put it this way: "The Ottoman Turks had numerous contacts with the new Western world. In fact, they were never out of contact with the West. They were aware of the rise of a new civilization, but they steadfastly remained aloof from Western developments because they were convinced of the superiority of their own system. It was only in the wave of doubt occasioned by certain events in the early eighteenth century that they began to realize that their assumptions were no longer absolute truths. They began to realize that they had been overwhelmed by a superior military power. The acknowledgement of defeat became the stimulus for the rise of a new attitude." In Niyazi Berkes, *The Development of Secularism in Turkey* (New York: Routledge, 1998), p. 24. Halil Inalcik, by contrast, attributes the Ottoman recognition of "the superiority of the West" to a period of defeats in Hungary at the end of the seventeenth century (1638–99), resulting in first military and eventually administrative reform. See Halil İnalcik, *Turkey and Europe in History* (Istanbul: Eren Yayıncılık, 2006; 2008), p. 63.

86. Elisabeth Özdalga, introduction to *Late Ottoman Society: The Intellectual Legacy*, ed. Elisabeth Özdalga (Abingdon: RoutledgeCurzon, 2005), p. 1.
87. Özdalga, *Late Ottoman Society*, p. 2.
88. Erik-Jan Zürcher, "Ottoman Sources of Kemalist Thought," in *Late Ottoman Society*, p. 19.
89. M. Şükrü Hanioğlu treats all three figures in "Blueprints for a Future Society: Late Ottoman Materialists on Science, Religion, and Art" in *Late Ottoman Society*.
90. Hanioğlu, "Blueprints for a Future Society," p. 33.
91. Hanioğlu, "Blueprints," p. 32. The debate in the Arab parts of the Ottoman Empire over evolution had started as early as 1876 via the journal *Maqtataf*, where the debate tended to split into Arab Christian intellectuals' defense of evolution and the Muslim ulema's rejection of it (32–3).
92. Hanioğlu, "Blueprints," p. 34.
93. Another example is Beşir Fu'ad.
94. Hanioğlu, "Blueprints," p. 40–1. Here, Cevdet writes about the Prophet, "You are the bright star that radiates in the ninth heaven of Islam," and not long after beginning medical studies scrawls in French, "Religion, ce faux et ravissant rayon, Emané de cerveaux ivres d'illusion . . ."
95. Hanioğlu, "Blueprints," p. 42.
96. Silverstein, *Islam and Modernity in Turkey*, p. 4. For his use and extended understanding of the concept of modernity see pp. 4–5 of the same work.
97. Charles Taylor, *Sources of the Self: The Making of the Modern Identity* (Cambridge, MA: Harvard University Press, 1989; 1992), p. 511.
98. This said, the terms "modernity" and "tradition," while understood differently by various Turkish theologians; nevertheless, often connote various polarities within the Turkish theological academy.
99. Silverstein, *Islam and Modernity in Turkey*, p. 10.
100. Quentin Skinner, "Modernity and Disenchantment: Some Historical Reflections," in James Tully (ed.), *Philosophy in an Age of Pluralism: The Philosophy of Charles Taylor in Question* (Cambridge: Cambridge University Press, 1994), p. 38. Skinner, in this citation, sums up Charles Taylor.
101. Anthony Giddens and Christopher Pierson, *Conversations with Anthony Giddens: Making Sense of Modernity* (Stanford: Stanford University Press, 1998), p. 94.
102. This was translated recently into Turkish by the academic theologian couple Bilal Baş and Selma Aygül Baş as *Benliğin Kaynakları: Modern Kimliği İnşası* (Istanbul: Küre Yayınları, 2012). The author has personally met Bilal Baş at

Marmara İlahiyat Fakültesi, where he generously offered me a copy of the monumental translation.

103. Taylor, *Sources of the Self*, pp. 510–11.
104. Taylor, *Sources*, p. 512.
105. Taylor, *Sources*, p. 514.
106. Taylor clarifies that even postmodern thinkers are rather modern in their insistence on freedom as final good in *Sources*, p. 489.
107. Taylor writes, "the demands of benevolence can exact a high cost in self-love and self-fulfillment, which may in the end require payment in self-destruction or even in violence." *Sources*, p. 518.
108. Bauer is certainly not the first to challenge this. Since the popularity of the secularization hypothesis has waned, it has become more common for scholars to recognize religious and textual fundamentalism as a product of modernity rather than a living fossil of some earlier traditional and superstitious time.
109. Jürgen Habermas, "An Awareness of What is Missing," in Jürgen Habermas et al. (eds), *An Awareness of What is Missing: Faith and Reason in a Post-Secular Age*, trans. Ciaran Cronin (Cambridge: Polity Press, 2010), p. 20.
110. M. Hakan Yavuz, *Toward an Islamic Enlightenment: The Gülen Movement* (Oxford: Oxford University Press, 2013), p. 10.
111. José Casanova, *Public Religions in the Modern World* (Chicago: University of Chicago Press, 1994), p. 26.
112. Casanova, *Public Religions*, p. 234.
113. Thomas Bauer, *Die Kultur der Ambiguität: Eine andere Geschichte des Islams* (Berlin: Verlag der Weltreligionen, 2011), p. 40: "Das Unbehagen an sprachlicher Ambiguität, das die westlichen Gesellschaften seit der Aufklärung kennzeichnet . . . ist . . . Teil des westlichen Sonderwegs."
114. Bauer, *Die Kultur der Ambiguität*, p. 35. My translation of the original: "Der Prozeß der Bürokratisierung und Technisierung verlangt nach vereinheitlichten Standards und betrachtet jede Ambiguität als Störung, und der Erkenntnis der Unvermeidlichkeit von Ambiguität stehen die Anstrengungen der Computerlinguistik gegenüber, ihre Strategien der Disambiguierung so weit wie möglich zu verfeinern. Anders als in der klassischen islamischen Welt, wo Ambiguität als unvermeidlicher Bestandteil des Daseins akzeptiert wurde, der gute und schlechte Seiten hat und deshalb beobachtet und gebändigt, nicht aber ausgemerzt werden muß und kann, gehen in der westlichen Moderne eine kleiner ambiguitätsfreundlicher intellektueller Diskurs und ein mächtiger ambiguitätsfeindlicher Hauptstrom nebeneinanderher. In der islamischen

Welt selbst hat diese Komponente der Modernisierung zu beträchtlichen Verwüstungen geführt."

115. Bauer, *Ambiguität*, p. 114. Alpyağıl in particular, treated in part two, also sees postmodern potential in Islam.
116. Bauer, *Ambiguität*, p. 124.
117. Another possible example of this phenomenon is legal reform in Muslim countries like Egypt and the Ottoman Empire in the nineteenth century. On Ottoman and Egyptian legal reforms of the nineteenth century, see chapter four of Wael B. Hallaq, *Shariʿa: Theory, Practice, Transformations* (Cambridge: Cambridge University Press, 2009). In Egypt of the 1860s, al-Ṭahṭāwī (1801–73) and his students undertook the translation of French codes. By 1876 there existed mixed courts in Egypt, and laws were even drafted first in French before being translated into Arabic. In the Ottoman Empire, the Humayun decree of 1856 gave non-Muslim minorities legal rights before the Ottoman state and the *Mecelle* (formally codified Islamic law, i.e., civil code), effective as of 1877, while inclusive of sharia norms, also marked a rise in state authority above sharia.
118. See Hallaq, *Shariʿa*. Throughout this work Hallaq endeavors to contrast of sharia law prior to colonialism and Western influence with a mutated and ruptured understanding of sharia that forms in the wake of such rupture. Hallaq argues fiqh was not originally a totalizing power/knowledge structure. But the story of sharia's transition into modernity is one of rupture, entexting, and reduction, where both Islamic states and those who see sharia as "other" construct a disconnected remnant of the old fiqh tradition(s) along Foucauldian lines of power and totalizing discourse.
119. Bauer, *Ambiguität*, p. 129.
120. Theology faculties still regularly carry works by Turkish scholars on Fazlur Rahman in their theology bookstores.
121. By variant readings, Bauer does not mean interpretations. He means the different possible vocalizations of the quranic text.
122. Bauer, *Ambiguität*, p. 46. He writes, "Der ambige *Text* schlechthin ist der Koran."
123. John Caputo has made a postmodern call for embracing ambiguity as an intellectual value, but this is, as Bauer notes, the less common position. See his "In Praise of Ambiguity," in Craig J. N. de Paulo, Patrick Messina, and Marc Stier (eds), *Ambiguity in the Western Mind* (New York: Peter Lang, 2005), pp. 15–34.

124. One interesting connection here is that between disenchantment and opposition to ambiguity. An ambiguous world is also an enchanted one—where one is not forced to settle on one mode of explanation or one narrative but is allowed the magic of combining cause and genesis. Arguably, Bauer's hypothesis that modernity is linked to a high intolerance of ambiguity goes hand in hand with debates over "disenchantment."
125. The titles are all given in (my) translation. I list the publications in Turkish in the order mentioned: Recep Alpyağıl, *Derrida'dan Caputo'ya: Dekonstrüksiyon ve Din* (İstanbul: İz Yayıncılık, 2010); Şaban Ali Düzgün, *Çağdaş Dünyada Din ve Dindarlar* (Ankara: Lotus Yayınevi, 2012; 2014); İlhami Güler, *Direniş Teolojisi* (Ankara: Ankara Okulu, 2010; 2011; 2015) and his *Dine Yeni Yaklaşımlar* (Ankara: Ankara Okullu Basım, 2011; 2014); Şinasi Gündüz, *Küresel Sorunlar ve Din* (Ankara: Ankara Okulu, 2005; 2010); Yaşar Nuri Öztürk, *Deizm: Tanrı, Akıl ve Ahlaktan Başka Kutsal Tanımayan İnanç* (Istanbul: Yeni Boyut, 2015); Burhanettin Tatar, *Felsefi Hermenötik ve Yazarın Niyeti: Gadamer versus Hirsch* (Ankara: Vadi Yayınları, 1999); and Zeki Özcan, *Teolojik Hermenötik* (Istanbul: ALFA Yayınları, 1998; 2000).
126. The Turkish original: *Din ve Modernizm*, 6th edn (Istanbul: Çıra Basın Yayın, 2012).
127. Again, the Turkish publications are as follows: Caner Taslaman, *Modern Bilim Felsefe ve Tanrı* (Istanbul: İstanbul Yayınevi, 2015); Tülin Bumin, *Tartışılan Modernlik: Descartes ve Spinoza* (Istanbul: Yapı Kredi Yayınları, 1996; 2015).
128. For instance, see the work of Adnan Aslan, *Religious Pluralism, Atheism and the Perennialist School: A Critical Approach* and Mehmet Bayrakdar, *Pascal's Wager: Betting on the Afterlife According to Ali, Ghazālī, and Pascal*. For more on these two authors, see chapter six, which includes edited sections from Taraneh Wilkinson, "Moderation and al-Ghazali in Turkey: Responses to Skepticism, Modernity and Pluralism," *The American Journal of Islamic Social Sciences* 32:3 (2015): pp. 29–43. The titles in Turkish are: Adnan Aslan, *Dinî Çoğulculuk, Ateizm ve Geleneksel Ekol: Eleştirel Bir Yaklaşım* (Istanbul: İSAM, 2010) and Mehmet Bayrakdar, *Pascal Oyunu: Hz. Ali Gazzâlî ve Pascal'a Göre Âhirete Zar Atmak* (Istanbul: İnsan Yayınları, 2013).

II

THE INDIVIDUAL AND AUTHORITY IN DIALECTICAL CONTINUITY

3

Alpyağıl's Case for Canon

Against all delicacy, it is far from an artificial synthesis; on the contrary it is creative.

—Recep Alpyağıl[1]

Beyond its original Christian context, the word "canon" broadly refers to the set of formative texts and accompanying concepts viewed as authoritative for an intellectual tradition—in this case Turkish Muslim intellectual tradition.[2] In this context, I define tradition by its appeals to these accepted texts and concepts, such as the Qur'ān, or even to a particular understanding of reason.[3] Authority is bound up with interpretation of these texts and concepts, and a successful interpretation is often marked by the authority it carries for others who identify as part of that same tradition. Canon, accordingly, entails not only the set of formative texts and concepts but also the process of validating authoritative interpretations of said texts and concepts within a tradition. A need to redefine and reexamine how authority and intellectual canon function bespeaks a crisis not only of authority but also of authenticity. As Turkish scholar Yasin Aktay writes, "Muslim society now no longer stands in an authentic condition isolated from the global impacts of Westernization."[4] If isolation is no longer a feasible or even authentic solution to crisis, then canon and authority will need to be rethought in relation to the challenges of modernity and "Westernization."

In Turkish theology, the concepts which inform authoritative interpretations of the Qur'ān and Prophetic tradition are drawn both from Muslim sources and from Euro-American intellectual sources. From this plurality of conceptual provenance arises the question of authenticity. Who determines the broader Turkish Muslim intellectual canon and on what terms? What counts as authentically Turkish and Muslim? To address these questions beyond the level of broad superficialities, I will focus on how one Turkish scholar's oeuvre both reflects the complexity of Turkish Muslim intellectual tradition and offers possible answers to its dilemmas. Recep Alpyağıl (b. 1977) is a Turkish theologian and philosopher of religion at Istanbul University's Theology Faculty. His work accords special significance to the question of "authenticity," particularly when it comes to matters of intellectual authority in Turkey.

In Alpyağıl's work authority, authenticity, and intellectual canon all go hand in hand. Across his oeuvre, he takes up the possibility and conditions of an authentically Turkish philosophy of religion and does so by arguing for an inclusive, multifaceted canon of legitimate sources for philosophy, inviting a veritable dialectic among potentially distinct intellectual traditions. Alpyağıl's creative and inclusive engagement with multiple authoritative traditions makes his work a prime example of how Turkish theology cannot be reduced to old dichotomies. His fundamental case is that an authentically Turkish (and Muslim) philosophical canon should *de facto* include a multiplicity of authoritative traditions. Alpyağıl's inclusive canon has implications for the role of the individual Turkish Muslim who seeks to engage this project of authentic philosophy of religion. With an inclusive and dialectical vision of what counts as authentic canon, this individual must reconstitute her own sense of continuity with an Islamic and Turkish past as well as future. Alpyağıl's quest for authenticity is at heart a call for the renegotiation of Turkish Muslim intellectual canon.

This chapter takes up the work of Recep Alpyağıl on issues of intellectual authority and canon. In making the case for individual authority, this chapter will lay out how Alpyağıl frames the problem of philosophy of religion in Turkey, his choice of Paul Ricoeur as an entry point for reclaiming the religious dimensions of philosophy, and his case for an inclusive canon. In exploring Alpyağıl's case for an inclusive canon in Turkish philosophy of religion, I take up the question as to why such a canon is needed in the first place. To answer this question, the discussion delves into the interrelatedness of authority, authenticity, and canon in Alpyağıl's work by building a case for the role of individual authority amid an authentic and inclusive intellectual canon.

The role of the individual, as I will treat in more depth in the following chapter, is central to Alpyağıl's case for authenticity.

At the start of this inquiry, I identified something I call the dialectical threefold schema, which I argue is a hallmark of much Turkish theology. This dialectical threefold schema is characterized by an ongoing and dynamic negotiation of Turkish theological identity with at least three broad intellectual traditions: Ottoman/Turkish, classical Arabic, and Western Christian. If this is the case, then how do Turkish theologians navigate claims to authority within such a dialectical threefold schema, marked as it is by competing authoritative intellectual traditions? I argue that Alpyağıl has addressed this issue in much of his own theological and philosophical output. The examination of Alpyağıl's case for an inclusive canon and individual authority takes up his explicit treatments of dialectical interplay between multiple authoritative traditions. While Alpyağıl does not use the language of "dialectical threefold schema," I argue that his project for an inclusive canon is, at heart, a case for the authenticity of Turkish theology's dynamic engagement with multiple traditions.

Alpyağıl recognizes the believing individual's dynamic relationship to sacred text, to tradition, to canons of authority, and to society. I argue that two common elements in each of these relations are their dynamism and reciprocity. For Alpyağıl, an individual is formed by scripture, tradition, various canons of authority, and the society she lives in;[5] however, an individual is never merely a product of these relations. As I will argue in the following chapter, for Alpyağıl, the individual exists not in a purely passive relationship to these outside sources, but in webs of ongoing dialectics, where she plays a defining though not absolute role.

Alpyağıl: An Introduction

Recep Alpyağıl (b. 1977) is a Turkish theologian and scholar of philosophy of religion. He completed his master's in philosophy of religion at the Ondokuz Mayıs Theology Faculty (2002) and went on to earn his doctorate in philosophy of religion at the Istanbul University Theology Faculty (2006). He has concentrated on philosophical hermeneutics and currently holds a post at Istanbul University Theology Faculty in philosophy of religion.[6] Alpyağıl has travelled extensively and has published in English as well as in Turkish. He often engages postmodern thought, with book titles including names and buzzwords like Wittgenstein, Derrida, Caputo, and "deconstruction." He is also known for his efforts to recover the Ottoman philosophical heritage and to found a modern Turkish philosophical tradition and for his endeavors to read classical Islamic thinkers in dialogue with postmodern thought.[7]

To better orient the reader, it may help to first take a broad overview of Alpyağıl's oeuvre along with some of his main conceptual starting points. Alpyağıl has worked extensively on philosophical issues related to Qur'ān hermeneutics. In his book *Whose History Which Hermeneutic? Essays on the Way to Understanding the Qur'an* (2003),[8] Alpyağıl expressly grapples with the "linguistic turn"—especially its consequences for sacred scripture.

As with Düzgün, a figure discussed in chapters five and six, Alpyağıl's enemy is not modernity but rather reductionism. His goal is to de-mystify the discourse of hermeneutics so popular in Turkish academic discussions, without over-insisting on either objectivism or subjectivism. That is, Alpyağıl does not wish to eliminate either the subjective or objective elements which may factor into an interpretative act. He recognizes that a reader's context is essential to meaning, but he also does not wish to reduce textual interpretation to subjective relativity.

When it comes to textual interpretation, Alpyağıl does not have merely any text in mind. Since Alpyağıl deals extensively with religious hermeneutics in a Muslim Turkish theological context, he ultimately grapples with a common polemical question in Turkish theology and beyond: is the Qur'ān historical or not? His response, in short, is that there is no neat answer.[9] In refusing to offer a pre-packaged answer on the question of quranic historicity, Alpyağıl raises the call for Turkish thinkers and especially philosophers of religion to develop their own ideas on what critical historicism should even entail.[10] The questions surrounding Qur'ān hermeneutics need reframing. To this end, Alpyağıl remarks that many of the recent and contemporary Islamic debates on the historicity of the Qur'ān feed upon an inferiority complex vis-à-vis Western civilization and, as a result, calcify imported categories into simplistic understandings instead of fully engaging in a lively re-negotiation of said categories.[11] Because of this tendency, he explains, the frameworks of many Muslim discussions of historicity are not equipped to move Muslim thinkers forward into independent and creative approaches equipped to address religious and intellectual identity today.

As a way forward, Alpyağıl calls for reformulation of debates on historicity and advocates for a more integrated discipline of philosophy of religion.[12] In addition, Alpyağıl's broader contributions also serve to develop the idea of Ottoman/Turkish intellectual authority, reframing debates on historicity, fideism, rationalism as well as other touch-points of modernity.

In short, Alpağıl's aim is to reframe old discussions on many fronts. His is a holistic, open-ended project. His wider oeuvre reflects the double task of seriously engaging Western philosophical tradition(s) and of using resources from these traditions along with Ottoman resources to rethink the classical Islamic sources and Muslim intellectual tools. Throughout, Alpyağıl's work exemplifies a consistent endeavor to negotiate between extremes, ask better questions, avoid reductionism, and maintain as much critical distance to his subject as possible.[13] In this way, he offers an especially self-conscious and dialectical example of Turkish theology's threefold engagement with Turkish, broader Islamic, and Western sources. Not only this, he also suggests Turkish philosophy of religion's strength and authentic future lie in critically embracing this multi-tradition engagement.

The Problem of Philosophy of Religion in Turkey

In his book *The Possibility of Creating an Authentic Philosophy in Turkey and Philosophy of Religion: An Investigation into the Example of Paul Ricoeur* (2010),[14] Alpyağıl makes a case for an authentic philosophy of religion in Turkey. This does not mean he aims to introduce the discipline to Turkish academic theologies, since philosophy of religion is in no way new to Turkish academia. Philosophy of religion exists already as a recognized discipline in Turkish theology faculties today.[15] Nor is philosophy of religion new to Turkish academics generally.[16] In fact, during the mid-twentieth century it was Mustafa Şekip Tunç (1886–1958) who first used the expression "philosophy of religion" systematically in Turkish thought.[17] Alpyağıl instead draws attention to a perceived stagnation, specifically, of Turkish philosophy of religion—one bemoaned by at least some scholars since the mid-1980s.[18] Without claiming to solve the dilemma of founding an authentically Turkish philosophy, Alpyağıl nonetheless suggests that scholars have consistently framed this issue in ways that do not help move the discussion forward. For example, the question of whether or not the Ottomans had an authentic philosophical tradition is biased from the outset. Behind this question lurk the specters of Orientalism, post-colonialism, crisis, and rupture, which—as we will see—he constructively addresses.[19]

Although Alpyağıl does not attempt to introduce philosophy of religion to Turkish academies or theology faculties (since it already exists there), he nevertheless envisions a more integrated discipline. This need for integration stems in large part from the structure of Turkish theology faculties themselves. In Turkish theology faculties there is a division between "philosophy of religion" (*din felsefesi*) and "Islamic philosophy" (*İslam felsefesi*).[20] A scholar specialized in one discipline will not necessarily be conversant in the other discipline. Philosophy of religion generally involves a curriculum built around European and Anglophone texts; whereas Islamic philosophy focuses on classical Islamic thought and increasingly on later Ottoman thought.[21] Given this compartmentalization, the very questions of canon and authority in Turkish theology must somehow address the resulting academic divide. Many of Alpyağıl's writings integrate the two disciplines, and he actively argues for a greater inclusion of Islamic texts within the to-date fairly Eurocentric discipline of philosophy of religion.[22] His own work represents an example of the kind of integration of traditions for which he argues, and the question of authenticity arises precisely amid this call for an integrated canon.

Authenticity of an academic discipline and of an entire intellectual canon raises the question as to which texts and whose academies carry authority. In his work *The Possibility of Creating an Authentic Philosophy in Turkey and Philosophy of Religion*, "authenticity" (*otantisite/otantiklik*) is Alpyağıl's word and discussion of choice. As a rough synonym to the European-derived *otantik* (authentic), he also uses the Arabic-derived *sahici*, which translates to "authentic" or "genuine." Alpyağıl's investigation into what makes a tradition authentic is both deconstructive vis-à-vis European intellectual heritage and constructive vis-à-vis the Ottoman/Turkish intellectual tradition.[23] He gestures toward the inevitable rootedness of the European and Anglophone philosophical tradition in its own specific religious heritage—regardless of whether it labels itself secular or atheist.[24] Here Alpyağıl's main argument is as follows: if those in European and Anglophone countries connect to their religious roots while doing philosophy, why cannot this also be the case in Turkey? Further, he urges Turkish intellectuals to not be satisfied with imitating Western philosophy or teaching philosophy of religion according to the perceived Western canon. Instead, scholars in Turkey should dare to discover their own approaches and canon(s) for doing philosophy of religion.

But what does the term "authentic" mean for Alpyağıl? He equates authenticity with self and selfhood.[25] The self that acts, owns, and moves with independence—that is, embodies an internal agency rather than an external one—is an authentic self.[26]

In addition to a sense of internal agency, authenticity also entails rootedness. Yet, Alpyağıl does not associate authenticity with a simple return to the past or a mere retrieval of lost identity. He cautions that authenticity is not something simply retrieved:

> However, it should not be forgotten that authenticity is not a pre-existing place that we can return to, it is [rather] an identity which we will be able to discover.[27]

Authenticity is active and creative. It is something a person moves towards and discovers—not something a person finds and uncovers. This does not mean that authenticity disregards the past. On the contrary, authenticity is profoundly rooted in the past. Alpyağıl goes on to define being authentic as having a clear root, not cut off. "*Authenticity* in its most basic and historical sense is related to having root or origin," he elucidates, "Accordingly, it can be said of *something with a clear root* that it is *authentic*."[28] At the same time, authenticity is not something that already exists, nor something that can be returned to.[29] Authenticity is again something that must be discovered, perhaps even constructed. This authentic self-discovery does not happen in a vacuum, however. Part of being authentic means having a living relation to place.[30] For Alpyağıl, authenticity is neither a myopic return to an idealized past nor a naïve attempt to start anew without sense of rootedness in the past. Authenticity—as Alpyağıl uses the term—lives in the present, is connected to the past, and looks creatively towards the future.

Alpyağıl also sees a certain irony in using the word *otantisite*, or authenticity. He writes:

> It is interesting that one of the ironies facing this topic is our not yet having an authentic term to discuss authenticity. In other words, with respect to the present discussion, the very term 'authentic' is not authentic.[31]

The Turkish words for authenticity are borrowed from French (*authenticité*) or constructed from Arabic roots (*saḥīḥ*): *otantik/otantisite* and *sahici*, respectively. In the context of an authentic Ottoman/Turkish philosophical tradition, Alpyağıl observes the very word he uses to frame this discussion (authentic/*otantik*) does not live up to its own meaning. It is a European import.

Nonetheless, authentic philosophy is a philosophy of roots.[32] While Alpyağıl makes a case for consciously recognizing Turkish and Islamic roots in Turkey's philosophical tradition, the fact of the matter is that philosophy of religion in Turkey involves European and Western roots. More precisely, contemporary philosophy of religion in Turkey takes its roots predominantly from Western sources. Alpyağıl argues for a stronger integration of Ottoman/Turkish and Islamic roots into this conversation. This means he must make the case for including more Islamic and Ottoman sources into debates and discussions that have hitherto been dominated by Western voices and framed in Western terms. In other words, his project entails a healthy admixture of rootedness.

Authenticity is not merely a concern in the Turkish context. Syrian scholar Aziz al-Azmeh (b. 1947) characterizes questions of authenticity in the Islamic world as a reaction to claims to universality posited by the "West" in the colonial encounter. According to al-Azmeh, this reactionary view of authenticity treats history as unreal, in the sense of not exhibiting real change. He criticizes this notion of authenticity as something constructed and negatively bound up with the reaction to Orientalism and Western cultural hegemony. In this reactionary model of authenticity, authenticity is a recovery of lost continuity, but, since history is not real, authenticity is also a denial of lost continuity. History is only understood as privation and corruption of the real, followed by a restoration of the real. What is real and authentic has an essence which the historical can at best obscure or obfuscate. This essentialism posits the other (i.e., those outside of authentic tradition) as accidental, and in this way reactionary forms of authenticity defend against the claim to universality posited by the "West," that is, by flagging the West's claim to universality as accidental.[33]

Because of the reactionary nature of existing discourses of authenticity, "the notion of authenticity is predicated on the notion of a historical subject which is at once self-sufficient and self-evident. Its discourse is consequently an essentialist discourse, much like the reverse it finds in Orientalism . . ."[34] Similar to Western discussions of the primitive and cultural otherness, "the discourse on authenticity postulates a historic subject which is self-identical, essentially in continuity over time, and positing itself in essential distinction from other historical subjects."[35] In this model of authenticity, change is seen as negative, contingent, inessential, and as a sign of outside interference.[36] While this may hold true for some Turkish debates on Turkish Muslim identity, this does not necessarily hold for Alpyağıl. Alpyağıl urges the Turkish philosopher of religion to move beyond mere retrieval and he does not dismiss "Western" sources as merely accidental or as inessential interference.

What then is the place of philosophy in Turkey and what does it reveal about Turkish notions of authencity?[37] In accordance with his project of forming a new, integrated, and more fruitful relationship with Ottoman/Turkish and Islamic roots, Alpyağıl argues for the necessity to retrieve in order to construct anew. Why is it still necessary to retrieve the Ottoman intellectual tradition? For Alpyağıl, the problem is that Turkish intellectuals have not been looking for a philosophy of their past due to a bias drawn from Orientalist views and perpetuated by Turkish scholars: the assumption that the Ottomans had no philosophical tradition.[38]

Alpyağıl starts by criticizing the assumptions behind asking whether or not there is a philosophy native to Turkey. He does not simply ask, "Does Turkey have its own particular philosophy?" His approach is subtler. He opens with this question in order to address its underlying assumption and to challenge it.[39] Similar assumptions date back as far as the early twentieth century. In the first decades of the Turkish Republic, it was commonplace for people to ask whether Turkey had its own particular brand of philosophy, and the standard response was to conclude in the negative.[40] Yet, asking whether Turkey or its Ottoman past had its own authentic brand of philosophy perpetuates a circular debate. This circular debate has continued to circle up to the present day, as Alpyağıl explains, painting the picture of a Turkish academy still stuck asking the wrong questions. As a way forward, he proposes one path out of this *cul-de-sac*—learning to ask new questions. Asking new questions is crucial for arriving at new answers.

The question of philosophy in Turkey naturally ties into a wider web of questions, particularly those involving identity in the wake of Western colonial mentalities. This is not surprising, as even European and Anglophone philosophies are bound up with questions that are colored by historical contingincy or questions that bleed into other disciplines. So, for a start, instead of asking *whether* Ottomans did philosophy, Alpyağıl suggests asking *what sort* of philosophy they practiced.[41] Instead of providing an outright answer, he underscores the significance of breaking out of limiting discussions. His aim is not to exhaust the topic, but to look at a seemingly static discussion from fresh angles. To the forefront of this exercise in seeking fresh angles, Alpyağıl brings the example of Paul Riceour.

Paul Ricoeur as an Example of Integrating Religious Tradition as a Source of Authentic Philosophy

His reader may find it curious that Alpyağıl begins with a European philosopher in order to make the case for an authentic Turkish philosophy. Yet, Alpyağıl is ultimately arguing for an inclusive canon that draws critically and freely from Western and non-Muslim examples even as it roots itself more authentically in Islamic sources. In this way, Alpyağıl's use of Paul Riceour supports the idea of a more inclusive Turkish philosophical canon. He has chosen the example of Paul Ricoeur to argue that *any* authentic philosophical tradition is legitimately and inevitably rooted in the *religious* tradition(s) and text(s) out of which it developed. Once the reader can accept this as a fundamental premise, Alpyağıl then makes the parallel case for including the Qur'ān along with classical Islamic and Ottoman traditions as legitimate sources for an authentic Turkish philosophy of religion.

Alpyağıl works with English, limited French, and numerous Turkish translations of Ricoeur's oeuvre.[42] Many of Ricoeur's works were published in Turkish translation in the late 2000s.[43] With recent significant translations of Ricoeur's work into Turkish, this also means that at least some of Ricoeur's work is directly accessible for Turkish scholars and readers who cannot read the French hermeneutical philosopher's works in English (or French). While it is hard to estimate the impact of these translations, it is still worth noting that the efforts to translate Ricoeur into Turkish are relatively recent and extensive, making Alpyağıl's choice of example timely.

Alpyağıl also explicitly addresses the reasons behind this choice of Ricoeur as an example for Turkish philosophy of religion. For Alpyağıl, Ricoeur's contribution to philosophy of religion serves as a positive case for the value of an inclusive yet still authentic philosophical canon. This inclusive move is one of the first steps needed to reconstruct broken ties with the past.[44] Alpyağıl stresses that Paul Ricoeur is a perfect case example, because, within European and Anglophone academies, he helped hoist philosophy of religion into mainstream philosophical discourse.[45] Alpyağıl rightly affirms that, for Ricoeur, thinking philosophically always entails thinking religiously.[46] Ricoeur's significance in pioneering the practice of tearing down walls between philosophy, hermeneutics, and theology elucidates in part Alpyağıl's own vision for the future of philosophy of religion and broader philosophical discussions in Turkey.[47] Alpyağıl writes:

> In [the context of] philosophical endeavors in Turkey, new topics are needed—topics that will speed up the development of philosophy and open up the possibility to establish an authentic [sense of] identity. And this will be possible through efforts to problematize the boundaries between religion and philosophy as in the example of hermeneutics. The best example of this is hermeneutic literature in contemporary philosophy.[48]

In other words, Alpyağıl thinks that Turkish philosophy needs new subjects, new horizons to establish itself authentically. For him, hermeneutics has problematized in exemplary fashion the boundaries of Western philosophy.[49] This is an example he wishes to take up and apply to a Turkish context.

To better grasp how Ricoeur's work speaks to the situation in Turkey, it is important to clarify two things. First, Alpyağıl speaks of crisis and rupture in the context of Turkey's intellectual tradition. Second, Alpyağıl approaches the Western tradition as a diverse whole that enjoys continuity between its past and present. For Alpyağıl, Ricoeur is a bridge as well as an indication of rupture within the Western canon—his work is an effort to expose and validate the seams intertwining theological and philosophical reflection. In parallel fashion, Alpyağıl thinks that Ricoeur represents a rupture as well as a bridge for the Turkish intellectual canon. On the one hand, Ricoeur is a European thinker whose Judeo-Christian heritage has been minimized in Turkish philosophical discussions, a double rupture, an authority from outside and an example of a thinker stripped of his roots. On the other, his integrated philosophy of religion is also a bridge—an example for greater integration of religious tradition and philosophical thought in Turkish philosophy.

How exactly does Alpyağıl frame the issue of rupture and crisis? Alpyağıl recognizes that the Turkish philosophical landscape still reels from a historical rupture with its Ottoman and, to some extent, its broader Islamic heritage. Turkey is, of course, not the only place to feel the effects of rupture and crisis. The effect of colonial encounters with the West has reached many non-Western cultures. Yet, how does one respond to crisis and rupture? Alpyağıl articulates a need to recognize and re-narrate. For a start, he reads the Tanzimat reforms (1839–76) as a typical manifestation of a dualistic East–West encounter.[50] This sort of dualism is harmful when it leads to false paradoxes and circular reasoning. For this reason, his aim is not to react against Western influence, but rather to find ways to reclaim agency in the process of re-narrating the Ottoman and Turkish encounter with the West. He also stresses the necessity of retrieval, with the remark, "Frankly speaking, it is necessary to re-establish the broken bridges and ruptured ties, if we ever wish to establish an authentic philosophy."[51] However, this would require a broader understanding of philosophy of religion. He clarifies, "[I] do not mean 'philosophy of religion' in a narrow sense, [but rather] in a broader, comprehensive sense."[52] Alpyağıl criticizes the narrow understanding of Turkish philosophy of religion, which relies heavily on Western academic discussions. So doing, Alpyağıl sheds light on how philosophy of religion as it is still practiced in Turkey fails to be authentically Turkish. What would render philosophy of religion in Turkey truly authentic, according to Alpyağıl, would be to embrace an inclusive intellectual canon and affirm the importance of individual efforts to creatively navigate this wider, richer canon. Alpyağıl faults Turkish academic theology, and its philosophy of religion, for failing to embrace its true potential for complexity and independent creativity. Turkish philosophy of religion may fall short of being truly dialectical and remain stuck in stagnant duality, but Alpyağıl presents efforts to change this. To move forward, he proposes a dialectic between philosophy and philosophy of religion. Why philosophy of religion? Philosophy of religion has the potential "to build bridges."[53]

In comparison to Western examples of intellectual continuity, Alpyağıl's treatment of Turkish philosophical authenticity strongly suggests that Turkey still stands in the wake of rupture with its own tradition. By contrast, he views academic cultures representative of the Western intellectual tradition as enjoying a relatively less problematic relationship to their past.[54] Not only this, he notes the ease with which Muslim thinkers make use of Western sources compared with the relative paucity of Islamically grounded philosophies:

> Decades after colonialization, the [continued] absence of authentic intellectual approaches directed towards Muslims, apart from superficial attributions, is a very surprising (!) situation.[55]

In his view, compared to Western (included with this: Christian) philosophers who enjoy relatively extensive recourse to their intellectual traditions, Muslim thinkers are far less likely to build philosophical approaches seriously grounded in Islamic traditions.[56]

In this discussion, Alpyağıl addresses the disparity between rupture and continuity. He shows there has arisen a double standard regarding whose religious tradition is considered a legitimate part of philosophical knowledge-production. As a prime example of this double standard, he points to Jesus and the Torah as inexhaustible sources for Western (including secular) thought even today.[57] By contrast, philosophy of religion in Turkey does not necessarily draw on Islamic sources with confidence.[58] To bring out the two-sided logic of this double standard, he points out that if philosophy is only legitimate when it is not grounded in religious tradition, then most medieval philosophy (and presumably many modern thinkers) are not real philosophers. That is to say, St. Augustine, St. Thomas, Ibn 'Arabī, and Ibn Sīnā—all of whom write from a context of religious conviction—are not real philosophers.[59] In this way, Alpyağıl uses an *ad absurdum* argument to highlight the fact that it is unrealistic to consider philosophy legitimate only when it has been stripped and sanitized of its religious roots. This stripping and sanitizing is asymmetrical, leaving Western philosophical roots in much more legitimate contact with their Christian elements than in the Muslim case, since, in his opinion, there historically has been much less concern for such sanitization when it comes to members of the Western philosophical canon.[60]

Alpyağıl's fundamental stance is that genuine philosophy, whatever the form, will pass through religion. The task is to apply this premise to Islamic sources in addition to Christian and other Western sources already part of the Turkish philosophical discussion. The precise admixture of this complex set of sources is in large part left up to the discretion of the individual philosopher. On this point, Alpyağıl firmly asserts:

> the path of an authentic philosophy, in some form—a form determined by the philosopher—will pass through religion.[61]

In sum, not only does Alpyağıl foresee the future of authentic philosophy as intricately bound up with its religious roots, he also warns that trying to deny these roots results in a harmful and stultifying form of intellectual reductionism. In short, when philosophy does not take account of religion, philosophy degenerates into reductive tendencies. It is this sort of reductionism which Alpyağıl considers an enduring obstacle in Turkey. Alpyağıl contrasts his assessment of philosophy of religion in Turkey with Ricoeur's example: Ricoeur's synthesis is neither superficial nor reductive—and for this reason it is precisely the sort of synthesis that interests Alpyağıl.[62]

One tactic Alpyağıl suggests for sidestepping stultifying reductionism is moving beyond false dichotomies and expanding past rigid binaries. In short, Alpyağıl argues for the value of moving past *either/or*. Such a move is especially important in the context of Turkish academia. Yet, how does this pan out in the concrete? Moving past *either/or* roadblocks entails reframing discussions to address issues in all their complexity. In Alpyağıl's diagnosis, Turkish philosophers have not identified the real problems and, as a result, Turkish philosophers are still as stuck as they were in 1986.[63] Not only that, Turkish philosophers are vividly conscious of being stuck. Yet, awareness of stagnation does not suffice for overcoming it. Turkey remains stuck, he argues, due to an oversimplification of the problem; it is not, as many try to frame the issue, a question of religion vs. science.[64] The religion vs. science dichotomy is a classic instance of an *either/or* mentality. Instead of approaching things with an *either/or* mentality, Alpyağıl proposes working through issues with a *both/and* attitude:

In the author's opinion, philosophy of religion's continuously thinking in terms of *both/and* could build a bridge across this compartmentalization.[65]

In other words, it is time for Turkish philosophy to get beyond the false assumptions that one can do philosophy without religion or that one cannot be *both* religious *and* a bona fide philosopher. It is possible to be *both* religious *and* think philosophically.[66] Specifically, it is possible to be Muslim and a philosopher, or use Muslim sources to build an authentic philosophy. To support his suggestion for a *both/and* mentality, Alpyağıl uses Ricoeur to stress antireductionism and openness.[67] In addition to a stress on openness, Alpyağıl insists that a theological turn is not necessarily a reactionary turn. It is in fact the reactionary turn of *either/or* that Alpyağıl spends so much intellectual effort trying to avoid. Theology is neither monolithic nor mere reaction—it too is in constant development. In a helpful visualization, he employs Ricoeur's language of circle to show how turning to theology means creative change, motion forward and plurality. Alpyağıl playfully explains:

> Theology, however, is not *a unity* such that it returns [to a point] and stops. Rather, it turns and turns, halts somewhere, and where it stops is never where it began—much has changed.[68]

This process of turning is also a process of change and collision. This sort of turning is an open circle—like a hermeneutic circle. Speaking of circles and centers, Alpyağıl also holds that despite Ricoeur's role as an example for philosophy of religion and even despite Ricoeur's own awareness of the dangers of Eurocentrism, Ricoeur still remains relatively Eurocentric.[69] Alpyağıl cites Ricoeur, who states, "In emphasizing the importance of the Greek or Judaeo-Christian traditions, we often overlook the radically heterogenious discourses of the Far East . . ."[70] and Alpyağıl asks whether it is not helpful to take this oversight more seriously.[71]

With Ricoeur's comments in mind, Alpyağıl looks at the languages, narratives, discourses, and traditions out of which specific philosophies emerge.[72] The question of language presupposes the texts which shape and wield authority in language. Thus, it is not merely a question of whose language but also a question of whose texts. In this light, he goes on to propose that Ricoeur's case for intertextuality (*metinlerarasılık*) be expanded beyond the European canon—especially since intertextuality can entail deep theological dimensions.[73] Being a text entails that in being read it is read in relation to other texts. This process is for Alpyağıl a hallmark of intertextuality.[74] As Alpyağıl notes, it is difficult to speak of real and robust intertextuality if the canon considered remains limited to Judaeo-Christian texts.[75]

For those among his Muslim readership afraid that this proposed soup of intertextuality will boil down to pure subjectivism, Alpyağıl retorts that reacting defensively against subjectivism only creates another form of subjectivism.[76] Intertextuality is a question of hermeneutics and addresses objective realities. Since everything humans do is through language, hermeneutics is what brings things together, uniting distinct discourses into one shared consideration. Hermeneutics is thus pervasive in its scope. Accordingly, it is neither a threat nor a perfect solution. On this he refers to Zeki Özcan, one of the pioneers of theological hermeneutics in Turkey. Z. Özcan explains that hermeneutics is neither Aladdin's lamp nor Pandora's Box but something extremely useful.[77] Why is hermeneutics useful in this case? Hermeneutics, Alpyağıl explains, is "a point of convergence" (*bir kesişme noktası*) between theology and philosophy.[78] In the space between theology and philosophy, Alpyağıl grants a positive function to both hermeneutics and to philosophy of religion.[79] He suggests that, "hermeneutics could be a meeting point between religion and philosphy for an authentic philosophy. I think that the best candidate for establishing this meeting point is philosophy of religion."[80]

What sort of questions would or could an authentic Turkish philosophy address? As one possible application of theological hermeneutics, Alpyağıl brings up the issue of quranic historicity. He criticizes the banality of Turkish discussions on quranic historicity, citing medieval Muslim thinker al-Ghazālī (d. 1111) to support his own position—a position that also takes Ricoeur's hermeneutics of revelation (*vahyin hermenötiği*) as a helpful reference point.[81] Regarding hermeneutics of revelation, Ricoeur emphasizes that when it comes to revelation, the believer's textual perspective allows for more "pluralism" and "polysemy" than the perspective of a philosopher trying to formulate a "monolithic" concept of revelation.[82] This emphasis on plurality exhibits strong parallels with Alpyağıl's work. Specifically, Alpyağıl insists, with Ricoeur, that the reader of the text is not master of the text, but a person open to being acted on by the text.[83]

Sacred scripture, or revelation, walks ahead of the reader open to encounter. This means that revelation works forward into the future, and as such is not something static. The text is always one step ahead of its commentator.[84] In this spirit, he baptizes Ricoeur's approach with some of al-Ghazālī's remarks in the *Niche of Lights*:

> One who considers the realities of these words may become bewildered by the multiplicity of the words and imagine many meanings. But one to whom the realities are unveiled *will make the meaning a root and the words a follower.* This situation is reversed in the weak, since they search for the realities from the words.[85]

Alpyağıl implies through al-Ghazālī's words that meaning lives and pours from revelation. This is a question of the direction and origin of meaning, where revelation always precedes and exceeds the believer's commentary or speculation. Revelation is not limited by one commentary or one interpretation. It opens up horizons in front of the reader, not as a fossil of history but as an ongoing address to the present moment. Using al-Ghazālī's analogy, just as the meaning is the root of the word, so too is revelation the living root of sacred commentary. In this context, Alpyağıl takes the phrase "believing to understand and understanding to believe" to denote not a fideist position but a dynamic (rather than objectified) relation to the text.[86]

In sum, Alpyağıl uses Ricoeur primarily as a starting point to engage and move beyond the (allegedly stalled) Turkish situation. Importantly, Alpyağıl takes pains to appreciate that while Ricoeur is known as a philosopher, Ricoeur also does serious theological work. Ricoeur holds the credentials of a philosopher and nevertheless remains in touch with and even builds philosophical reflections on Judeo-Christian roots. Ricoeur's example resists those who insist philosophy must steer clear of theology. Further, Ricoeur serves as a point of passage to talk about philosophy of religion in Turkey, treating him as an example rather than an absolute authority. Finally, Alpyağıl portrays Ricoeur as a voice calling for opportunity amid crisis.[87] Alpyağıl approvingly notes of Ricoeur, that he, "soundly draws together a number of opposing poles that seem distant from one another," and being philosophically equipped to deal with dichotomies and dialectics, Ricoeur "saw dilemmas as an opportunity and not as a crisis."[88] For Alpyağıl, just as Ricoeur saw dilemmas between theology and philosophy as opportunities, so too should Turkish philosophers of religion. Amidst a crisis of authenticity it is still possible to move beyond passivity, eclecticism, and false dichotomies to seize the chance to do something fresh and non-reductive. Let us pass now to the question of what an authentic Ottoman/Turkish canon looks like in practice.

Notes

1. Recep Alpyağıl, "Trying to Understand Whitehead in the Context of Ibn 'Arabi," in *Ishraq: Islamic Philosophy Yearbook No. 3* (Moscow: Vostochnaya Literatura Publishers, 2012), p. 223.
2. The Western Christian understanding of canon generally includes "an agreed list of authoritative sacred texts," as Diarmaid MacCulloch writes in his *Christianity: The First Three Thousand Years* (New York: Penguin Books, 2010), p. 127.
3. Daniel A. Madigan has compellingly argued against the simple equation of quranic revelation with notions of "text" or "book." Nevertheless, for the sake of simplicity, I use the term "text" broadly, as Alpyağıl does himself in his discussion of Paul Ricoeur and religious hermeneutics. See Daniel A. Madigan, *The Qur'ān's Self-Image* (Princeton: Princeton University Press, 2001); in this work he argues that the quranic use of the term *kitāb* cannot be equated with current understandings of "book."
4. Yasin Aktay, "The Historicist Dispute in Turkish-Islamic Theology," in Sinasi Gunduz and Cafer S. Yaran (eds), *Change and Essence: Dialectical Relations Between Change and Continuity in the Turkish Intellectual Tradition* (Washington, DC: The Council for Research in Values and Philosophy, 2005), p. 82.
5. The Turkish language does not have gender or gendered pronouns. For the sake of this discussion my default translation of "*o*" (he/she/it) is "she."
6. His educational background and academic position is posted on the Istanbul University Theology Faculty website: <http://ilahiyat.istanbul.edu.tr/?p=6485> (last accessed January 14, 2017).
7. On this, see his article on deconstruction. For his work in English, see Alpyağıl, "Derrida and Islamic Mysticism: An Undecidable Relationship," in Z. Direk and L. Lawlor (eds), *A Companion to Derrida* (Oxford: Wiley Blackwell, 2014), pp. 480–9. In Turkish, see Alpyağıl's book *Derrida'dan Caputo'ya Dekonstrüksiyon ve Din* [*From Derrida to Caputo: Deconstruction and Religion*] (Istanbul: İz Yayıncılık, 2007; repr. 2010). This work will reappear in chapter seven's discussion of skepticism.

8. Recep Alpyağıl, *Kimin Tarihi, Hangi Hermenötik? Kur'an'ı Anlama Yolunda Felsefesî Denemeler I* (Istanbul: İz Yayıncılık, 2003; repr. 2013). Cited as KTHH.
9. KTHH, p. 135.
10. KTHH, p. 136. Debates on historicism carry some history within Turkish theology faculties. For a thorough overview, see Yasin Aktay's "The Historicist Dispute in Turkish-Islamic Theology" in *Change and Essence*. In short, Aktay presents Turkey as a case of self-colonization, with Turkish Muslim theologians at the forefront of the challenges of modernity and specifically Ankara at the center of the polarizing historicist discussion. The mid-1980s onward saw many Turkish translations of non-Turkish Muslim views on the problem of historicity as applied to the Qur'ān, but wider attention was not given to some of these non-Turkish authors until the 1990s. Felix Körner has looked at the question of historicity in Qur'ān hermeneutics in the late 1990s and early 2000s.
11. KTHH, p. 146. I take up his critique of quranic historicity in Turkey below.
12. Alpyağıl is not the only philosopher of religion who thinks Turkish philosophy of religion is a discipline well-situated to address core challenges associated with modernity. Philosopher of religion Cafer S. Yaran, for instance, posits philosophy of religion as a crucial tool in questions of religion vs. science. Cafer S. Yaran, *Bilgelik Peşinde* [*In Pursuit of Wisdom*] (Istanbul: Ensar Neşriyat, 2011), p. 112.
13. KTHH, pp. 7–8.
14. The Turkish title: *Türkiye'de Otantik Felsefe Yapabilmenin İmkanı ve Din Felsefesi: Paul Ricoeur örneği üzerinde bir soruşturma* (Istanbul: İz Yayıncılık, 2010). Cited as TO.
15. The formal teaching of philosophy of religion in Turkish theology faculties started in the mid-1970s, according to Cafer S. Yaran. C. S. Yaran, "Non-exclusivist Attitudes towards Other Religions," in *Change and Essence*, p. 18.
16. While there was extensive intellectual exchange between European intellectuals and the Ottomans of the nineteenth century, this exchange continued on into the twentieth century. For a detailed account of the names and contributions of European scholars (including philosophers and scholars in the humanities) who sought refuge and employment at Istanbul University during the garrulous first half of the twentieth century, see Gürol Irzik, "Hans Reichenbach in Istanbul," *Synthese* 181 (2011): pp. 157–80.
17. TO, p. 29. See Mustafa Şekip Tunç, *Bir Din Felsefesine Doğru* [*Towards a Philosophy of Religion*] (Istanbul: Türkiye Yayınevi, 1959). For an earlier work of his on philosophy of religion, see Tunç, *Felsefe-i Din* [*Philosophy of Religion*] (Istanbul, 1927).

18. TO, p. 67.
19. Even as late as 2005, Turkish Muslim theologians themselves might take up the Oriental view that Ottoman thought made few if any original philosophical contributions. For instance, Ömer Aydın asserts that Ottoman madrasahs failed to make significant philosophical contributions without critically examining the criteria for judging a significant philosophical contribution in his "*Kalam* between Tradition and Change: The Emphasis on Understanding Classical Islamic Theology in Relation to Western Intellectual Effects," in *Change and Essence*, p. 106.
20. The division between Islamic philosophy and philosophy of religion struck me especially on my late 2015 visit to the Ankara Theology Faculty. In the faculty canteen, I had the pleasure of sitting with several graduate students and faculty. Some of us inquired about one another's research. In the process, it became clear that some of my references and questions were appropriate *either* for those in philosophy of religion *or* for those in Islamic philosophy. I asked about the division, and it was later confirmed to me by other theologians. There are some parallels between religion and theology in Anglophone academies, but the division here is also specific to Turkey and mapped out between two subdepartments nested under one shared department (i.e., The Department of Religious and Philosophical Sciences).
21. For a concrete sense of this division, visit the Ankara Theology Faculty website and click on Academic Departments (*Akademik Bölümler*) and you will see both Philosophy of Religion (*Din Felsefesi*) and Islamic Philosophy (*İslam Felsefesi*) listed as separate departments, each with their own faculty members. See the Ankara University Theology Faculty website: <http://www.divinity.ankara.edu.tr/> (last accessed September 17, 2018).
22. It may be worth noting that the Ankara University Theology Faculty page for the Department of Philosophy of Religion stresses the existence of the discipline among late Ottoman thinkers. Among those mentioned are Memduh Süleyman and Eşref Zade Muhammed Şevketi. See the Ankara University Theology Faculty webpage for the Department of Philosophy of Religion, <http://www.divinity.ankara.edu.tr/?page_id=234> (last accessed September 17, 2018).
23. By deconstructive and constructive, I do not mean critical and uncritical. Alternately, Alpyağıl positively appreciates many of the European and Anglophone authors which he treats and at the same time criticizes his own academy.
24. Şaban Ali Düzgün holds a comparable position. The notion that *all "Western" intellectual product reflects a Judeo-Christian heritage regardless and sometimes by virtue of its claim to secularism* seems to be, in various forms, a widely held

assumption in Turkish theology faculties. While this association is explored further in chapter seven, an analysis of the full extent of this association goes beyond the scope of this project.

25. TO, p. 168. He here says "*otantik*" is the same as "*kendi*." This second word can mean self and be part of the noun for selfhood, but it can also be used as a type of pronoun or possessive pronoun to emphasize personal agency. "I did it *myself*," would be, "*kendim* yaptım." Or "I live in my *own* house," would read, "*Kendi evimde oturuyorum*." Given the broad uses of "*kendi*" it is both hard to translate and important to stress that it designates personal agency, ownership, and independence along with the more abstract idea of selfhood.
26. TO, p. 168.
27. TO, p. 168: Turkish: "Ancak unutulmamalı ki, otantiklik, zaten varolan ve kendisine dönebileceğimiz bir yer değil, keşfedebileceğimiz bir kendiliktir."
28. TO, p. 33. Turkish: "*Otantiklik*, en basit ve tarihsel anlamıyla kök-le, kökenle alâkalıdır. Buna göre *otantik* olan, *belli bir kökü olana* denebilir."
29. TO, p. 37.
30. TO, p. 39.
31. TO, p. 33. Turkish: "İlginçtir, bu konuyu bekleyen en önemli ironilerden birisi de, otantikliği tartışmak için henüz otantik bir kavramımızın olmayışıdır. Yani, *authentic* kavramının kendisi konuştuğumuz bağlam için otantik değildir."
32. TO, p. 34. He also references Heidegger's "*Eigentlichkeit*" in the course of this discussion. While this does not play a major role in his overarching argument, he does note the German phenomenological roots of authenticity (*Eigentlichkeit*)— here as elsewhere displaying a broad awareness of Western philosophical tradition.
33. Aziz al-Azmeh, *Islams and Modernities*, 3rd edn (London: Verso, 2009), p. 105.
34. Al-Azmeh, *Islams and Modernities*, p. 99.
35. Al-Azmeh, *Islams and Modernities*, p. 100.
36. Al-Azmeh, *Islams and Modernities*, p. 100.
37. For the reader interested to know who he means when he addresses philosophers of religion in Turkey, Alpyağıl engages and draws on various Turkish philosophers who contribute to the discussion of hermeneutics and philosophy of religion. These include Zeki Özcan, Mehmet Aydın, Nilgün Toker, Zeynep Direk (Turkish translator of Levinas), Ahmet İnam, Cafer S. Yaran, Betül Çotuksöken, Latif Tokat, Mustafa Günay, Nurettin Topçu, Nermi Uygur, Arslan Kaynardağ, and Necip Taylan (TO, pp. 24, 38–53, 84, 89, 90, 93–4, 115, 119, 131–5, 140, 146). From an older generation active in the mid-twentieth century, in TO he cites Mübahat Türker Küyel (author of *Türkiye'de Cumhuriyet Döneminde Felsefe*

Eylemi, 1946) on pp. 83–4 and 122–3 as well as the later Doğan Özlem (who wrote *Tarih Felsefesi* in the 1960s, first published in 1984) in TO, p. 85, and in KTHH, p. 149. From those writing at the end of late Ottoman period and in the early days of the Republic, he cites Mustafa Şekip Tunç and Elmalılı Muhammed Yazır; he also cites İsmail Hakkı Baltacıoğlu, whose written production spans both the end of the Ottoman Empire to well into the late twentieth century (TO, pp. 14–15, 29–30, 52). This is not an exhaustive list but it is meant to be a starting point for orientation. Throughout his treatment Alpyağıl offers a critical digest of differing opinions. For instance, he notes Kaynardağ rejected the claim that there was any Ottoman philosophical thought (TO, p. 119), whereas the earlier Küyel thought there already existed a potential to create an authentic philosophy from Ottoman sources (TO, p. 122).

38. Recently scholars even outside the Turkish context have argued for a reassessment of Ottoman intellectual contributions. See, for instance, Khaled El-Rouayheb, *Relational Syllogisms and the History of Arabic Logic, 900–1900* (Leiden and Boston: Brill, 2010). In his introduction, El-Rouayheb challenges the previous scholarly trend to dismiss the post-thirteenth century Arabic logical tradition. The course of his argument stresses the ongoing contributions of Ottoman scholars to the Arab/Islamic philosophical tradition in logic.

39. TO, p. 17. Turkish: "Türkiye'de, kendine özgün bir felsefe var mıdır?"

40. TO, p. 38. As an example of the types of figures Alpyağıl may be broadly referencing, Macit Gökberk (1908–93) was a Turkish "Westernist" and was only interested in the intellectual contribution of the West, dismissing Islamic philosophy altogether. For a summary of his life and views, see Ömer Mahir Alper, "The Conceptions of Islamic Philosophy in Turkey," in *Change and Essence*, pp. 134–6.

41. TO, p. 18.

42. In TO, pp. 54–105, which looks in depth at the example of Paul Ricoeur, he cites Ricoeur's English works, limited reference to his French work, and multiple Turkish translations. These include *The Rule of Metaphor: Multi-disciplinary Studies of the Creation of Meaning in Language*, trans. Robert Czerny, Kathleen McLaughlin, and John Costello (Toronto: University of Toronto Press, 1977); *The Philosophy of Paul Ricoeur*, ed. Lewis Edwin Hahn (Chicago: Open Court, 1995); *Reading Ricoeur*, ed. David M. Kaplan (Albany: State University of New York Press, 2008); *Histoire et verité* (Paris: Seuil, 1964); *Être, essence et substance chez Platon et Aristote: Cours professé à l'université de Strasbourg en 1953–1954* (1957), now available in a 2011 edition by Seuil; and an extensive citation of *Yorumların Çatışması* [*The Conflict of Interpretations*], vols 1–2, trans.

Hüsamettin Arslan (Istanbul: Paradigma Yayıncılık, 2007 and 2009). See footnote below (n43) for Turkish translations of Ricoeur's works. I have not included the articles cited, since Alpyağıl sometimes cites a European/Anglophone article and gives a Turkish title without a translator.

43. These works include Paul Ricoeur, *Yorumların Çatışması: Hermenoytik Üzerine Denemler I* [*The Conflict of Interpretations* (1974)], trans. Hüsamettin Arslan (Istanbul: Paradigma Yayıncılık, 2009); *Zaman ve Anlatı: 2* [*Time and Narrative, Vol. II* (1984)], trans. Mehmet Rifat (Istanbul: YKY, 2009); *Çeviri Üzerine* [*On Translation*, trans. Eileen Brennan (2006)], trans. Sündüz Ö. Kasar (Istanbul: YKY, 2008); *Zaman ve Anlatı: 1* [*Time and Narrative, Vol. I* (1984)], trans. Mehmet Rifat and Sema Rifat (Istanbul: YKY, 2007); *Yorum Teorisi: Söylem ve Artı Anlam* [*Interpretation Theory: Discourse and the Surplus of Meaning* (1976)], trans. Gökhan Yavuz Demir (Istanbul: Paradigma Yay., 2007); *Yoruma Dair: Freud ve Felsefe* [*Freud and Philosophy: An Essay on Interpretation* (1970)], trans. Necmiye Alpay (Istanbul: Metis Yayınları, 2006). Not yet translated at the time of Alpyağıl's treatment of Ricoeur stands Paul Ricoeur, *Başkası olarak Kendisi* [*Oneself as Another*, trans. Kathleen Blamey (1992)], trans. Hakkı Hünler (Ankara and Istanbul: Doğubatı Yayınları, 2010). All but the last are either cited by Alpyağıl or included in his bibliography.

44. TO, p. 21.

45. TO, p. 20. It may be easier to claim that Ricoeur's work built bridges between philosophy of religion and theology than to speak of his impact on mainstream philosophical discourse. On Ricoeur's contribution to philosophy of religion, see, for instance, the relatively recent work: Boyd Blundell, *Paul Ricoeur Between Theology and Philosophy: Detour and Return* (Bloomington, IN: Indiana University Press, 2010). Kenneth A. Reynhout evaluates Ricoeur's contribution to interdisciplinarity in "Ricoeur and Interdisciplinarity," *Literature and Theology* 27 (2013): pp. 147–56. See also Justin Sands, "Passing through Customs: Merold Westphal, Richard Kearney, and the Methodological Boundaries between Philosophy of Religion and Theology," *Religions* 7 (2016), 83, doi:10.3390/rel7070083.

46. TO, p. 21. For this claim, he refers to Ricoeur, *Main Trends in Philosophy* (New York: Holmes & Meier Publishers, 1979). In this work, Ricoeur specifically addresses the question of philosophy of religion at the end of this work, pp. 372–92, a discussion which begins with the following statements: "It is impossible to treat the *foundations of humanism* without entering into the discussions in regard to the significance of the religious fact for philosophy. We have given our survey of these the title 'Philosophy of Religion,' which simply means: How is the

religious fact accounted for in philosophical discourse?" (p. 372). Ricoeur goes on to evaluate ontological, analytic, linguistic, and hermeneutical approaches to religion. Ricoeur recognizes that many reject a religious ground for humanism, but states there are also dissenting voices that affirm the necessity of a religious grounding of philosophical humanism; Ricoeur lists: Aldous Huxley, Paul Tillich, Reinhold Niebuhr, Gabriel Marcel, Karl Jaspers, and Arnold Toynbee (p. 391).

47. TO, p. 25.
48. TO, p. 26. Turkish: "Türkiye'deki felsefe faaliyetlerinde, felsefenin ivmesini hızlandıracak, otantik bir hüviyet kazanmasına imkân tanıyacak yeni mevzilere ihtiyaç vardır. Bu da, hermenötik örneğinde olduğu gibi dinle felsefe arasındaki sınırları sorunsallaştıran teşebbüslerle mümkün olacaktır. Bunun en güzel örneği çağdaş felsefedeki hermenötik literatürdür."
49. Within his treatment of the problematic bounds of Western philosophy, he mentions the divide between Continental and Analytic philosophy. It may be worth noting that this divide is also treated ambitiously in Ricoeur's *Main Trends in Philosophy*, which moves from a history philosophy of mathematics and logical positivism towards new cases for ontology, hermeneutics, and humanism.
50. TO, p. 28. The Tanzimat reforms were, among other things, an Ottoman attempt to modernize the empire and to legally establish greater equality of non-Muslim minorities in the Ottoman Empire. Alpyağıl does not elaborate on how he thinks the Tanzimat reforms manifested a harmful East–West encounter, but in their day the reforms were not viewed positively by all, often seen as a product of foreign influence.
51. TO, p. 28. Turkish: "Açıkçası kopan bağların, yıkılan köprülerin yeniden kurulması gerekmektedir, eğer otantik bir felsefenin ortaya çıkması isteniyorsa."
52. TO, p. 28. Turkish: "biz 'din felsefesi'ni dar bir anlamda değil, daha geniş ve kuşatıcı bir anlamda ele alıyoruz."
53. TO, p. 29.
54. While the question of modernity may be a question of rupture for many cultures, even Western cultures; arguably the rupture which Western societies experience is not always analogous to the rupture other societies subjected to Western cultural and technical norms have experienced. The discussion of double standards is drawn out, occurs most explicitly in TO, pp. 43–57, 67–80, 83–100, and continues as an ongoing thread. Alpyağıl does not offer counter examples to the assumption that Western cultures experience continuity; his focus instead lies with his Turkish audience.

55. TO, p. 101. Turkish: "Onca yıllık sömürünün ardından, Müslümanlara yönelik hâlâ, yüzeysel atıfların dışında, sahici düşünsel yaklaşımın olmaması çok şaşılacak (!) bir durumdur." In this same paragraph he contrasts this gap with the continued dependence of Muslim intellectuals on Western sources.
56. While there is a subdepartment in Turkish theology faculties devoted to Islamic philosophy, Alpyağıl does not seem satisfied with partitioning Islamic philosophical sources into a discipline sheltered from broader discussions of philosophy. Since he is advocating for an authentic, even creative, Turkish philosophy of religion, he addresses a broader audience—Turkish philosophers inside and outside of the theology faculties. His argument puts more emphasis on including Islamic sources in these broader philosophical discussions than on interjecting these broader discussions into the Turkish discussions of Islamic philosophy. This may be in large part due to the fact that he has been trained and holds a position in Philosophy of Religion and not Islamic Philosophy.
57. TO, p. 44. Another example he lists is secular French philosopher Alain Badiou's work on the Christian figure of St. Paul. See his *Saint Paul: la foundation de l'universalisme* (Paris: Universitaires de France, 2002). Alpyağıl cites this secular philosophical use of the Christian tradition in TO, p. 80. For a parallel viewpoint on the subject of Western continuity, Talal Asad writes: "The West defines itself, in opposition to all non-Western cultures, by its modern historicity. Despite the disjunctions of modernity (its break with tradition), 'the West' therefore includes within itself its past as an organic continuity." Talal Asad, *Genealogies of Religion* (Baltimore: The Johns Hopkins University Press, 1993), p. 18.
58. Alpyağıl notes of only one attempt in Turkey to create a philosophy based on the life and teachings of Muhammad—Cemil Sena's *Hz. Muhammed'in Felsefesi* [*The Philosophy of Muhammad*], 1984 (TO, p. 80).
59. TO, p. 45.
60. Though Alpyağıl does not mention this debate, the contemporary debates on whether medieval Muslim thinker al-Ghazālī (d. 1111) was a philosopher embody the double standard that Alpyağıl wishes to move beyond. For a concise literature review on varying scholarly opinions of al-Ghazālī's status in this regard, see the introduction of Frank Griffel's *Al-Ghazali's Philosophical Theology* (Oxford: Oxford University Press, 2009). In his introduction, Griffel treats and challenges al-Ghazālī's assumed role in the now heavily challenged theory of philosophical decline in post-classical Islam.
61. TO, p. 50. Turkish: "Kanaatimizce, sahici bir felsefenin yolu, bir şekilde, -ki şekline filozof karar verecektir-, dinden geçecektir."

62. TO, p. 27.
63. TO, p. 67. He cites Necla Arat et al., "Felsefe Forumu," *Felsefe Dergisi* 1 (1986): p. 103.
64. TO, p. 68. The temptation to frame religion and philosophy in terms of a question of religion versus science is a common tactic in Turkey (and elsewhere). Arguments and qualities of approaches vary from the infamous Adnan Oktar (also known as Harun Yahya) to serious academic theologians like Şaban Ali Düzgün, whom we will treat in the coming chapter. Adnan Oktar is famous for bringing a lawsuit against Richard Dawkins, who responded with a mocking public retort. Michael Ben Sims brought my attention to Oktar, whose caricatured take on religion and science has made prevalent appearances in Turkish popular media.
65. TO, p. 70. Turkish: "Kanaatimizce, sürekli *ve ile* düşünen din felsefesi bu bölünmüşlük arasında bir köprü kurabilecektir."
66. It is worthwhile noting that while Alpyağıl draws on Paul Ricoeur's work, there is another major European thinker who challenged the boundaries between theology and philosophy—Paul Tillich. While Paul Tillich is known in Turkish theology faculties, it is possible that Alpyağıl prefers Paul Ricoeur because Ricoeur made serious efforts to establish his legitimacy within the discipline of philosophy and so helped legitimize and bring awareness to the religious roots of philosophy. Paul Tillich, on the other hand, is more known for philosophical theology and for his contributions to theological discourse. It is worth noting that Zeki Özcan, whom Alpyağıl cites and sometimes relies on, translated some of Paul Tillich's works. Also, Şaban Ali Düzgün, whom we will treat in the next chapter, offers a brief treatment of Tillich's contribution.
67. TO, p. 71.
68. TO, p. 78. Turkish: "Oysa teoloji de *yek* değildir ki, döner, durur. Yani döner döner, bir yerde durur, durduğunda ise yer asla eski yer değildir, çok şey değişmiştir." The verb *dönmek* can mean "to turn" or "to return" in Turkish. I have translated it alternatively based on context. I have also translated "*yek*" or "one" as "a unity" for this context.
69. TO, p. 100. In this criticism, Alpyağıl cites Ricoeur, "The Creativity of Language," an interview with Richard Kearney. See Paul Ricoeur, "The Creativity of Language," in Mario J. Valdés (ed.), *A Ricoeur Reader: Reflection and Imagination* (Toronto: University of Toronto Press, 1991), pp. 463–81. In this interview, Ricoeur also takes up an evaluation of Lévi-Strauss. Riceour thinks Lévi-Strauss was right to designate some (non-Western) societies as "cold" societies who are

both resistant to historical and interpretive thought and to designate "Greek and Hebraic" along with "Western culture" as "hot" societies for whom interpretation and historicity are internal elements of meaning-making (p. 471). Though Alpyağıl does not cite this discussion from the same work, it supports Alpyağıl's criticism of Eurocentric aspects to Ricoeur's perspective.

70. Ricoeur, "The Creativity of Language," p. 473.
71. TO, p. 100.
72. TO, pp. 99–101.
73. TO, p. 101.
74. TO, p. 101.
75. TO, p. 102. This goes especially for philosophers of religion who are writing in a primarily Muslim context, i.e., the context in which Alpyağıl writes.
76. TO, p. 130.
77. TO, p. 131; Zeki Özcan, *Teolojik Hermenötik*, 2nd edn (Istanbul: ALFA Yayınları, 2000), xix–xx. Notably, Özcan begins the preface to the first edition of this work with a citation attributed to Newton, "The world is a book written in the language of hermeneutics." He begins with this in order to assert both the prevalence of hermeneutics in how we "read" the world and to affirm that meaning is not an individual human creation, rather it is handed down through culture. At the same time, to live means to play the game of assigning meaning to reality, suggesting subjectivity is not at odds with receiving what is handed down to the individual by culture. This discussion appears on pp. xvii–xviii of the second edition.
78. TO, p. 132.
79. TO, p. 133.
80. TO, p. 133. Turkish: "Hermenötik, otantik felsefe için, din ve felsefe arasındaki bir buluşma noktası olabilir. Bu buluşmayı sağlamaya en fazla aday olan, öyle zannediyoruz ki, din felsefesidir."
81. It is perhaps worthwhile speculating that Ricoeur's hermeneutics of revelation is especially suitable to a Turkish theological concept, in that Ricoeur expresses a desire to uphold reason and revelation without equating the two and condemns the Christian magisterium or church authority for the corruption of the concept of revelation. Paul Ricoeur expresses this in his "Toward a Hermeneutic of the Idea of Revelation," *Harvard Theological Review* 70 (1977): pp. 1–2. As we will see in the following chapter on Şaban Ali Düzgün's work, when approaching Christian thinkers, Turkish theologians tend to criticize church authority even when they appreciate other aspects of Christian thought.

82. Ricoeur, "Toward a Hermeneutic of the Idea of Revelation," p. 3. Ricoeur also writes (and this seems to lie at the core of his argument) that rather than referring to speculative thought, "A hermeneutic of revelation must give priority to those modalities of discourse that are most originary within a community of faith" (p. 15). The modalities Ricoeur has in mind are prophetic, narrative, prescriptive, wisdom, and hymnic discourses.
83. TO, p. 137. Ricoeur deals with this question of "actant" (agent) and text in several ways—through modes of revelation, a critique of philosophical speculation's presumed role in receiving revelation, and a turn to the appeal of poetry. See Ricoeur's "Toward a Hermeneutic of the Idea of Revelation."
84. TO, p. 137. Among various works cited, Alpyağıl includes Paul Ricoeur, "Toward a Hermeneutic of the Idea of Revelation," in Lewis S. Mudge (ed.), *Essays on Biblical Interpretation* (Philadelphia: Fortress Press, 1980), pp. 73–118, a later printing of the original article.
85. Al-Ghazālī, *The Niche of Lights*, trans. David Buchman (Provo, UT: Brigham Young University Press, 1998), p. 26. Alpyağıl, on pp. 137–8 of TO, uses a Turkish translation of the same work: "Lafızlardan hakikatlere giden, onun kesretinden şaşkınlığa düşer ve manaların çokluğunu tahayyül eder. Ancak hakikatin kendisinde inkişaf ettiği kimse *manaları asıl ve lafızları bu manalara tabi kılar*. Zayıf olan kimse hakikatleri lafızlardan talep eder." Ebu Hamid Gazzali, *Mişkatü'l-envar: (Nurlar Feneri)*, trans. Süleyman Ateş (Istanbul: Bedir Yayınevi, 1966), p. 27.
86. TO, p. 137. Turkish: "anlamak için inanmakla, inanmak için anlamak." Elsewhere, Alpyağıl does a sustained critique of Christian fideism. This critique will be discussed under "Christianity and Skepticism" of chapter seven.
87. TO, p. 57.
88. TO, p. 57. Turkish: "[Ricoeur], birbirine uzak görünen birçok kutbu [. . .] sağlam bir biçimde kaynaştırmıştır. [. . .] O, ikilemleri bir kriz olarak değil her zaman bir şans olarak görmüştur."

4

Inclusions and the Role of the Individual

The previous chapter presented Alpyağıl's case for an inclusive and authentic canon. What does his inclusive canon say about Turkish theology? How does a believing individual navigate this canon? What is the believing individual's relationship to history, tradition, and sacred text? The present chapter will look at what Alpyağıl's inclusive canon entails and how it functions by taking up his views on narrative, history, and what it means to be in hypoleptic continuity with the past. As seen in the previous chapter, Alpyağıl freely engages with European/Anglophone, Turkish, Ottoman, and contemporary Arab and classical Islamic counterparts. This engagement makes Alpyağıl a strong example of how Turkish theology can move beyond dichotomies and creatively forge new theological insights with the help of a canon that integrates Turkish, Arab-Islamic, and Western sources. I argue that the role of the believing individual in mediating claims of authority stands at the center of Alpyağıl's creative push beyond stale dichotomies.

Beyond a Reactionary Canon—Inclusions and Re-narrations

Alpyağıl's proposed sense of intellectual canon is organic and inclusive. Alpyağıl does not argue for the value of Islamic and Ottoman sources in order to exclude what would be considered Western sources from an authentic Turkish intellectual canon. Instead, his project is one of restoration, integration, and re-narration. In the previous chapter, the discussion touched on the topic of crisis—a crisis of authenticity. Alpyağıl does not stop with a story of crisis; rather, he emphasizes the opportunity present in the ongoing crisis of identity and advocates for a positive search for authentic roots. The previous chapter focused primarily on Alpyağıl's use of Paul Ricoeur to argue for an inclusive Turkish canon of philosophy of religion. To better illustrate the concrete content of Alpyağıl's inclusive canon, this chapter offers a sample of the plurality of voices that both inform Alpyağıl's sense of intellectual canon and serve as his critical dialogue partners.

Canon

Canon refers to the set of formative texts and accompanying concepts viewed as authoritative for an intellectual tradition. In a situation like that of contemporary Turkish theology, discussions are often *de facto* intertextual, based on several distinct intellectual traditions. Yet, in the discipline of philosophy of religion, the authentic connection to formative Muslim texts is underdeveloped. As we saw in Alpyağıl's engagement with Paul Ricoeur, Alpyağıl asserts that for intertextuality to be truly intertextual, the canon of texts considered formative must expand to include those outside Western thought and religion. In particular, he makes a case for the legitimate inclusion of the Qur'ān and pious Muslim perspectives.[1] Alpyağıl does not make his case in a vacuum. He recognizes that Turkish scholars in academia have made some progress in re-appropriating their philosophical roots, yet he nevertheless stresses the continued need to wriggle out of the trap of Eurocentrism.[2] On this point, he defers to Mustafa Günay's relatively recent remarks on the matter. Mustafa Günay writes:

> It appears necessary for us to get out of Eurocentricism. [. . .] We must not think in terms of reducing philosophy merely to local and national elements.[3]

Yet, how does one ever break free from the nearly ubiquitous "circle" of Euro*centr*icism? Alpyağıl provides us with a simple yet appropriate visual model: the move from circle to *spiral*.[4] Let us keep in mind that Alpyağıl does not argue for an exclusive or reactionary philosophy of religion in Turkey.[5] On the contrary, he both engages and draws upon Western philosophical and theological traditions. A spiral contains within itself the motion of a circle, but unlike a circle it is not doomed to always repeat itself. The spiral also moves forwards and backwards. Alpyağıl refuses to limit authenticity to a static relation to the past, rejecting a purely circular understanding of authenticity. For him, authenticity and rootedness do not involve simply returning to a lost path; they are essentially motions that integrate past, present, and future, or motions that reach backwards and forwards to establish living continuity. Similarly, a spiral includes within it a circle but reaches out behind and in front of the circle. In this way, a spiral is an elegant symbol for Alpyağıl's take on authenticity, which requires both rootedness in the past and openness towards the new. In other words, the question of an authoritative canon among Turkish academic philosophers hinges on this image of simultaneous rootedness and openness, offering the Turkish philosopher of religion the chance to sublate the inevitable Eurocentric intellectual pressures into a higher, more authentic venture. Philosophy in Turkey, it appears, must pass through both religion and the Western canon. This passing through is productive, since it stops *neither* at static reactionary claims to an idealized past *nor* at the bounds of what is considered authorative in a Eurocentric intellectual canon.

A productive canon is both rooted and open. A canon can and should be this way, because the very notion of a tradition (which in turn informs the canon) is not monolithic. As Alpyağıl asserts, tradition is not a monolith; it is by nature multifaceted. He writes:

> [T]he relationship between problem and history is not one-dimensional or drawn only with one line—there are many dimensions and many lines. As a matter of fact, tradition itself is not a monolithic structure, it is a whole that is constantly changing, revolving and expressing plurality in relation to us.[6]

Here we see that Alpyağıl emphasizes the relational and organic aspect of tradition. Tradition exists in relation to communities. Communities have diverse and changing needs, and a living tradition can develop to meet these needs. On this note, he questions why Turkish philosophers do not include more thinkers of the Arabic and Ottoman traditions. Would this not better reflect the needs, history, and rootedness of their Turkish readers?

Alpyağıl advocates a practice of philosophy of religion that consciously includes a broad spectrum of Islamic sources. Some of his examples include Muslim thinkers whose legitimacy as authorities does not need as much arguing for, since they have already gained authority in the Western canon, like

Avicenna or Averroes. While Alpyağıl includes such figures, he does not limit his canon to these figures. In addition to stressing the importance of an Avicenna or an Ibn Rushd, he points to as yet untapped resources available to the Turkish canon, writing:

> Is there a place in philosophy departments close to those deservedly recognized as philosophers such as Augustine, Aquinas or Abelard for someone like a Taftazani or a Jurjani, who in fact are no less [deserving of such rank]? Or are the names Molla Fenari, Sarı Abdullah, Gelenbevi, Saçaklızade, etc.... remembered?[7]

Alpyağıl references post-classical Islamic figures less recognized by Western philosophy and includes among them Ottoman thinkers. To better appreciate the above comment, it is perhaps helpful to recall the division between Islamic philosophy and philosophy of religion in Turkish theology faculties—not to mention the existence of separate philosophy departments outside of theology faculties altogether. While there increasingly exist Turkish theologians who produce scholarly studies of such figures as listed above, what is lacking is an integration of these figures into the wider philosophical canon in Turkey. He cites Necla Arat, who pointed out in 1986 that philosophy done in Turkish philosophy departments is simply Western philosophy.[8] What was true for Turkish philosophy in the 1980s is, in Alpyağıl's view, still at least largely true in Turkish philosophy today. Alpyağıl argues for a change of this status quo.

According to Alpyağıl, an authentic philosophical canon in Turkey ought to include sacred scripture, classical Islamic thinkers, Ottoman thinkers, Turkish thinkers, and European/Anglophone thinkers. Among classical Islamic thinkers, he suggests incorporating those like al-Fārābī (d. 950/951), Ibn Sīnā (980–1037), and Ibn Rushd (1126–98) along with those who came after, like Fakhr al-Dīn al-Rāzī (1149–1210), Naṣīr al-Dīn al-Ṭūsī (1201–74), Ṣadr al-Dīn al-Qūnawī[9] (1210–74), and Athīr al-Dīn al-Abharī[10] (1200–64). He also points to the value of late Ottoman figures and thinkers of the early Republic like Ziyaeddin Fahri Fındıkoğlu (1901–74), Babanzâde Ahmed Naim (1872–1934), and Elmalılı Muhammed Yazır (1878–1942).[11] Alpyağıl does not have to argue for the inclusion of Western philosophers in Turkey's philosophical canon. Western thinkers have and continue to dominate the philosophical landscape in Turkey and they also play an integral role in Alpyağıl's own scholarly production.[12] Rather, the argument needs to be made for the inclusion of Muslim and Ottoman sources which currently are not formative voices in the Western philosophical canon, but which are nevertheless potentially authentic roots for contemporary Turkish philosophical production. For a visual illustration of Alpyağıl's inclusive canon, one need only to look at the cover of his book *Difference and Commentary: Philosophical Essays on the Way to Understanding the Qur'an*.[13]

From top left to bottom right (figure 4.1), the reader is met with a kaleidoscope of philosophical representatives: Avicenna (980–1037), Averroes (1126–98), the Moroccan Mohammed Abed al-Jabri (1935–2010), the Iranian Abdolkarim Soroush (b. 1945), the Egyptian Nasr Hamid Abu Zayd (1943–2010), the English Don Cupitt (b. 1934), the Scottish William Montgomery Watt (1909–2006), and the Austrian Ludwig Wittgenstein (1889–1951).[14] Notice that all but the first two names are figures from the twentieth and twenty-first centuries. The cover of this book visually illustrates his most basic move: affirming not a reactive canon of authority, but an inclusive canon of authority—one that freely mixes Ottoman, Arab, Persian, and European faces.

Alpyağıl not only argues for an inclusive canon across religious traditions, he also argues for inclusiveness of the canon within the Islamic philosophical tradition. In his book *Difference and Commentary*, he concludes by taking up Moroccan philosopher Mohammed Abed al-Jabri's (1935–2010) treatment of Eastern and Western Islamic traditions. Al-Jabri harshly criticizes what he sees as the Eastern Islamic branch of thought—believing it to be philosophically unsound due to its stress on mystical knowing (*'irfān*). Al-Jabri traces the root of the problem to Ibn Sīnā (also known as Avicenna) and al-Ghazālī, the latter of whom al-Jabri considered a blind follower of the former. Alpyağıl concedes to al-Jabri that Andalusian (here: Western Islamic) thought is valuable and representative of the Islamic tradition, but he also asks: do we have to throw out Ibn Sīnā?![15] Alpyağıl points to the Ottoman strands of the Avicennan tradition and asks whether these sources would not carry equal value or merit. He resists al-Jabri's insistence on dividing up Islamic tradition between East and West to decide which one is more authentic. For Alpyağıl, it is not necessarily a question of *either/or* when faced with Western and Eastern Islamic traditions; there is room for both.[16] By critically engaging al-Jabri on the

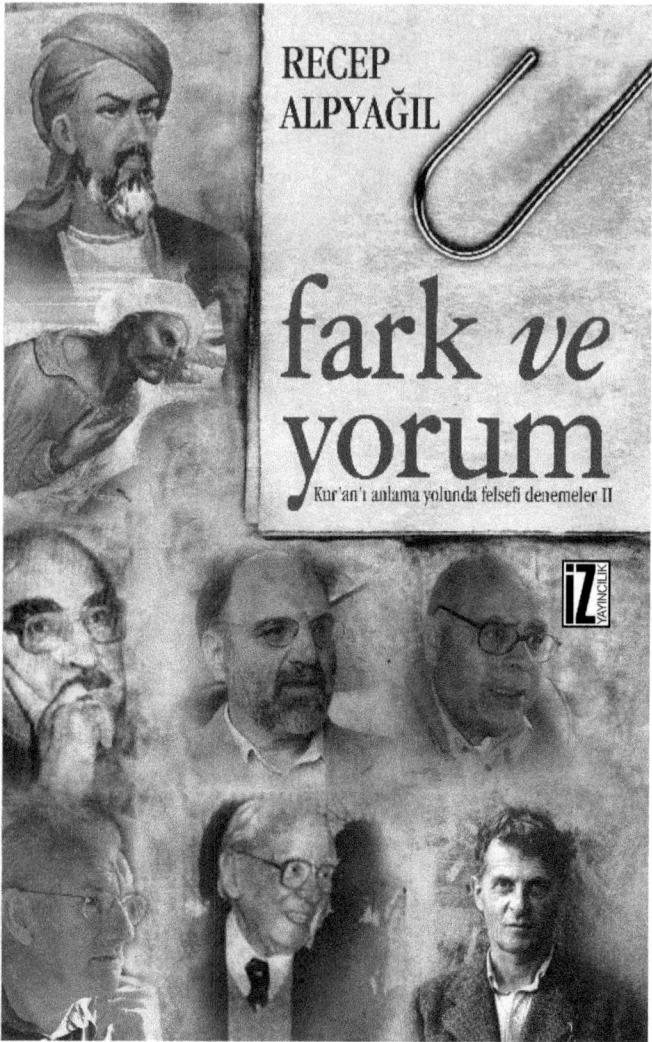

Figure 4.1 Cover of *Difference and Commentary*. (Source: Recep Alpyağıl kindly sent me the image of his book cover, ennumerated the identities of the figures, and helped me obtain permission from İz Yayıncılık to use this image. The author thanks İz Yayıncılık for generously granting permission to use this image.)

question of an authentic Islamic tradition, Alpyağıl offers his reader a direct example of the power of saying *both/and* when it comes to recognizing and narrating the roots of a specific philosophical tradition.

Let us look at one more example from Alpyağıl's inclusive canon before turning to the question of narrative and to his comments on Gadamer's mark on Turkish academic self-understanding. Remarking on the influence of Gadamer in modern Turkey, Alpyağıl states that the Turkish reader is accustomed to Gadamer.[17] Gadamer's basic thesis is well establised in Turkey, and this thesis, in simple summary, is that there is really no such thing as prejudice-free reading.[18] Because of Gadamer's influence on the Turkish academy, the savvy Turkish reader is less amenable to the notion that a reading can be purely objective.[19] Alpyağıl then introduces a related term, "narrative," and explains how this term has proliferated in the humanities. His explanation of the English term is clear, brief, and to the point:

> *Narration*, a word whose Turkish equivalent is *"anlatı,"* simply put, means the transmission of *a specific explanation* of the past or present.[20]

Closely related to dynamics of authenticity and continuity, this definition of narration also applies to history. He argues there is no absolute way to represent the reality of the past.[21] In fact, a plurality of possible historical truths is a good thing.[22] Narratives, whether factual or fictional, play an important role.[23] He thus encourages the reader to accept (the admittedly Gadamerian thesis) that there is no neutral perspective from which to narrate history.[24] With this turn, the issue now becomes how "we" narrate "our" philosophical past. What should this new narration should look like, he asks, from what point in history should it begin, and what roads should it pass through?[25] Whatever roads are taken, the task at hand is no doubt a living synthesis of past and new. In Alpyağıl's words, "We must formulate a new narrative in relation to the philosophical tradition of our past."[26] This re-narration is unfinished and ambitious. For the outside inquirer, the whirl of names and references can be hard to follow. Yet, Alpyağıl's stated goal was not to definitively answer old questions but to lay the groundwork for asking new and better questions. I will now turn to his use of narrative and address its function in his overarching project.

Narrative

Now it is time to move away from the broader sense of intellectual canon to the question of how a sacred text is mediated within intellectual tradition. To do this, we will look specifically at Alpyağıl's treatment of narrative. Alpyağıl does not simply address narrative as a philosophical concept, he offers a sincere engagement with narrative theology and its attempts to read sacred text for meaning in the face of modernity.[27] Narrative theology is a Christian theological movement that arose in the latter half of the twentieth century and it stresses narratives from sacred text over dogma and systematic formulations of faith. Rather than engaging with Christian dogmas or debates on theological details, Alpyağıl takes up narrative theology as a dialogue partner for Muslim reflection on how to read the Qur'ān.

He delves into the question of narrative and narrative theology his book *Difference and Commentary*. With some regret, he remarks that this book "is part of an unfinished story of Islam's modernity."[28] Reflecting on Islam's encouter with modernity, Alpyağıl starts with several key discoveries of the past century. I list these in figure 4.2.

Alpyağıl draws attention to an increasing recognition in Muslim quranic scholarship that the Qur'ān can be read to say many things, and this does not threaten its centrality to all Muslims, regardless of their individual interpretations. Moreover, Alpyağıl does not cite the above examples of discovery as proof that Muslims are already beyond the current crisis, nor is moving out of the current crisis his immediate goal.[29] His purpose is to investigate how people try to understand the Qur'ān.[30] He warns his reader not to expect all the answers from him but to approach the book as an exploration.

Among his numerous dialogue partners in this book are Hans Frei (1922–88), Wittgenstein (1889–1951), Don Cupitt (b. 1934), and the Egyptian modernist Muhammad Ahmad Khalafallah (1916–91).[31]

Alpyağıl does not spend too much time with any thinker, but Frei and Wittgenstein are both figures influential for Christian narrative theology. Moving from one figure to the next, Alpyağıl resists approaching religious narratives as if they were strictly historical narratives. He suggests, rather, that a religious narrative should be evaluated by its function, even if some of his readers might object that stories are less effective than historical facts when it comes to

1) The Qur'ān, like the New Testament, is a big basket where the interested reader can find almost anything, including at times seemingly contradictory principles.

2) Different ideologies can find things that support their ideologies in the sacred text – this includes socialists, capitalists, Islamic calls for peace, and Islamic calls for war.

3) The Qur'ān can be read across various topics. While the Qur'ān is important and what it says is central to all Muslims, different people inevitably read different things out of the Qur'ān.

Figure 4.2 Key Milestones in Islam's Narrative of Modernity. (Source: FY, 9–10. This table title is my own and is based on Alpyağıl's text.)

convincing a reader to commit to moral action.[32] While Alpyağıl draws on the work of famous Egyptian scholars of the Qur'ān and narrative like Abu Zayd (1943–2010) and Khalafallah, he does not borrow without critical distance.[33] Alpyağıl explains that Khalafallah, in his rejected dissertation *Narrative Art in the Holy Qur'an*,[34] identifies the question of historicity as a pitfall diverting reflection away from the quranic message and liable to drive readers away from seriously reading the sacred text, just as many Christian readers lost faith in the Bible with the rise of historical criticism.[35] Rather than allow historical criticism to dominate readings of the Qur'ān, Khalafallah proposed drawing on literary methods. Although Alpyağıl disagrees with Khalafallah on multiple points;[36] he, nevertheless, positively appraises Khalafallah's argument that reading quranic narrations primarily for historical value is tantamount to a misreading of the text insofar as historical debates have siphoned away attention to the quranic message. Rather than view talk of narrative as merely an attack on the integrity of the Qur'ān, Alpyağıl agrees with Khalafallah that the Qur'ān might tell stories for good reasons.[37] Further, setting up a narrow focus of interpretation can produce harmful results; as Alpyağıl notes, the more the reader limits the bounds of her interpretation, the easier it becomes to attribute error to the Qur'ān.[38] Thus, a narrow conception of narrative function, while seemingly protective of the Qur'ān's sacred status, could unintentionally cause an interpreter to attribute errors to the text. Alpyağıl does not stop at this point, however.

Alpyağıl makes a further move that challenges the assumed dichotomy between narrative and history. While many readers assume that narrative is purely fictional and history is purely factual, history itself, as Alpyağıl points out, is a kind of narrative. Therefore, even history is not necessarily realistic.[39] He writes, "History, with respect to other literary productions, does not contain more truth/reality (*gerçeklik*)."[40] Who you are determines how you view history.[41]

Having effectively nested the category of history under the broader concept of narrative, Alpyağıl goes on to highlight narrative's importance in life generally.[42] Whether factual or fictional, narratives are important to people. Not only are narratives important, they also perform many functions. As such, the Qur'ān may contain fictional narratives; and if it does contain them, this does not subtract from its sacredness.[43] More importantly, whether fictional or factual, a sacred narrative does not merely bend to human expectation.[44] He stresses that both literary and historical perspectives have something to offer.[45] While the Qur'ān may make use of fictional stories, these narratives may yet be based on real happenings—Alpyağıl reminds his reader that it is important to keep in mind that the Qur'ān is still more realistic than other scriptures.[46] He does not propose a great map to God or a model that explains all, but rather exposes the limitations of the fact/fiction dichotomy and recognizes the positive value of various approaches, including literary approaches to reading sacred text.[47] And while he affirms various popular methods for reading the Qur'ān, he reminds the reader that these methods do not exhaust the meaning of the Qur'ān.

History, Tradition, and Text

Alpyağıl's views on history, tradition, and sacred text are deeply related. Across all three categories, Alpyağıl stresses mediation, dialectic, and navigation of extremes. Consistent with his stance on a plurality of authentic sources and a plurality of useful narratives, he opposes the outright rejection of history or tradition as well as the fetishization of any one particular historical interpretation or any narrow understanding of sacred text.

History

Recall that Alpyağıl understands history to be a kind of narrative. His reflection on the category of history does not stop there. He also proposes a dialectical idea of the sacred. This dialectical sense of the sacred is not meant to usher in a new conservativism. It is not posited as a reaction against the profane, but in dialectical relation to it. Between the event of the text and the text itself, there exists a profane relation. This profane relation is the historical dimension. It is through this historical or profane relation that the sacred manifests. This act of the sacred appearing in and through the profane relation places the text in history and simultaneously constitutes the event of revelation.[48] Alpyağıl writes, "For no matter how profane the period in which revelation is sent down, it differs from other historical periods in that it contains a manifestation of what is sacred."[49] To support his position, he draws on Kenneth Cragg's work on the Qur'ān. Cragg asserts that something eternal cannot enter time without doing so at a specific point and time.[50] Moreover, Alpyağıl views the relationship between the sacred and profane as a shared problem applicable to any sacred scripture.[51]

Tradition

A text, especially a sacred text, is intricately tied to the community of readers that read it and seek meaning in it. This community's readings over time forms a tradition around the text. Alpyağıl is philosophically sensitive to this dynamic in his treatment of the idea of tradition. The work where he delves most critically and extensively into the notion of tradition is his book *Whose History, Which Hermeneutic?*[52]

In *Whose History, Which Hermeneutic?* (2003), Alpyağıl starts with a very simple concept—rule following. He asks: what role does tradition play in following a rule? His answer: a large one. He defines tradition in terms of the consensus among people applying a rule, where belief is not equivalent to following a rule.[53] On this point, Islamic law, or fiqh, has already recognized a distinction between faith and following a rule and has condemned examples of rule following without faith. Yet, faith is still bound up with the discussion of rule following. For those who view faith as a purely personal matter, Alpyağıl contests that rule following is an act that points beyond the single individual, as it is not the individual but predominantly the society in which the individual lives that determines whether one is following a rule. At the same time, an individual retains the power to interpret a rule, since individual interpretation is necessary for any specific application of a rule.[54] In this manner, Alpyağıl slowly teases out the dynamic reciprocity between individual interpretation and societal consensus.[55] To explain it differently, the application of a rule is not something that can be determined in advance.[56] Because of this indeterminability of a rule that has not yet been applied to a concrete situation, no rule's meaning is entirely definitive (*kati*).[57] The dance of determining how to follow a general rule in a specific instance necessitates the mediation of both the individual and that individual's community. There is no escaping individual interpretation. Nonetheless, each individual act of interpretation is still subject to judgment of the community.[58] Meaning, in this dance, transcends the individual and points backwards to a pre-existing social context; meaning entails something prior.[59] Yet this "prior" is not something that predetermines all future outcomes. When he asserts that rules point to something prior, Alpyağıl nowhere claims that this something prior can predetermine individual acts of interpretation. Rules are necessary but not sufficient for understanding, for giving meaning.[60] The process of applying rules and finding meaning is necessarily dynamic. Addressing this double and irreducible dynamic between the individual and her social context, he suggests a double (*ikili*) hermeneutic—one that navigates the two extremes of absolute objectivity and absolute relativity.[61]

Alpyağıl then turns from questions of rule following and meaning to sacred text and the role of tradition in interpreting that text. According to Alpyağıl, encountering the Qur'ān is similar to an encounter with a work of art, though not reducible to an aesthetic encounter. In a work of art, the art acts on the viewer, producing a reaction. Similarly, the Qur'ān also acts on the reader, illuminating the passive aspect of encountering revelation.[62] At this point, Alpyağıl raises an important question: when a believer reads the Qur'ān, is the reader truly the subject and the text merely an object?[63] He answers that a believer who reads the Qur'ān is both subject and object with respect to the text.[64] And this is where his analogy of aesthetics no longer applies.

For this reason, believers cannot merely read the Qur'ān like any other text.⁶⁵ The encounter with revelation necessitates a heavier or more "intensive interaction" (*yoğun iletişim*) between the reader and text for the text to function as sacred.⁶⁶ In an unusual conjunction of voices, he touches on the positions of the Egyptian Sayyid Qutb alongside German thinkers Heidegger and Gadamer, to finally claim, "The Qur'ān should be approached above all as a dynamic, living document that urges [believers to action]."⁶⁷ Or, in other words, the Qur'ān's aim is to be read and to drive the reader to action, not simply to be analyzed or intellectualized.⁶⁸ Reading the Qur'ān means reading for action and giving life to word.⁶⁹ Following this analysis, there are two clear ways in which the quranic encounter differs from, for instance, an experience of art: 1) the presence of faith in the reader and 2) the reader's consciousness of her nothingness before God.⁷⁰ Other necessary tools for reading the Qur'ān are common sense (*sağduyu*) and good will (*iyi istenç*).⁷¹ Important to note, Alpyağıl does not espouse that the reader can simply approach the text and take from it whatever meaning she desires.⁷² Further, the Qur'ān is not something a believer reads once and exhausts, but rather it exists as an ongoing guide for the reader.⁷³ Finally, the tools for understanding a text, even a sacred one, depend on the existence of readers who will use them.⁷⁴

Text

As for what it means for the Qur'ān to be a historical text, he stresses firmly that there are no prepackaged answers.⁷⁵ In Turkey, theologians have tended to understand the historical nature of sacred text to mean that "the text has been left in history" ("*metnin tarihte kalmış olması*") along with its rulings.⁷⁶ This, he points out, does not satisfy many Turkish readers. With a sacred text left behind in history, it is hard to imagine the injunctions and rules of that text remaining relevant to the present age. It starts to sound as if a universally valid message sent by God for all people and all times has actually been nullified. This contradiction results in part from the limitations of discussions on historicity. Alpyağıl criticizes the narrow discussions this approach has produced—in the discipline of fiqh and among the debates of the moderate historicists.⁷⁷ Even if one follows the "soft historicism" of Fazlur Rahman that has historically dominated Turkish discussions of historicism⁷⁸ and accordingly upholds the existence of an eternal kernel held in the historical husk of a historically situated text, the question still arises as to what this essential and eternal core message is when stripped of its historical baggage.⁷⁹ Alpyağıl expresses his skepticism concerning such an "historical" approach, asking:

> Can we [even] speak of a text's concrete message outside of the social and political identities of those trying to understand it?⁸⁰

His answer to this question is a firm no. As far as Alpyağıl reads the debate, neither radical nor moderate historicists break away from the narrowness of the discussion. For this reason, he has tried to offer alternative ways of thinking through history.⁸¹ The question finally becomes, "whose discussion" (*kimin yorumu*) are we even having?⁸² Drawing on the thought of Foucault, Derrida, Habermas, J. Caputo, and Edward Said, Alpyağıl argues that we inevitably read into a text.⁸³ Yet, good intentions alone do not guarantee good or valid readings.⁸⁴ Drawing on Gadamer, he reminds the reader that even good intentions can be shaped by political, economic, and power instincts.⁸⁵

Turning to Pakistani thinkers Aziz Ahmed and Fazlur Rahman, Alpyağıl points out these thinkers, as well as those making similar moves in Turkey, tend to problematize the historicity of the text so much so that they ignore the historicity of their own readings of the text. Looking at Aziz Ahmed's readings, he points out how they inevitably reflect his own situation in Pakistan/India. He does the same with Fazlur Rahman, who has been widely influential in Turkish discussions of quranic historicity. Fazlur Rahman speaks of a double movement in interpreting sacred text in history.⁸⁶ This movement involves looking at the historical moment at which the Qur'ān was revealed, finding the universal kernel of a quranic injunction, and then applying it to the present moment. Alpyağıl does not discount the readings of Aziz Ahmed or of Fazlur Rahman, but he challenges them as facile instances of "historical" interpretation. In reality, there are two historical moments—the moment being interpreted and the moment behind the act of interpretation, that is, the historical prejudices the reader brings to the text. Rahman's method, in Alpyağıl's view, does not fully grapple with the historical lens endemic to the moment of interpretation. Such interpretations are not worthy of condemnation; nevertheless, he calls his reader to greater self-reflection on the impact of her own historical context upon her reading of the Qur'ān.⁸⁷ Fazlur Rahman, whose historical approach has long been established in Turkey, does not in Alpyağıl's view offer an adequately nuanced understanding of historicity.

Alpyağıl further argues with sophistication that historicity is an issue of authority. He laments that much of the hype over historicity feeds on Muslims' "backwardness complex" ("*geri kalmışlık kompleksi*") in encounter with Christian/secular Western civilization.[88] To better illustrate what he might mean, let us look directly at a statement by Fazlur Rahman. Rahman not only bemoaned scientific and technological lack but also stressed that Muslim societies are more spiritually impoverished than they imagine:

> There is little doubt that most Eastern societies have been laboring under the false and totally self-deceptive impression that they suffer from an over-plentitude of spirituality and spiritual insights while the West, barren in this respect, has outstripped them in material technology and that now they need only get the latter. That the West has outstripped the East in science and technology is correct; what seems to be a fiction is that the East is replete with spirituality, for, if this were so, why should the East—or the Muslim societies—suffer from the mental and spiritual dichotomy of which I have mainly been speaking here?[89]

Fazlur Rahman's above lament over the state of "Eastern" societies showcases the very backwardness complex which Alpyağıl seeks to uproot and eradicate.

For Alpyağıl, the discourse of historicity (*tarihsellik*), as it is often carried out, is *de facto* a discourse of defeat.[90] However, he does not want to be overly essentializing or reductive in this claim.[91] It is, nonetheless, important to keep in mind that the question is more than "whose hermeneutic?" it is also and always a question of "whose affair?"[92] There is no narration of history which is not entangled in a socio-political context. As Alpyağıl puts it, "A history without ideology is nothing but a clump of events."[93] This is significant especially since in the Turkish theological context, the question of historicity has strong political roots.[94] In stressing the inescapable matrix of historical context, Alpyağıl takes a stance similar to that of Turkish theologians before him like İlhami Güler, a student of Hasan Hanafi, and Ömer Özsoy.[95]

For Alpyağıl, there is no getting out of the political aspect of hermeneutics.[96] Inevitably, the manner in which guidance is derived from the Qur'ān is a historically and politically entangled affair. This does not mean, however, that the Qur'ān's guidance is historically limited to the point it cannot still address and guide its reader.[97] The Qur'ān may not have a clear ruling for everything but it is nonetheless guidance. As such, the quranic examples should not be dismissed as outdated, on the one hand, nor should they be treated as a manual of rulings on all future human problems, on the other. To explicate his point, Alpyağıl draws partially on Gadamer, who remarks that a text is a stage in the event of communication.[98] Alpyağıl appropriates this, claiming the Qur'ān is not merely a fecund object.[99] Not only is the text not a passive object, moreover, neither historical scrutiny nor an over-literal reading of the text can secure revelation's (*vahiy*) relation to the believer.[100] Reading with faith, by contrast, prevents the believer from objectifying the text.[101]

Alpyağıl is open about not attempting to solve all the problems he delves into. His stated aim is to ask better questions and approach these old problems in new ways.[102] His work expresses an openness combined with rigorous inquiry, which both engages and invites the reader to struggle towards independent conclusions, new questions, and lived answers. Since he is not interested in determining his reader's answers to these big questions, his approach places the burden of reflection and responsibility squarely on his believing reader. In other words, where there is no easy answer, it is up to the individual to mediate competing claims of authority in matters of meaning seeking. Let us now turn to the role of the individual in mediating the authority of an inclusive canon with a plurality of possible narrative readings.

Dialectic of the Sacred: The Individual in "Hypoleptic" Continuity

As discussed above, for Alpyağıl, not every text exists merely for contemplative pleasure—sometimes we read for action. We read to give life to word.[103] In reading for action, the agency of the individual and the individual's own mediated authority come to the fore, as it is ultimately the individual who acts. Specifically, Alpyağıl envisions an active reader in living relation to the Qur'ān and points forward to an empowered Muslim—not one at the mercy of Western criticism, but one confident and able to actively dialogue with many voices and many authorities.[104] Modeling what he hopes to see flourish, Alpyağıl's work provides the reader with one example of what an empowered Muslim voice in active dialogue looks like, leaving his readers with the humble invitation to do the same.

As discussed above, reading with faith is crucial in the struggle not to render sacred text a dead object with no power to influence the subjectivity of its reader. When it comes to reading the Qur'ān, reading with faith includes using the believer's intellectual capacities to take the initiative on working out how to apply the quranic address to her own time and place. Alpyağıl draws on Turkish Islamic philosopher Burhanettin Tatar, who writes:

> The Qur'an is not a text which speaks directly about something: it is a text that incites people to come into communication [with it] on clear topics and questions by calling out to the human faculties of understanding.[105]

This vision of the reader's relationship with the Qur'ān implies a deeply engaged, personal dynamic. In stressing such a dynamic, Alpyağıl emphasizes the role of individual engagement and authority. This engaged quality of readership stresses the living and dynamic relationship an individual believer brings to the encounter with the Qur'ān. As scripture is both object and subject, so too does the believer in the encounter with the Qur'ān act as both object and subject.

As Alpyağıl stresses, questions of interpretation tend to eschew ready answers.[106] This does not mean that any interpretation whatsoever is valid or that the reader takes from or reads into the text whatever she desires.[107] Neither is the process of encountering the text as straightforward as reading an instruction manual or a metro map, even if such an individual encounter is (rightly) still deeply embedded in social rules and interpretive voices from tradition. Without a ready map for action, the uniting thread in Alpyağıl's careful discussion of history, sacred address, and tradition is *the individual*. For, it is the individual who mediates tradition and lives out the sacred call of the text. Let me take a moment to better elucidate how Alpyağıl envisions the role of individual authority, where his key word is "hypoleptic."

Hypolepsis is a Greek word that appears in Aristotle's discussion of the soul and is taken to mean assumption, roughly synonymous with reputable and widespread opinion.[108] For Alpyağıl, hypolepsis entails continuity with variation rather than strict recapitulation.[109] It serves as a locus for the dialectical idea of the sacred rather than a naïve idea of the sacred.[110] As he explains it, hypoleptic continuity is a way of mediation between rejection of tradition and uncritical acceptance of tradition. To be in hypoleptic continuity means the believer does not have to reject tradition, but at the same time, she does not have to use tradition uncritically either—by avoiding these extremes, the believer develops a "hypoleptic awareness" (*hipoleptik bir bilinç*).[111] In this way, believers are not always starting from scratch. The authority of tradition is taken into account; while, at the same time, the value of individual (and hence new) authority is still upheld.[112] This is a mediated individual authority, where the individual stands in a critical but positive relation to tradition and stands also in reflective relation to her own social and historical context. Moreover, this critical relation to tradition is not directed solely towards Islamic tradition. This critical relation also addresses the traditions of the European Enlightenment and other Western sources. Alpyağıl remarks that since there is no universal agreement on Enlightenment claims to universality, it also makes sense to enter into critical dialogue with Enlightenment criticism.[113] Such an individual, having rooted herself authentically in her own context and religious identity is "secure in her past and future"[114] and, as such, is capable of critical reflection and dialogue with various canons of authority. She is like the spiral that Alpyağıl mentioned earlier. She is not stuck in a dead end, a static return to the past, nor is she trapped in stultifying false dichotomies. Instead she is reaching forwards into the future and backwards in dialectical continuity with her past. Although Alpyağıl's approach puts greater responsibility on the individual believer, this does not mean that the believer cannot err in interpreting scripture or tradition. He acknowledges that it is often an open question as to when an interpretation counts as bankrupt.[115] Thus, an individual is active, aware, and ethically responsible in interpreting sacred scripture.

To tie this in to the wider discussion, Alpyağıl uses Scottish philosopher Alasdair MacIntyre's definition of humanity: humans are a story-telling animal.[116] This definition is important for the individual Muslim's relation to the Qur'ān. Alpyağıl stresses the significance of the Qur'ān in Muslims' self-narratives today, writing:

> Above all else, the Qur'an is what represents us (Muslims) in the face of other paradigms. [. . .] It is our history; it is the history—the narrative—that makes us who we are.[117]

Narrative, including history, is an inescapable and constitutive part of identity. This sense of context and belonging provides a formative relationship for individual identity. For Alpyağıl, the believing individual does not stand outside looking in at the Qur'ān and tradition, but stands already in relationship to the Qur'ān, as a text that offers the believing individual her fundamental narrative and history as a Muslim.

A dialectic spans across the narrative space between self-understanding and historical understanding. Failing to engage in this dialectic results in a kind of paralysis. In order to illustrate the effect of this paralysis, Alpyağıl draws on Oliver Sacks' *The Man Who Mistook His Wife for a Hat*.[118] Sacks brings up the case of Jimmie, the 49-year-old who still thinks he is nineteen and is incapable of forming new memories. According to Alpyağıl, twenty-first-century Muslims run the risk of exhibiting the same symptoms as Jimmie.[119] A Muslim who relates to the Qur'ān and the history of her tradition in the way Jimmie does to his life is a Muslim stuck with a truncated memory of her own tradition. Such a Muslim may have a naïve understanding of history and, as a result, be incapable of fully connecting with her tradition in such a way as to contribute actively and meaningfully to it.[120] In other words, a believer who cannot engage in this dialectic is impeded from coming into her full agency and identity as a Muslim.

At heart, Alpyağıl addresses a crisis of memory and, by extension, a crisis of identity (*kimlik*). The failure to engage in dynamic continuity with the past and authentically claim one's Muslim identity moving into the future is a kind of trauma, one bound up with historical realities of Muslim encounters with the Christian West in colonial contexts. This trauma is a result of—or characterized by—a crisis of identity and memory, and it is now a question of getting beyond this trauma. He states, "In sum, our present moment is a situation where we have suffered a very heavy trauma." Then he asks, "Well, is there a way out of this trauma?"[121] As we have seen throughout, the way out for Alpyağıl is—without getting stuck in the past—embracing history as something that gives Muslim Turkish philosophers and believers identity today and helps them imagine utopias for tomorrow.[122] This way out is also a dynamic and dialectical dance between individual authority, collective identity, and profound formation through encounter with the sacred text. He writes, "Reading the Qur'an as a narrative that makes us 'us' means that it is a source still in the process of forming us."[123]

This dynamism is also present in Alpyağıl's treatment of intellectual canons of authority. As a prime example of one who found dialectical balance between individual efforts and the guidance of tradition, Alpyağıl holds up medieval philosopher al-Fārābī (c. 872–950). In the latter's *Kitāb al-Burhān*, Alpyağıl praises al-Fārābī's careful yet critical appropriation of Aristotle— al-Fārābī is able to appreciatively study Aristotle without blindly accepting Aristotle's position on every subject. Al-Fārābī shows exemplary intellectual engagement as well as confidence in his own judgment of what to take from Aristotle and what to reject.[124] This is the sort of attitude Alpyağıl wishes to see in Turkey. Philosophy is not made by simply translating.[125] Translation is not enough to engage in critical dialogue.[126] There must be dynamism and criticism. For this to occur, a dialectical relationship between individual authority and various canons of intellectual authority must be fostered.

The dialectic at work here is a dialectic of *both/and*. *Both* the individual *and* tradition matter. *Both* narrative *and* history have a place in discussions of sacred hermeneutics. Sometimes it is even appropriate to say *both* yes *and* no. Alpyağıl at one point even calls this a "yes-no dialectic."[127] Further, he does not claim that the yes-no dialectic is new to Islamic tradition and he even suggests that the yes-no dialectic has some foundations in Islamic tradition.[128] In short, being able to mediate extremes with authenticity is crucial to moving into a new phase in Turkish philosophy. And to mediate authentically requires rootedness in the past; Alpyağıl reminds his reader:

> In the author's opinion, regarding philosophy's relation with the past, it is an overly simple preference to jettison [philosophical] heritage and try to save oneself in this manner.[129]

In other words, rejecting the past or the valuable contributions of prior Islamic tradition will not save Turkish thought from its current identity crisis. Blind acceptance of this or that interpretation or blind acceptance of this or that philosophical canon is not enough either. Sometimes it is not a question of yes *or* no, but a matter of saying yes *and* no—and this is an attitude that, according to Alpyağıl, could be useful for Turkish philosophy.[130]

Yet who or what stands at the heart of these extremes? Who mediates and directs these dialectical spaces? What Alpyağıl seems to be saying is that it is the individual who must bravely use her own faith, intellect, context, and judgment to navigate extremes, external authorities, and the crisis of identity. To borrow a phrase from Fazlur Rahman, "There is no such thing as a societiless individual."[131] Ultimately, Alpyağıl's view of an individual is a deeply relational one. This individual has no intention to exercise absolute authority since she does not suffer from the illusion that her individuality can exist in a purely objective, abstract sense distinct from her relations to other beings in the world. She understands she is as much her own product as she is the product of the world around her. Moreover, this individual recognizes the value of tradition, of society, of her relations to others, and of the call of sacred text. This individual consciously and carefully exercises dialectical and mediated authority in order to navigate and establish her place in a world of many voices and many claims.

Only an empowered and hypolectically aware believing individual is equipped to creatively bring new answers and questions out of the mixed canons of intellectual authority which Turkey has inherited. Instead of reacting against any one part of Turkey's intellectual heritage, Alpyağıl's response is to bring them all in the mix—whether they are Turkish/Ottoman, Arabic, or Western. Thus, Alpyağıl is a prime exemplary of the threefold complexity and internal dialectics which I find characteristic of Turkish theology. Alpyağıl looks to the creative potential of authentic Turkish philosophy as something that includes and combines voices from Islamic intellectual tradition, Western intellectual tradition, and from Turkey's own recent history. For Alpyağıl, authentic Turkish philosophy bespeaks an inclusive canon and an ongoing dialectic of authoritative traditions.

Notes

1. TO, p. 90. He shies from claiming that the Qur'ān should be systematically used to underpin a whole philosophy, and, in this, his position is similar to Ricoeur's, who also resists the notion of a purely speculative and secondary appropriation of sacred text.
2. TO, p. 84.
3. TO, pp. 84–5. Mustafa Günay, "21. Yüzyılda Türkiye'de Felsefe Yapmak," in B. Çotuksöken and S. İyi (eds), *Kimin İçin Felsefe* (Istanbul: Heyamola Yayınları, 2006), pp. 79–80. Turkish: "Avrupa-merkezcilikten sıyrılmamız zorunlu görünmektedir. [. . .] felsefeyi yalnızca yerel ve ulusal unsurlara indirgemek

anlamında düşünmemek gerekir." On a related note, Fazlur Rahman also spoke of a "vicious circle" when he took up the inversion of the relation of politics to Islam, lamenting that the latter unfortunately served the former instead of vice versa and calling this inversion a major challenge for Islam in the face of modernity. In his view, the issue is not to save religion from modernity, which is a purely partisan interest, but to save modern human beings from themselves through religion. To do this Rahman wished to separate normative from historical Islam—a distinction Alpyağıl's own approach complexifies. Fazlur Rahman, *Islam and Modernity: Transformation of an Intellectual Tradition* (Chicago: University of Chicago Press, 1984), pp. 140–1.

4. TO, p. 88. To compare, Pakistani-American Qur'ān scholar Asma Barlas also speaks of a spiral in her discussion of reading the Qur'ān from a holistic, non-relativistic, polysemic hermeneutical approach. This similarity of approach may in large part be due to the influence of Fazlur Rahman in the Turkish context and on Barlas' work. Asma Barlas, *"Believing Women" in Islam: Unreading Patriarchal Interpretations of the Qur'ān* (Austin: University of Texas Press, 2002), especially pp. 19 and 24. In this work, Barlas engages both the Qur'ān and Western theories but rejects the language of synthesis between the two (p. 25).

5. TO, p. 82. Alpyağıl strongly rejects a strict notion of turn/return (*dönüş*) to the past—as he sees it, this does not work philosophically.

6. TO, p. 41. Turkish: "sorun ve gelenek ilişkisi, tek boyutlu ve tek çizgili değil, çok boyutlu ve çok çizgilidir. Zaten geleneğin kendisi monolitik bir yapı değil, bizlerin ilişkisiyle sürekli olarak değişen, dönen, çoğullaşan bir bütündür." Even Pakistani scholar Fazlur Rahman stressed that the endeavor of Qur'ān interpretation was never monolithic, not even in the early Muslim community. Rahman, *Islam and Modernity*, p. 144.

7. TO, p. 48. Turkish: "felsefe bölümlerinde Augustinus, Aquinas veya Abelard'ın felsefeci olarak hak ettikleri yere yakın, hatta onlardan hiç de farklı olmayan sözgelimi bir Taftazani'nin, Cürcani'nin yeri var mıdır? Ya da Molla Fenari, Sarı Abdullah, Gelenbevi, Saçaklızade vd. Bunların adları anılır mı?" The works of al-Taftāzānī (1322–90) and al-Jurjānī (1339–1414), Ottoman scholar Halil Inalcik notes, were foundational to the Ottoman medrese tradition. Halil Inalcik, *The Ottoman Empire* (London: Phoenix Press, 2000), 175–6. The last four names Alpyağıl lists represent Ottoman Islamic figures: 1) Molla Fenari (1350–1431) was an Ottoman polymath in the school of Ibn 'Arabī, 2) Sarı Abdullah Efendi (d. 1661) is famous for his commentary on Rumi's *Masnavi*, 3) Gelenbevi Ismail Efendi (1730–90/1) was a mathematician who applied his expertise to

Ottoman military interests, 4) he presumably refers here to scholar Saçaklızade Osman Efendi whose death dates are placed in the mid-sixteenth century.
8. TO, p. 48. Necla Arat et al., "Felsefe Forumu," *Felsefe Dergisi* 1 (1986): 129.
9. In Turkish, *Konevî*.
10. In Turkish, *Ebherî*.
11. TO, p. 88.
12. One interesting subtlety to note is that Alpyağıl not only uses Western thinkers but he also uses Western critiques of Eurocentrism (while also pointing out their limits as we saw with Paul Ricoeur's notion of "intertextuality"). In short, he uses the assumed voice of Western authority to put in question its assumed authority. This element is particularly prevalent in Alpyağıl's *The Possibility of Creating an Authentic Philosophy in Turkey and Philosophy of Religion* (TO).
13. *Fark ve Yorum: Kur'an'ı Anlama Yolunda Felsefî Denemeler II* [*Difference and Commentary: Philosophical Essays on the Way to Understanding the Qur'an II*] (Istanbul: İz Yayıncılık, 2009; 2014). Cited as FY.
14. For this list I am indebted to Recep Alpyağıl—I could not visually identify all figures without aid.
15. FY, p. 176.
16. This discussion raises the question of an assumed discourse here. Why is a Ghazālian interpretive schema suspect? Or why should an overly philosophical (Avicennan) or mystical (Akbariyya/Ibn 'Arabī's school) approach be suspect? His choice to end his book, *Difference and Commentary* (FY), on this discussion might indicate his sensitivity towards a larger case of disputed intra-Islamic authority. Outside of Turkey, these same strands are sometimes held suspect.
17. For an overview of Turkish theological hermeneutics, see Burhanettin Tatar, "The Hermeneutical Turn in Recent Turkish Intellectual Thought," in Sinasi Gunduz and Cafer S. Yaran (eds), *Change and Essence: Dialectical Relations Between Change and Continuity in the Turkish Intellectual Tradition* (Washington, DC: The Council for Research in Values and Philosophy, 2005), pp. 145–58. Tatar writes, "responses to Western hermeneutics on the Turkish intellectual scene are mainly three: 1) Descriptive and historical; 2) Critical and reactional; 3) Hermeneutical. [. . .] Hermeneutical studies are the ones which propose discovering hermeneutical aspects of Turkish or Islamic thought by staging them as a play with Western hermeneutical conceptions" (p. 145). Tatar mentions Alpyağıl in the third category (p. 157).
18. FY, p. 155.
19. FY, p. 156.

20. TO, p. 107. By "explanation" I aim to translate "*anlatım*," which is a slightly different word than "*anlatı*"—the one he is already defining. Turkish: "'*Narration*' ın Türkçesi olarak dilimize girmiş olan anlatı, basitçe, geçmişin ya da şimdinin *belli bir anlatım* yoluyla aktarımını ifade eder."
21. TO, p. 111.
22. TO, p. 112.
23. TO, p. 113.
24. TO, p. 115.
25. TO, p. 116.
26. TO, p. 118. Turkish: "Geçmişteki felsefe birikimimize ilişkin yeni bir anlatı oluşturmalıyız."
27. Narrative theology is a development of the late twentieth century and focuses on narrative, especially biblical narratives, rather than systematic doctrine.
28. FY, p. 9. Turkish: "İslam modernizminin henüz tamamlanmamış öyküsünün bir parçasıdır."
29. FY, pp. 9–10.
30. FY, p. 11.
31. FY, pp. 51, 54–7, 61–81. Frei is known for his work on biblical hermeneutics and serves only as an entry point for Alpyağıl. Frei's work is important in the development of narrative theology. Khalafallah, whom Alpyağıl engages for over fifteen pages (TO, pp. 65–81), is known for his work on quranic narrative; a student at al-Azhar University in Cairo, he was never able to defend his 1947 thesis on narrative in the Qur'ān and had to write a non-religious thesis in order to obtain his doctorate.
32. FY, pp. 63–4.
33. In his discussion of Khalafallah he does not engage the work of Nasr Hamid Abu Zayd; he engages Abu Zayd in a preceding work, the first part of his two-part discussion of Qur'ān hermeneutics, entitled *Whose History, Which Hermeneutic?* (2003, 2013), abbreviated throughout as KTHH.
34. The Ankara School publishing house (Ankara Okulu Yayınları) published a Turkish translation of this work in 2002, which Alpyağıl cites from: Muhammed Ahmed Halefullah, *Kur'an'da Anlatım Sanatı*, trans. Şaban Karataş (Ankara: Ankara Okulu Yayınları, 2002).
35. FY, p. 66.
36. FY, pp. 69–74. Alpyağıl criticizes Khalafallah for incorrectly reading the quranic address to make use of mythology in debates with polytheists, for having too narrow a view of literary methodology, for maintaining the Qur'ān was only

affirming previous books of revelation rather than also correcting them, for underplaying quranic references to historical events, and for overall lack of clarity as to how the literary method can benefit a believer reading the Qur'ān.

37. FY, p. 67.
38. FY, p. 68. His argument for openness and rootedness in engaging a living sacred text (discussed in chapter three) may support his criticism of narrow readings of the Qur'ān. That is, one might understand a narrow reading as one too heavily predujiced by human ideas and standards to be receptive to the full richness of sacred address.
39. FY, pp. 77–9. He cites H. White (from the English) and R. Chartier (from Turkish translation) to talk about history as a fiction-making operation (*kurgu oluşturma işlemi*). See Hayden White, "The Historical Text as Literary Artifact," in B. Fay and P. Pomper (eds), *History and Theory: Contemporary Readings* (Oxford: Blackwell, 1998), pp. 15–33. H. White argues that the bounds between history and narrative are necessarily blurry.
40. FY, p. 79. Turkish: "Tarih diğer edebi ürünlere oranla daha fazla gerçeklik içeriyor değildir."
41. FY, p. 80.
42. FY, p. 82.
43. FY, p. 87.
44. FY, p. 89.
45. FY, p. 89.
46. FY, pp. 93–5.
47. FY, p. 93. Here he explains that just like in geography it is not a question of finding the best map of the land but making maps that best help us recognize and understand the land, so too should the reader understand quranic narrative. He stresses it is important not to look for one single "mega model" but look instead for models that will best help us understand the quranic message.
48. KTHH, pp. 108–9.
49. KTHH, p. 109. Turkish: "Çünkü vahyin nazil olduğu dönem, her ne kadar profansa da, kendisinde kutsalın tezahür etmekliğiyle diğer olağan tarihsel dönemlerden farklıdır" (translation into English not overly literal).
50. Kenneth Cragg, *The Event of the Qur'an: Islam and Its Scripture* (Oxford: One World, 1994), p. 112. Cited in KTHH, p. 128.
51. KTHH, p. 129.
52. Recep Alpyağıl, *Kimin Tarihi, Hangi Hermenötik? Kur'an Anlama Yolunda Felsefi Denemeler I* (Istanbul: İz Yayıncılık, 2003; repr. 2013). Cited as KTHH.

The title bears similarity in structure to MacIntyre's *Whose Justice, Which Rationality?* (1988). KTHH does contain citations of MacIntyre but not references to this 1988 work.
53. KTHH, p. 14.
54. KTHH, p. 15.
55. KTHH, pp. 9–25. This position he builds from a discussion of Wittgenstein's linguistic theory. To note, this position is incidentally reminiscent of Schleiermacher's characterization of the individual, who is both relatively independent and dependent on the world around (and by extension society). He does not bring in Schleiermacher here, but he does touch on Gadamer and Habermas.
56. KTHH, p. 19.
57. KTHH, p. 22.
58. KTHH, p. 24.
59. KTHH, p. 35.
60. KTHH, p. 53.
61. KTHH, p. 55.
62. KTHH, p. 59.
63. KTHH, p. 63.
64. KTHH, p. 64. It may be helpful to supplement Alpyağıl's position on this with some words of Ricoeur, whose treatment of revelation Alpyağıl has elsewhere drawn on. Ricoeur, in an article that Alpyağıl elsewhere draws upon, also portrays the one who reads revelation in a way that resists the objectification of the text. He writes, "Reflection is never first, never constituting—it [tradition] arrives unexpectedly like a 'crisis' within an experience that bears us, and it constitutes us as the subject of the experience." Riceour, "Toward a Hermeneutic of the Idea of Revelation," p. 29. In the same article, Ricoeur further claims, "the pretension of consciousness to constitute itself is the most formidable obstacle to the idea of revelation" (p. 30). Ricoeur and Alpyağıl are in agreement that the human mind is not the only subject in the encounter with revelation; revelation, too, is a subject which acts upon the believer.
65. KTHH, p. 64.
66. KTHH, p. 65. As quranic indications of this intense relation between believer and revelation, he cites Q13:31 and Q18:01.
67. KTHH, p. 67. Turkish: "Kur'an, her şeyden çok sevk edici, dinamik ve canlı bir belge olarak algılanmalıdır."
68. KTHH, p. 68.

69. KTHH, pp. 102–3.
70. KTHH, p. 68. Şaban actually pushes back on characterizing the encounter with God and revelation as one that reduces the believer to a sense of nothingness—see part three. Alpyağıl's quranic resources for the point made here are: Q6:81, Q11:24, Q9:109.
71. KTHH, p. 75.
72. KTHH, p. 77.
73. KTHH, p. 78.
74. KTHH, p. 79.
75. KTHH, p. 135.
76. KTHH, p. 135.
77. KTHH, p. 135. I take him to refer to those influenced by Fazlur Rahman's method when he speaks of moderate (*ılımlı*) historicists.
78. I use Yasin Aktay's reference to Fazlur Rahman's "soft historicism." Aktay, like Alpyağıl after him, also criticizes the superficiality of some historicist discussions in Turkey, going so far as to criticize Pakistani intellectual Fazlur Rahman for oversimplifying Gadamer. Yasin Aktay, The Historicist Dispute in Turkish-Islamic Theology," in *Change and Essence*, pp. 75–7.
79. Note a parallel debate in Christian thought, not referenced in Alpyağıl's discussion: Troeltsch critically responded to Adolf von Harnack's thesis that the message of Christ and the New Testament must be shorn of its historical husk to reveal the essential meaning of Christianity. In his famous article "What Does 'Essence of Christianity' Mean?" (1903), Troeltsch astutely pointed out that, since truth comes to us by way of history and we ourselves are also in history, it is rather tricky to determine what is "husk" and what is "essence." In short, his response to von Harnack was that truth does not work in such a way that one can claim an "essence" free of historical "husk." Alpyağıl's position on historicity seems more or less in agreement with Troeltsch's basic objection.
80. KTHH, p. 135. Turkish: "Bir metnin, onu anlamaya çalışan kişilerin ait oldukları siyasal ve sosyal kimliklerinin dışında, somut bir *mesaj*ından söz edilebilir mi?"
81. KTHH, p. 136.
82. KTHH, pp. 136–7.
83. KTHH, pp. 137–43. He especially draws on Foucault's emphasis on power in discourse. The connecting theme between these figures is postmodernism and

post-colonialism. Here and elsewhere, it is difficult to provide adequate context for all the authors he uses without detracting from the flow of his own argumentation. Alpyağıl often provides minimal context for the figures he engages and sometimes none at all, making high demands on his reader.

84. KTHH, p. 143.
85. KTHH, p. 143.
86. Fazlur Rahman is known for expressing many of his views on historicity in his *Islam and Modernity*, first published in 1982. In this same discussion, Rahman starkly criticizes the "Atatürkish" attempt to reform a community without real connection to the past as impossible. Rahman, *Islam and Modernity*, p. 126.
87. KTHH, p. 145. In terms of Qur'ān commentaries, Alpyağıl makes use of Mohammad Asad's commentary translated into Turkish. He is somewhat critical of M. Asad and prefers al-Suyūṭī on matters of literal interpretation (KTHH, p. 156). For M. Asad he uses the following Turkish translation: M. Esed, *Kur'an Mesajı: Meal-Tefsir*, trans. Cahit Koytak-Ahmet Ertürk (Istanbul: İşaret Yay., 1996). On al-Suyūṭī (1445–1505), Alpyağıl refers to his *El İtkan fi Ulumi'l-Kur'an* (Damascus: Darub-u Kesir, 1987), vol. 1, p. 92.
88. KTHH, p. 145.
89. Rahman, *Islam and Modernity*, p. 137.
90. KTHH, p. 145.
91. KTHH, p. 145.
92. KTHH, p. 147. In the discussion of whose affair, he uses the phrase "which affair" or "*hangi maslahat*." The word "*maslahat*" means "business" or "affair" in modern Turkish. In Arabic, in the context of fiqh, it has a specific meaning of benefit or good. One way of translating it here might be "vested interest."
93. KTHH, p. 167. Turkish: "İdeoloji olmaksızın tarih, bir olaylar yığından başka bir şey değildir."
94. Aktay, "The Historicist Dispute in Turkish-Islamic Theology," p. 68.
95. Aktay, The Historicist Dispute in Turkish-Islamic Theology," pp. 74, 77. Özsoy takes historical concerns a bit further than Güler, according to Aktay's summary of both. Aktay summarizes Özsoy on historicity: "As human beings we have no chance to look from an over, beyond or trans-historical point of view. Our perception is by its very nature tied with history. Man exists within history, and his consciousness cannot be treated as isolated from history" (p. 77).
96. KTHH, p. 148.

97. KTHH, p. 157.
98. KTHH, p. 148. In his discussion, Alpyağıl cites the Turkish translation of Gadamer. H. Arslan has translated "Metin ve Yorum" ["Text and Commentary"] in *Hermeneutik ve Humaniter Disiplinler* (Istanbul: Paradigma Yay., 2002). Turkish theological scholar Burhanettin Tatar has also translated some Gadamer: "Aristo'nun Hermenötik İlgisi" ["Aristotles' Hermeneutic Interest"] in *Siyasi Hermenötik* (Samsun: Etüt Yay., 2000).
99. KTHH, p. 158. Alpyağıl draws on Gadamer to make this point, even if he does not fully agree with Gadamer.
100. KTHH, p. 161.
101. KTHH, p. 163. Despite his insistence on faith for reading the Qur'ān as more than an object, Alpyağıl in no way espouses an arational or fideist position. In another publication, *Doing Philosophy of Religion Moving from Wittgenstein to Kierkegaard* [*Wittgenstein ve Kierkegaard'dan Hareketle Din Felsefesi Yapmak*], he distances himself from recent and current Christian arguments for fideism. He believes that faith needs to remain open to rational inquiry, but does not claim to have all the answers, nor does he think people will ever agree on a single answer. This book will be taken up in chapter seven's discussion of skepticism and fideism.
102. Alpyağıl suggests that one way of tackling the tricky business of reading a text from a different time and context for universal meaning is to approach the Qur'ān like an anthropologist. In saying this, he does not mean all anthropological approaches are appropriate. He stresses that using one's own culture as a reference does not have to entail negating the culture behind the text. He even suggests that late Ottoman *mufassir* Elmalılı Muhammad Yazır does an anthropological reading of the Qur'ān with Anatolian culture as his own touch point. See his discussion in KTHH, pp. 152–5.
103. KTHH, pp. 102–3.
104. KTHH, p. 165.
105. Burhanettin Tatar, "Kelam'a Göre Öteki Dinlerin Konumu," in Cafer S. Yaran (ed.), *İslam ve Öteki* (Istanbul: Kaknüs Yay., 2001), p. 201. Cited in KTHH, p. 126. Turkish: "Kur'an doğrudan bir şey hakkında konuşan değil; beşeri anlama yeteneklerine seslenerek insanları belli konu veya sorunlar üzerinde iletişime geçmeye sevk eden bir metindir."
106. KTHH, p. 134.
107. KTHH, p. 77.

108. For more on this term in its Aristotelian context, see Werner Theobald, "Spuren des Mythos in der Aristotelischen Theorie der Erkenntnis: 'Hypolepsis' bei Aristoteles, *De anima* und *Anal. post*," *Archiv für Begriffsgeschichte* 44 (2002): pp. 25–37.
109. KTHH, p. 124.
110. KTHH, p. 108.
111. KTHH, p. 130.
112. KTHH, p. 129. This move might have a parallel in Christian theological attempts to rehabilitate dogma/doxology, words etymologically related to *doxa*, the rough synonym for hypolepsis. Rather than a dead and unthinking profession of rote or uncritical belief, there is a shared sense of stressing a believer's dynamic and connected relationship with tradition.
113. KTHH, p. 130.
114. KTHH, p. 165. Taken from this Turkish sentence: "geçmişine ve geleceğine güveni olan, kendisini ötekinin karşısında konumlayan ve de bu cezayı Allah'ın hududu biçimde tanımlayan bir kimlik çıkar."
115. FY, p. 102.
116. See MacIntyre's *After Virtue* (1981; repr. Notre Dame, IN: University of Notre Dame Press, 1984).
117. KTHH, p. 167. Turkish: "Kur'an her şeyden önce, bizi (Müslümanları), diğer paradigmalar karşısında temsil eden bir metindir. [. . .] . . . bizim tarihimizdir; bizi biz yapan bir tarihtir, anlatıdır."
118. He cites the Turkish translation of this work: *Karısını Şapka Sanan Adam*, trans. Çiğden Çalkılıç (Istanbul: Yapı Kredi Yayınları, 1997).
119. KTHH, p. 168.
120. This I am inferring from the example. I have the sense that he is criticizing both extremes—those who reject tradition for an idealized pristine religious past (like many Salafists) and those who reject tradition and the call of sacred scripture in the face of modern skepticism.
121. KTHH, p. 169. Turkish: "Özetle içinde bulunduğumuz an bizi ağır bir travmaya uğratmış durumdadır. [. . .] Peki, bu travmadan bir kurtuluş yolu var mıdır?"
122. KTHH, p. 169. He points to the Jewish tradition as an instance of successful mediation between embracing history and utopic vision.
123. KTHH, p. 170. Turkish: "Kur'an'ı bizi biz yapan bir anlatı olarak okumak, onun hala bizi oluşturmaya devam eden bir kaynak olduğu anlamına gelir."
124. TO, pp. 94–5.
125. TO, p. 90.

126. TO, p. 92.
127. TO, p. 138. Turkish: "evet ve hayır diyalektiği."
128. TO, p. 139. For a work in which Alpyağıl looks at potential postmodern resources already endemic to Islamic tradition see his "Derrida and Islamic Mysticism: An Undecidable Relationship," in Z. Direk and L. Lawlor (eds), *A Companion to Derrida* (Chichester: Wiley Blackwell, 2014). Broadly speaking, his answer is a yes and no as to whether one can claim postmodern ideas were already present in Islamic mystical thought.
129. TO, p. 99. Turkish: "Kanaatimizce, felsefenin geçmişle olan ilişkisinde *mirası atmak* ve bu yolla ondan kurtulmaya çalışmak oldukça basit bir tercihtir."
130. TO, p. 141.
131. Fazlur Rahman, *Major Themes of the Qur'an* (Chicago: University of Chicago Press, 2009), p. 37.

III

A THEOLOGICAL ANTHROPOLOGY OF EMPOWERMENT

5

Düzgün's Case for a Religion of Freedom

In the previous discussion of Recep Alpyağıl's work, *mediated individual authority* came to the fore. In Alpyağıl's case, the argument for authority was inferred from his larger project of reclaiming and re-narrating an authentic philosophical canon along with a living, dynamic Muslim identity. In the next two chapters, the aim is to address a more direct argument for individual authority. I locate this argument for individual authority in one theologian's theological anthropology. Turkish theologian Şaban Ali Düzgün's theological case for individual agency offers an integration of concerns and sources from both Islamic and non-Islamic discussions, while still remaining in an Islamic framework. Taken together as a whole, his theological project vigorously affirms and defines individual agency, without being reduced to binary schemes of Islam vs. the West, religion vs. secularism, or tradition vs. modernity. The present chapter will give an overview of his thought, a treatment of his views on modernity, and a sketch of his theological anthropology.

Şaban Ali Düzgün (b. 1968) is a well-known and prolific professor at Ankara University's theology faculty, where he entered and completed his theological studies.[1] After earning his doctorate in *kalām* (Islamic theology) on the subject of the God–world relation in Islamic philosophy (1996),[2] he went on to participate in an academic exchange with the Gregorian University in Rome (2000–1) and was a visiting academic at Georgetown University (2003–4). He is the head of Ankara Theology Faculty's *Kalām* department. Travelling internationally, he has earned broader recognition for his efforts to address the question of religion and violence. His theological reflections display a mixture of the modern and postmodern,[3] as well as roots in classical Islamic thought and the Qur'ān.[4]

Düzgün's use of traditional Islamic sources alongside Western philosophical and theological scholarly works, a practice that I have argued is characteristic of many Turkish theologians, offers an example of the multiplicity of authoritative traditions at play in Turkish theology. While only closer engagement with specific arguments will be able to answer the question of how Düzgün uses his sources, this section offers a brief overview of what he typically cites as sources. Broadly speaking, Düzgün draws from several bodies of intellectual tradition: Christian theology, Western philosophy, along with Arabic, Ottoman, and other Islamic sources. A cursory glance at his theological dialogue partners within European and Anglophone scholarship shows at least nominal familiarity with a range of important theological voices from the nineteenth and twentieth centuries: Karl Barth (1886–1968), Friedrich Schleiermacher (1768–1834), Rudolf Bultmann (1884–1976), Bernard Lonergan (1904–84), Sallie McFague (b. 1933), Paul Ricoeur (1913–2005), Paul Tillich (1886–1965), Rudolph Otto (1869–1937), Jacques Maritain (1882–1973), Kevin J. Vanhoozer (b. 1957), George Lindbeck (b. 1923), Stanley J. Grenz (1950–2005), Thomas M. Kelly (b.?), Anders Nygren (1890–1978), Graham Ward (b. 1955), David Tracy (b. 1939), Janet Soskice (b. 1951), Ian Ramsey (1915–72), and Gordon Kaufman (1925–2011), to name a few.[5] As the names suggest, Düzgün cites contemporary academics and icons of theological history alike. Among European and Anglophone philosophers, he engages (with varying degrees of intensity) Blaise Pascal (1623–62), René Descartes (1596–1650), John Locke (1632–1704), Immanuel Kant (1724–1804), Georg W. F. Hegel (1770–1831), Auguste Comte (1798–1857), Ernst Cassirer (1874–1945), Hans Reichenbach (1891–1953), A. J. Ayer (1910–89), J. L. Austin (1911–60), Karl Popper (1902–94), Ludwig Wittgenstein (1889–1951), Willard V. O. Quine (1908–2000), Alasdair MacIntyre (b. 1929), Paul Feyerabend (1924–94), Martin Buber (1878–1965), Hans-Georg Gadamer (1900–2002), and Jacques Derrida (1930–2004).[6] Düzgün does not, however, rely solely on Western sources. Often, Western sources tend to offer occasions for broader discussions rather than fundamentally shape or determine the scope of his project.

In addition to Western sources, Düzgün frequently cites the Qurʾān and offers his interpretation or an explanation of the significance of various verses. Added to this list are classical Arabic authors like the Shāfiʿī scholar Abū Manṣūr ibn Ṭāhir al-Baghdādī (980–1037) and theologian Abū Manṣūr al-Māturīdī (853–944), whose work is often associated with Ḥanafī thought. In addition to classical Islamic sources he draws on modern Muslim thinkers; for instance, the Iranian intellectual icon Ali Sheriati (1933–77), the modernist Pakistani Fazlur Rahman, Indian Syed Ahmad Khan (1817–98),[7] Tunisian Mohamed Talbi (b. 1921), late Ottoman Ahmet Cevdet Paşa (1822–95), and the Ottoman-Turkish Hilmi Ziya Ülken (1901–74).

Beyond his sources, it may be helpful to start with an overview of Düzgün's thought before looking at any one position in detail. Düzgün's sources reflect an internal conversation of authoritative tradition with Arabic, Ottoman/Turkish, and Western sources, and Düzgün's conceptual repertoire also reflects a similar dynamic. While many of his positions are in line with values associated with the tradition of the European Enlightenment, these values are grounded in an Islamic framework and are often defined with the help of Islamic concepts. This overview aims to give a holistic sense of his integral use of traditions and concepts.

Düzgün considers himself a universalist. He affirms that human beings share a common constitution, both religious and moral, regardless of other human variations (such as culture, appearance, gender, class, etc.). Each human being possesses a *fiṭra*, a conscience (which is itself a reflection of *fiṭra*), the use of reason, and a propensity to seek true religion.[8] In several of his books, as well as in public talks, Düzgün argues for the authority and agency of the individual. He does so within a combined Islamic and Enlightenment framework. His appeals to the universality of human experience and language are consistent hallmarks of the positive influence of Enlightenment values in his work. These appeals are often made in the name of common sense and reason.[9] Yet, his theological project as a whole resists being reduced to a potpourri of Enlightenment values. Undergirding this universalist framework of Enlightenment values stands a theological anthropology which is avowedly Muslim. I shall argue that the foundation of his case for individual agency is his premise that true religion does not stand in the way of human values and individual agency, but indeed provides the healthiest grounds for true individual agency.

This individual authority is not the authority of a decentered self à la Charles Taylor.[10] Rather, the individual, according to Düzgün, bears authority precisely because God has outfitted each human being with an original nature that points back to God. In other words, God is the source and outfitter of individual authority.

Further, a closer examination of Düzgün's theological case for individual authority shows how his work often resists dualities of tradition vs. modernity, Islam vs. the Western intellectual tradition, or even modernity vs. postmodernity. Instead of dualities, his case for individual authority highlights the creative, constructive, and synthesizing elements at play in the Turkish theological context of competing as well as cooperating sources of intellectual authority.

Of his many writings, one of his more recent books *Religion and Religious [People] in the Contemporary World* (2012)[11] directly engages the concepts of modernity and postmodernity. In this work, Düzgün stresses the importance of religion in the continuity of cultural values. Religion, ideally, keeps culture striving for universal standards.[12] For this reason it is important not to see religion as something opposed to all other facets of human existence.[13] The diversity of cultures—even within the scope of a single religion—is a *sine qua non* for a living, fecund religious life. Islam, as the best example of this, embraces and thrives on cultural diversity. To force the entire Islamic world into one single culture would be to sterilize it.[14] In this way, Düzgün appreciates both universality and particularity. Religion urges individuals and cultures to strive for universal ideals and standards while simultaneously thriving amid diversity.

Since Düzgün views religion as a force that pulls people out of local hegemonies and cultural tunnel vision, he also defines religion as something that one can come to without an institution. Religion transcends individual human institutions and can be found in an individual's primal nature (*fıṭra*), conscience (*vicdan*), reason (*akıl*), and in common sense (*sağduyu*). These faculties equip any human being with the ability to discover divine, natural, or universal values.[15] Yet, if this is the case, then what additional purpose does revelation or the birth of a new religion serve? Düzgün's answer is that, in the course of history, revelation's purpose has been to restore society to universal values and principles; that is, revelation has instigated the reformation of society.¹⁶ To put it another way, religion functions to establish values and social equality as Islam did when it first appeared. Düzgün writes:

> For this reason, the fundamental purpose for religions being revealed is to create the structure of society anew within a framework of basic universal values like justice, freedom, equality of rights, and mutual respect.¹⁷

As the reader may note from the quote above, Düzgün's definition of religion and its function is very modern. Yet, he himself acknowledges this modern aspect, claiming that real religion has always carried within itself modernizing and reforming elements.¹⁸ Düzgün, citing Western Christianity as a primary example, also concedes that in the wrong hands, religion can be sterilized and used as a tool of an unjust state.¹⁹ Because religion can be misused, Düzgün offers the following standard for discerning when religion is being used for appropriate ends:

> Believers must test whether the relations of the society in which they live are configured in light of concepts like basic human rights, justice, freedom, and trust—using forms of critical conscience, creative imagination, utopian [regulative] ideals, and dialectical thinking.²⁰

This standard may sound like a rehashing of modern humanist values; however, it is grounded in his theological understanding of Islam. Düzgün affirms the positive values of modernity by pointing to the existence of such values in Islam and in religion regardless of time or place. While appreciative of many values associated with modernity, Düzgün does criticize modernity's reductionist tendency to strip religion of its ability to transcend time and place, effectively reducing religious values to a cultural or institutional hegemony. In short, Düzgün does not demonize modernity *per se*, but rather the reductionism associated with modernity. For the theologian, reductionism is not a necessary attribute of modernity; however, it has been a historical outcome in Western modernity.

While Düzgün recognizes values such as justice and equanimity as "modern," he distinguishes between various modernities.²¹ Western modernity, as he sees it, exhibits a harmful desire to homogenize human diversity.²² The culture of monopoly on truth and salvation are for Düzgün rooted in Judeo-Christian culture. In his view, this way of looking at reality is embodied in the Western cultural prevalence of *center-periphery* modes of thinking.[23] On the one hand, Düzgün views the reductionist and monopolizing discourses of Western modernity as central causes of violence and intolerance. On the other, Düzgün embraces some aspects of postmodernity, hailing it as a much-needed critique of the Western modern's desire to package all human experience into metanarratives.[24] In his view, postmodernity offers some tools for moving forward and out of what he sees as the sterilizing singlemindedness of Western modernity's tendency towards intellectual hegemony; to this end, Düzgün drops names associated with the critique of modernity, such as Michel Foucault (1926–84), Theodor Adorno (1903–69), and Max Horkheimer (1895–1973).[25] While his direct engagement with postmodern thought is limited, he still admits of postmodernity's value as a tempering force to Western modernity's false claims to universality.

One of Düzgün's most consistent and fundamental theological arguments is to stress the authority of the religious individual and the importance of her agency in the world, over and above materialistic or fatalistic paradigms. Far from arguing for rugged individualism, Düzgün builds this call for individual authority on the basis of what I deem to be his Islamic theological anthropology.[26] This theological anthropology is founded on a universalist position on human morality, an Islamic affirmation of the plurality of human life, a view of religion as both constructive and deconstructive, the claim that true religion is fundamentally modernizing, and a view of human agency that is not in competition with divine agency. He also argues in various contexts for the authority of *'aql* (a combination of heart and thought, as he uses the term),[27] common sense, human intuition, and conscience.[28]

The complexities of mediating various traditions and voices of authority inform Düzgün's theological project as a whole. By looking at how the pieces of his theological project fit together, it is possible to trace not only superficial engagements with distinct voices and tradition but to also shed light on the deeper fault lines of tension and on creative moments of synthesis.

Modernity—A Question of Avoiding Reduction and Affirming Plurality

Düzgün makes a case for the religious importance of individual agency, authority, and responsibility in the modern world. His case is not an account of the religious person disconnected from the crisis of modernity, globalization, secularism, or the horizons of science and technology. Instead, Düzgün embeds his discussion of the role of the individual within a larger, nuanced discussion of modernity. This section takes up questions of hegemony, post-colonialism, the authority of sacred text, hermeneutics, and the global context of science and pluralism. Due to the constructive and holistic nature of his thought (i.e., he does not tackle issues in isolation with one another), it is not possible to grasp his views on the role of the religious individual without first placing these views into context. As I will argue, Düzgün does not reject modernity or react against it; he criticizes what he sees as Western modernity's tendency to reduce the necessary and healthy plurality of human experience.

Hegemony and Post-colonialism

Düzgün marks 1839 as the beginning of intellectual modernism.[29] This coincides with the beginning of the Ottoman Tanzimat period (1839–76), which signaled a significant change in Ottoman state policies, including the increasing recognition of the rights of non-Muslims and the opening of the first modern universities (*darülfünun*). However, Düzgün does not restrict himself to the Ottoman experience of modernity. He speaks to a broader discussion of modernity beyond the Ottoman context. Within the scope of this wider discussion, he more than once delves into the post-colonial and dependency theories (*post-kolonyal tez/sömürge sonrası tezi* and *bağımlılık tezi*, respectively).[30] For this discussion, he draws heavily on Talal Asad's work.[31] Düzgün references post-colonial theory to indicate the thesis that non-Western societies can develop their own modernity; whereas, he references dependency theory to indicate the thesis that liberal modernity as exemplified in Western societies is the only modernity.[32]

For his part, Düzgün champions plural expressions of modernity against the monolithic idea of a single modernity. Although he does not believe human beings are essentially different or foreign to one another at a basic level, he points to diversity as a divinely willed and necessary element in human survival and flourishing. Further, Düzgün actively investigates and appraises different assumptions and associations lurking behind the concept of modernity, and he simultaneously employs modernity as a unifying concept and as a concept to be broken down and critically analyzed—stressing both the unity and plurality of a concept is one of the hallmarks of Düzgün's intellectual style of inquiry.

While modernity may have various expressions, Düzgün stresses that modernity as exemplified by Western societies belies a tendency towards hegemony. This tendency, whether expressed in secular or religious forms, he traces to the Western expression of Judeo-Christian history. For Düzgün, even an aggressively secular West reflects origins in a certain history of institutional religion.[33] Düzgün further notes that truth and salvation monopolies tend to get tied up with ethnocentrism, especially in the Judeo-Christian tradition. This tendency includes what he deems the "ethnocentric truth monopoly" of positivism.[34] He accuses positivists of not being consistent in their universal values. And what is the destructive element of positivism? Düzgün answers: monopolizing tendencies. Positivism's underlying ethnocentrism stems from its Judeo-Christian "genetics" of center/periphery, I/other modes of thought—all this is problematic. It creates a false and oversimplified division of West and other—as if all non-Western humanity fits into one category.[35]

Düzgün also speaks of a "Western truth monopoly" (*Batının hakikat tekelciliği*).[36] In other words, he notes there is a Western tendency to homogenize the world.[37] This is most evident in Western portrayals of non-Western societies, portrayals which often rest on a center/peripherary discourse.[38] The very structure of a center/periphery discourse implies the centrality of one position relative to all others. When this centrality is taken for granted and pervasively informs socio-politial realities, it operates as a kind of truth monopoly. For Düzgün, examples of this in Western society include the medieval crusades and more recent colonial history. In short, there is a bloody side to the West's truth monopoly.[39] This truth monopoly can manifest in religion, philosophy, or politics; this truth monopoly is not limited to religion even if he views the source of Western truth monopolies as a particular, faulty mutation of religion, citing Hegel as a typical example of a truth monopoly in philosophy.[40] These center/periphery frames of thinking have also helped create a tendency to view non-Western societies as arational.[41] And although this center/periphery mode of thinking infiltrates even secular modes of thought, Düzgün envisions the Western truth monopoly as a kind of quranic punishment for Christians and Jews.[42] Yet even this truth monopoly is not absolute. Within Western thought, post-colonial, deconstructive, and postmodern authors point to resources for a more authentic plurality. On this point, he touches on the works of Frantz Fanon (1925–61), M. Foucault, T. Adorno, and M. Horkheimer; as Düzgün sees it, the positive value of postmodernity is that it has brought an end to the supremacy of metanarratives.[43] Postmodernity helps deconstruct the false center/periphery discourses that characterize Western monolithic views of modernity.

For Düzgün, part of the problem lies in reigning Western metaphysical assumptions that produce a falsely divided sense of reality. Materialists value only the material world. Many Christians value only the non-material world. Both groups fail to look at existence as a whole. By contrast, Islam—unlike materialism or Christianity—does not divide the world into material and non-material realms in such a way as to deny the worth of only part of creation.[44]

Moreover, Islam embraces and thrives amid cultural diversity—so much so that to force the Islamic world into one homogenous culture would be to sterilize Islam. Rather than trying to contain Islam within the bounds of institutional religion, he stresses the importance of respecting the individual's ability to discover truth through common sense and by connection to her authentic nature. In his judgment, it is precisely this aspect of the Islamic understanding of the individual that makes it more resistant to the negatively homogenizing effects of institutionalization which so ravaged European religious history. He writes:

> It must be recognized that a human person is able to discover truth with her *fitra* and common sense even before being part of the structure of an institutional religion.[45]

The individual's authentic orientation to God takes precedence over institutional religion. Düzgün functionally equates institutional religion, in the negative sense, with a monopoly on God. In speaking out against institutional religion (his preferred example being the Catholic Church), he resists the idea of any human monopoly on God. Nevertheless, he still believes different individuals should have access to common means for discussing religion. Yet a shared discussion of religion cannot start from revelation (*vahiy*), as this is not commonly accepted by all.[46] Since people cannot agree on God, secular thinkers instead insist on conscience.[47] Düzgün too starts with conscience as a source of religious authority.

Epistemology in Modernity: The Authority of Theology and Sacred Text

This brings us to the question of epistemology. What sort of knowledge is considered valid in a modern world? If common discussions about religion cannot be grounded on specific revelation, what other options are there? Düzgün references the crisis of theology in Western academia as well as issues of scriptural hermeneutics. In accord with modernity's high estimation of human reason, Düzgün argues for the validity of independent human reasoning in making sound ethical decisions, but he also points to a broader spectrum of human faculties for knowing right and wrong, including conscience, grounding them all in God's plan for humanity.

Düzgün tackles this modern epistemological challenge to theology in his book *God, History and Nature: The Problem of Method in Theology and Theology's Meta-paradigmatic Foundations* (2005).[48] In this work, Düzgün points out that theology is often reduced to rationalism, empiricism, or to sacred texts. He then traces the reason for this reduction to the modern philosophical crisis of knowledge. He claims modern philosophy's concern for epistemology is at the heart of theology's search for method.[49]

In Düzgün's view, one major feature of modern epistemology is its tendency to discard the value of "*kashf*" (Turkish: *keşf*). *Kashf* can be translated to mean revelation or unveiling, but what precisely does Düzgün mfean by *kashf*? Süleyman Uludağ, in the *Turkish Encyclopedia of Islam*, defines *kashf* as "a Sufi term which refers to the mind and senses' direct acquisition of knowledge on religious topics where [formally revealed] instruction is lacking."[50] Düzgün uses the term more or less in this sense, making occasional but not overfrequent references to Sufis where appropriate.[51] *Kashf* functions as an instance of individual authority, since it designates direct knowing by means of an individual's insight and perception (for instance, as in dreams). By current theological standards, religious knowledge comes only through history and formal revelation and not through *kashf*.[52] Düzgün resists this modern devaluing of *kashf*, arguing instead that humans need spiritual vision to see reality as a whole and that religious knowledge should not be reduced to empiricism, rationalism, or agnosticism.[53] Modern rationalism, true to its reductionist tendencies, dumps "*nous*" for "*logos*."[54] *Nous* designates, for Düzgün, a broader idea of comprehension and conceptualization (with room enough for something like *kashf*), whereas *logos* means reason in the strict, mechanical sense. Rather than using Arabic or Islamic concepts, he uses ancient Greek distinctions in rationality to criticize modern Western epistemology—employing terms that have traditionally defined Western intellectual self-image to evaluate that same self-image.

Düzgün positively applies Gadamer's "fusion of horizons" (*ufukların birleşmesi*) to the status and function of scripture.[55] He uses "fusion of horizons" to point to the crucial contribution the reader brings to the act of meaning-making: "the text exists solely in the act of being read."[56] Thus, the role of the individual and the question of individual authority become paramount in the act of interpreting. Counter to popular trends that conflate the authority of individual and literal interpretation,[57] Düzgün opposes limiting readings to the literal sense. For him, a literal reading is too restrictive;[58] it is hard to draw a hard line between experience and textual commentary.[59] In a more recent work entitled *Humans Surrounded by a Precipitous Slope* (2016), Düzgün clarifies that his method for understanding stresses agency rather than passivity—on the part of sacred text and on the part of the reader: the Qur'ān is not to be read as a passive text reduced to historical detail; rather, the act of reading the Qur'ān should be understood as a heavily interactive process.[60] To read the Qur'ān as a document that historically addressed only its first interlocutors overlooks the creative purpose the Qur'ān serves in its interaction with the present-day reader. The Qur'ān is more than a book bound to the Prophet's time.[61]

Just as the reader is actively interpreting, so too is the Qur'ān purposefully acting on the reader. To illustrate this mutual relation Düzgün turns to a Christian scholar of scriptural hermeneutics. Düzgün agrees with Kevin J. Vanhoozer that commentary is a theological duty.[62] Vanhoozer, a Christian theologian and hermeneuticist, is known for writing a "theology of interpretation" but, unlike Gadamer, he argues that in the case of sacred text meaning is independent of the individual reading or interpretation of the text.[63] Düzgün appears to agree with Vanhoozer on the sacred text's independent agency and simultaneously concords with Gadamer on the relational quality of any one interpretation. Here Düzgün dwells less on what Gadamer's views on interpretation mean for the question of correct interpretation and focuses more on the relational and interactive elements of interpretation entailed in Gadamer's general thesis.[64]

Globalization and Questions of Pluralism and Science

Globalization is yet another face of modernity. Düzgün neither uncritically acclaims nor unequivocally condemns globalization. On the positive side, globalization pushes for more universal values. On the negative side, it provokes a profound loss of identity and foundation, resulting in a disorienting and paralyzing relativism (*görecelik*). Düzgün writes:

> People are everywhere but nowhere at home. This feeling of insecurity is the most significant factor pushing people to seek a new source of meaning.[65]

Globalization produces displacement and uprootedness. The displacement and loss of rootedness leads to a quest for meaning. While people may feel increasingly drawn to seek out meaning; at the same time, religion's sense of being threatened is also a response to globalization.[66] When it comes to the negative aspects of globalization, Düzgün assures his reader they are not the result of intentional conspiracies—the world simply developed in this manner such that it produced the challenges we face today.[67] Nevertheless, deformed/secularized Protestantism poses an ongoing threat to world religions.[68] Although Düzgün approves of the Protestant trend to put greater emphasis on individual responsibility rather than religious hierarchies, he strongly condemns individualism devoid of a sense of greater responsibility as something that devolves quickly into totalitarian and imperialist selfhood. In other words, the problem with some Protestant understandings of Christianity is that they did not stop at a call to individual responsibility, but, voided of their original values, these models devolved into systems that promoted a totalitarian and imperialist sense of self.[69] A self unchecked quickly takes on demonic qualities, or as Düzgün explains, absolute hegemony demonizes a person, making destructive individualism one of the many challenges of globalization.[70]

Globalization is also inextricably marked by the experience of postcolonialism. Düzgün uses the word trauma to speak of the colonial experience.[71] Insofar as the effects of Western power are felt, he writes, it is possible to say that no well-rooted reform has been achieved.[72] As with Alpyağıl, there is a clear reference to trauma and a recognition of the need to find new modes of responding to this trauma. Düzgün's initial call is for Muslims to get out of the rut of reflexive or reactive responses to colonialization.[73] He asks Muslims and other non-Western societies to move beyond the perceived tendency merely to react to colonialism and its aftereffects.[74] New forms of action are needed that do not reflect old colonial power structures. In this context, Düzgün hails Q16:125 as a quranic prescription for West–East relations.[75] The verse reads:

> Call [people] to the way of your Lord with wisdom and good teaching. Argue with them in the most courteous way, for your Lord knows best who has strayed from His way and who is rightly guided.[76]

With this quranic verse as a foundation, Düzgün points to dialogue, critical discussion, and re-evaluation of terms as ways of moving beyond the trauma of colonialism and other shocks of globalization. As part of the task of critical re-evaluation of terms, he highlights the pressing need to redefine words like racism, difference, otherness, and tolerance.[77] Düzgün further cautions the reader to place critical distance between his own prescriptions and the common tendency to stress center and periphery ways of categorizing issues.[78] Such binary modes of discourse only serve to essentialize and obfuscate complex issues. On this point, Düzgün also identifies a new form of Orientalism: essentializing anything a Muslim says as particular of Islam.[79] While he himself will speak for Islam and about Islam, he does remind his reader that individual Muslims express different aspects of Islam differently. Muslims in different places and contexts face very different challenges. For instance, he notes that Muslims in the West are increasingly faced with challenges of identity and belonging.[80] In this context, he stresses the importance of seeing Islam not as a foreign belief (not periphery, not other) but as a natural, value-producing well-spring wherever it is found.[81]

Düzgün's Theological Anthropology: Fiṭra (*fitra*)

Düzgün's view of quranic purpose for humankind is what I call Düzgün's "theological anthropology." For Düzgün, the divine purpose entails affirming freedom (especially religious freedom), affirming individual agency (i.e., humans are not subservient to either jinn or hierarchical religion), and the divine outfitting of humans with the interrelated faculties of intuition (*sezgi*), common sense (*sağduyu*), conscience (*vicdan*), and reason (*akıl*). For Düzgün, divine purpose affirms human purpose. This is because the affirmation of human purpose and agency goes hand in hand with the affirmation of inherent meaning in all of creation: God creates purposefully. Human beings are created with a purpose and equipped with faculties tailored to help them fulfill that purpose. So, by Düzgün's "theological anthropology," I mean what he claims to be the divine purpose for humanity as well as the divinely willed constitution of the human being to fulfill said purpose.[82]

Let us return to the term *fıṭra*, an Islamic concept of central importance. The term is often translated as primordial nature, innate nature, or natural disposition. Ebrahim Moosa describes *fıṭra* as something humans are equipped at birth with—"a natural state and with a built-in disposition for the truth (*fıṭra*)."[83] Moosa explains that for an earlier scholar of Islam like al-Ghazālī, "the role of innate nature (*fıṭra*) [functions] as a receptacle in the heart for the light associated with divine mercy and grace."[84] In short, the *fıṭra* is an original openness and orientation towards truth. Seyyed Hossein Nasr, whose work is relatively well known in Turkey, describes *fıṭra* in the following way. According to Nasr, a human being (*insān*), whether male or female, is "a being who still carries his primordial nature (*al-fıṭrah*) within himself, although he has forgotten that nature now buried deep under layers of negligence."[85] Here we note an image of estrangement from humankind's original disposition. Düzgün's understanding of *fıṭra* is similar to both Moosa's and Nasr's definitions, as estrangement from one's *fıṭra* or natural disposition plays a central role in his thoughts on society's relation to religion and the individual.

Düzgün develops these themes in his written opus as well as in popular talks. In a talk given in early 2014, Düzgün summarizes some of the most fundamental elements of his theological anthropology. This talk, roughly translated as "Building Identity based on Value," treats the question of human nature, or in Islamic terms *fıṭra* or "disposition."[86] Exploring an Islamic perspective on the fundamental identity and nature of a human being, Düzgün remarks that this original disposition is something individuals lose touch with over time, describing how politics, religion, culture, and other societal pressures drive people to act out two-faced behavior and, as a result, become alienated from their *fıṭra*.

In the talk, Düzgün further maintains that society often alienates an individual from her *fıtra*, and his portrayal of society emphasizes the corrupting nature of civilization, especially its institutions. For Düzgün, questions of authority and human values are especially precarious in societies that depend on law (*kanun*) and legal standards to ensure morality. This does not mean he opposes legal structures or institutions. Law is good in the sense that it provides rule of law and base-line standards, but it is better for individuals to have the space to freely negotiate these standards rather than to reduce their moral values to statutes and rulings. Statutes and rulings alone simply cannot take the place of individuals striving for and negotiating values among themselves.

For Düzgün, civilization can estrange an individual from her original nature, and legal standards fail to ensure morality. Thus individual authority is best understood in contradistinction to external authority or authority imposed from without by society, government, and legal strictures. Since the individual has an irreplaceable role in the process of building a society founded on shared values, individual authority is indispensable to society's moral fiber. A world run only in terms of institutional authority cannot be a world of living values. A world where individual discretion and expression of values has no formative place is also a world where authority comes entirely from the outside. Authority imposed solely from the outside restricts us. Such authority is dry and procedural and lacks authentic vitality. It also requires no active cooperation from the individual. To illustrate this aspect of outside authority, in "Building Identity based on Value," Düzgün gives the example of a government collecting taxes. When a government collects taxes, it makes no efforts to convince citizens to cooperate. The act is a demand accompanied by a strict expectation of compliance. This sort of externally imposed and potentially oppressive authority is the polar opposite to what he characterizes as inner authority.

From external authority of the stultifying variety, Düzgün turns to an ideal of authority that comes from within. Conscience, or in Turkish *"vicdan,"* is the inner authority we all possess.[87] When we act on our conscience, this exemplifies authority from within. However, this is no individualistic authority accountable merely to some vague and egotistical sense of self. On the contrary, this inner authority is inextricably linked to a higher authority, transcending the laws of states and societies. According to Düzgün, God acts through the human conscience, that is, through and not counter to an individual's sense of inner authority. The authority of conscience comes simultaneously from God and from human nature; it has a distinctly participatory and cooperative bent. For this reason, Düzgün intimates that the authority of conscience is more essential and fundamental to human flourishing than any particular manifestation of external, institutional authority.

In this same talk, Düzgün explains that true religion (*din*) is not about compulsion (*zorlama*); rather, it is about persuasion (*ikna*). Where there is compulsion (*zorlama*), one cannot be in true religion (*din*).[88] The Qur'ān itself does not force religion but works instead to convince—it is, in his words, a "book that works to convince."[89] Faith (*iman*), in turn, is like a motor. It powers and undergirds ethical striving. Faith does not evince compulsion but it does encourage us to do good things. By that same token, faith alone does not amount to much by itself unless a believer is already striving to be a good person and to do good works.

Original human nature and authority are closely related concepts for Düzgün. Düzgün, here and elsewhere, speaks against the constrictive and suffocating sides of dry legalism or institutional religion run amok. Nevertheless, in "Building Identity based on Value," he still affirms that individuals, while valuable as single entities, have even more worth as parts of greater wholes. Significantly, he does not say individuals have worth only when detached from society and structures, which may contain various external authorities. Instead, he affirms individual worth, first by affirming the value of the individual conscience, and then remarks that those individuals who exercise their conscience have even more impact as active members of larger societies. Individuality is enhanced and not diminished by conscientious participation in society. While society can and often does estrange an individual from her *fiṭra*, there exists no exclusionary binary between individual and communal existence. In sum, Düzgün's concept of an individual includes the individual's relationship to society and community. Because of this, I stress the centrality of "mediated" individual authority in his works in order to underscore the fact that his concept of the individual is not that of a lone, disconnected automaton.

Düzgün's views on the importance of internal authority also play out in his written works. In an earlier work *Religion, Individual, and Society*,[90] he starts with al-Māturīdī (d. 944), the importance of *fiṭra*, and a call for universal religious values. In this book, Düzgün's fundamental claim is that humans are by nature religious,[91] and the claim persists into his more recent scholarly activities. While al-Māturīdī is not a major influence in Alpyağıl's work, al-Māturīdī figures prominently in Düzgün's theological project. Here, Düzgün is not an isolated case. Al-Māturīdī serves as a major source of authority and orientation for many Turkish theologians—a trend going back to at least the mid-twentieth century.[92] Broadly speaking, Turkish Ottoman history favored Ḥanafī jurisprudence; and since Ḥanafī jurisprudence often went hand in hand with Māturīdī theology, al-Māturīdī's reception history in Turkey has deep historical roots.[93] As for Düzgün, he draws primarily on al-Māturīdī's Qur'ān commentary (*Ta'wīlāt al-Qur'ān*)[94] and from al-Māturīdī's *kalām* work *Kitāb al-Tawḥīd*. Düzgün, elsewhere,[95] writes on a follower of al-Māturīdī from a subsequent generation—Abū al-Muʿīn al-Nasafī (d. 1114/15), famous for his *Kitāb Tabṣirat al-Adilla*.[96]

Düzgün stresses the practical significance of subtle variations between Māturīdī and Ashʿarī theology. Compared with Ashʿarī (or "Ashʿarite") theology, Māturīdī theology places greater importance on human free will, strongly affirms human ability to come to knowledge of God and morality apart from prophecy, and considers God's creative act as eternal and ongoing despite the finite nature of creation.[97] These distinctions carry over strongly into Düzgün's work and all have direct implications for Düzgün's theological evaluation of *fiṭra*.[98] Such distinctions point to a human being who possesses free will and an innate orientation towards God and towards moral truths, a human being who is both given space and responsibility to choose and to act but is nevertheless not abandoned by God. God has created human beings with qualities of the divine attributes; independently, they can recognize God's oneness and can come to consciousness of the gratitude they owe their creator.[99]

For Düzgün, a human being is complete insofar as she is able to preserve and remain true to her *fiṭra*; she is primitive insofar as she has become estranged from her *fiṭra*.[100] His use of the word "primitive" (*ilkel*) is a conscious re-association of the term as it was used in early and mid-twentieth century anthropology.[101] Rather than designating people outside of urban civilizations or at perceived peripheries as "primitive," he marks those who have lost touch with their original disposition as primitive regardless of whether they live in Tokyo, New York, Minnesota, or Botswana. Further, he states the idea of God is so bound up with humanity's innate nature that the very concept of God came into existence together with the rise of humanity.[102] Accordingly, religion is something an individual can come to without an institution, through *fıtra* and common sense. Düzgün further parses individual authority and ability to discern into an array of God-given faculties: common sense, conscience, and reason. Yet, Düzgün does not mean reason (*akıl*) in a limited or narrow sense, putting reason in close connection with human intuition instead. For instance, in *Religion and Religious [People] in the Contemporary World*, he states that both reason (*akıl*) and intuition (*sezgi*) are what allow us to recognize good from bad.[103] He also invokes the quranic talent of intuition (*sezgi*) "*ilhām*," or inspiration, linking his argument for the independent authority of reason and intuition with what he sees as a quranic argument for individual authority. He cites Q91:8 as quranic indication of human authority: "and [God] inspired it [that is, the soul] with [the ability to discern] between its immoral action and its piety."[104] Note that the word "inspired" in the quranic Arabic comes from the same root as "*ilhām*," which Düzgün elsewhere translates as intuition (*sezgi*).[105] Düzgün aligns this interpretation with Ḥanafī thought on morality and contrasts it with Ashʿarī reasoning. His explanation of Ḥanafī moral reasoning is as follows: for Ḥanafīs, something is forbidden because it is bad, not bad because it is forbidden. By contrast, Ashʿarī positions on human morality emphasize that something is good or bad because God enjoins or forbids it. In contrast with Ashʿarī emphasis on the importance of revelation in determining moral good and moral evil, it makes sense from a Ḥanafī perspective that human beings can determine bad and good without the direct aid of revelation. Düzgün stresses that Ḥanafīs hold knowledge of good and bad can exist independently of sharia, that is, revealed Islamic law. Revelation itself addresses its interlocutors with the assumption they already know good from bad.[106] What then is the purpose of revelation in this instance if the human being is already equipped with moral discernment? Düzgün explains that revelation serves to educate the will (*irade*).[107] It would seem that, in comparison with the human mind and conscience, human will is less naturally equipped to recognize and pursue moral good.[108]

In addition to the importance of reason (*akıl*) and intuition (*sezgi*) in the process of human moral discernment, Düzgün stresses the role of the conscience. He points to the Arabic etymology of the Turkish word for conscience (*vicdan*) to underscore the intimate relationship between conscience and an innate orientation to truth:

> Conscience, which comes from the same root as existence (w-j-d), and reason [whose root is ('a-q-l)], which hints at the unbreakable tie binding human beings to the source from which they came, give human beings the power to distinguish between right and wrong (judgment [*furkan*] and insight [*basiret*]). Humans with both conscience and reason can discover divine/natural/universal values and, in light of these, can live a life codified (guidance [*hidayet*]) towards goodness and beauty.[109]

In short, *fıtra*, which entails reason, intuition, and conscience, bespeaks a relationship to something beyond the human individual and reflects universal values. As Düzgün puts it, *fıtra* is a tendency towards the real.[110] On this point, he is not Gadamerian to the extent that Alpyağıl may be.[111] Orientation to the real, as a concept, is less complex for Düzgün than it is for philosopher of religion Alpyağıl. The former builds from the premise that humans are fundamentally oriented towards the real, rather than delving into the philosophical grounds for and challenges of making this claim, as does the latter. According to Düzgün, God gave humans the ability to distinguish good from bad, the ability to reason abstractly, and the gift of common sense.[112] However, these gifts are not inviolable; humans also need to protect their *fıtra*. Since life is full of pressures and forces that estrange humans from their *fıtra*, it is often necessary to make a conscious return to this *fıtra*. This conscious return, he explains, is repentance: "Repentance [*tövbe*] is the return to a sound *fıtra*."[113] Further, piety (*takva*)[114] is what keeps humans within the healthy bounds of *fıtra*. In other words, he defines piety and repentance in terms of the individual's relationship to her innate disposition. Piety is the attitude which preserves a believer's innate disposition. Repentance is an act or state that restores this disposition.

As we have seen, one important aspect of *fıtra* is the human capacity for reason and common sense. In *God, History, and Nature* (2005), Düzgün expands upon what he means by rationality and reason. He argues that rationality is much broader than a theory of *'aql* (the Turkish adaptation of the Arabic being "*akıl*").¹¹⁵

'Aql is sometimes translated into English as "intellect" or understood generally to designate the faculty of reason. Classical and modern scholars differ on its exact use and function. For instance, Deborah Black, scholar of classical Arabic philosophy, explains the various philosophical divisions of *'aql* or "intellect" common in classical Arabic:

> The framework for all Arabic theories of the intellect was provided by Aristotle's distinction in book III of the *De Anima* between the agent and potential intellects. But the Arabic philosophers also identified a number of additional stages of the intellect, a practice which they inherited from the later Greek tradition.¹¹⁶

While the classical philosophical understanding of *'aql* and its ties to Greek philosophy is still significant to the contemporary use of the word, Düzgün more likely has modern and modernist assumptions about the function of human reason in mind. These assumptions—for instance, faith's diametrical opposition to reason—he subsequently wishes to challenge. Humanity's faculty of thought is not limited to reasoning as it is captured in the term *'aql* (Turkish: *akıl*).¹¹⁷ He lists understanding (*anlama*) or conceptualizing (*kavrama*) as another function of thought.¹¹⁸ Moreover, he lists intuition as part of human cognition; intuition works alongside more abstract reasoning associated with *'aql* (Turkish: *akıl*). He writes:

> For human "knowing" to be labelled religious or theological, or in other words, for the cognition of theological knowledge, it is necessary for reason [*akıl*], intuition, and other faculties of knowing to be used as a whole and in such a way as to support one another.¹¹⁹

Summarizing, intuition (*sezgi*) and reason (*akıl*) together play significant roles in human cognition. Düzgün defines intuition (*sezgi*) and explains how it supports reason:

> The concept that the Sufis used to get beyond the chain of cause and effect, however, was "intuition [*sezgi*]." [. . .] The author proposes that instead of "reason" and "intuition" being formed as opposing concepts, the two of them

found a cognitive subject–objective relationship in which they both function in tandem.[120]

For Düzgün, intuition is a complementary faculty alongside reason. Human intuition and reason work together to furnish a more complete relationship to reality. The significance of this argument lies in Düzgün's affirmation that abstract reason alone is insufficient to be mindful of God. Human reason may be a divine gift and part of our innate nature; however, abstract reason is not the only faculty humans require in order to live meaningfully. Nor does abstract reason exhaust the complex process of human cognition. While reason is a source of internal authority, it is nevertheless incomplete on its own. More complete insight and understanding is possible when reason as well as other aspects of human cognition (like intuitive grasping) are given due credit.

In order to be truly mindful of God, intuition, experience, and emotions all have a role to play. For those individuals forgetful of their original nature and unmindful of God, Düzgün refers to Q59:19: "Do not be like those who forget God, so God causes them to forget their own souls . . ."[121] He takes this quranic verse and expands on the character of those who have forgotten God and, as a result, their own souls. Those who have forgotten God are paralyzed in life; he likens them to butterflies that have become victims of their own silken cocoons, unable to open their wings and seize their true identity. Such individuals darken the world in their efforts to save themselves from it.[122]

By contrast, those who remember God are bound to God and live with a foundational feeling of trust, which allows them to rise above paralysis and face the world. As Düzgün puts it, God's most basic creation within the human being is the feeling of trust (*güven*).[123] This feeling of trust is available to all humans in touch with their original disposition. He thus affirms the value of human beings dependent not on intelligence and good deeds *per se* but rather insofar as they are in touch with their original, God-trusting disposition. Not only do all humans have value, but they also need and seek purpose.[124] To this end, human beings are the only living creatures saddled with true responsibility, a claim which is grounded in the Qur'ān.[125] In their special relationship with God, humans are given real responsibility and are even endowed with God's attributes—seeing and hearing.[126]

In addition to reason, intuition, and physical senses like seeing and hearing, humans are also outfitted with freedom. This freedom, Düzgün argues, is non-trivial and is not nullified by God's oneness or power. Nonetheless, while human freedom is real, human freedom is not without limit. Human freedom is common to us all, but it is not absolute.[127] According to Düzgün, freedom is 1) tied to the person, 2) cannot be transferred to another, and 3) cannot be taken away.[128] Further, this freedom extends to matters of faith. Faith cannot be forced. On this point Düzgün strongly grounds his position with quranic verses. He cites Q10:99–100, which reads, "Had your Lord willed, all the people on earth would have believed. So can you compel people to believe? No soul can believe except by God's will, and He brings disgrace on those who do not use their reason."[129] He also cites the oft-quoted Q2:256, which states there is no compulsion in religion.[130] Düzgün stresses that, in Islam, God's freedom and human freedom do not conflict.[131] It is not religion but human tendencies to resist real freedom that reduce the free individual to a divided slave.[132]

The free individual whose freedom comes from God contrasts starkly with the superficial and false freedom of the individual as defined by liberal society. Düzgün writes, "The error of liberal thought lies in its failure to understand the human being."[133] The negative traits of a liberal individual include selfishness and a feeling of powerlesnes.[134] This liberal individual is divided up by her own superficial and decentered desires. Because she cannot orient herself to the One God, she becomes a slave of every whim in creation. And in today's consumer culture, this image is not difficult for the reader to flesh out. By contrast, submitting to God means freedom in this world. Not submitting to God means submitting to others.[135] Moreover, one who submits to God, while remaining truly free, is not estranged from the world around her. Far from some mythical ascetic or isolated monk, the truly free individual is one who lives out her piety actively in society:

> This individual who has acquired true freedom in being God's slave [. . .] is the person who carries in her mind the awareness and courage to shoulder the responsibility that falls upon her in society at every turn.[136]

Otherwise stated, a truly Islamic society takes as its fundamental basis the individual and her individual accountability, or, in Düzgün's words, "Islam takes the individual as its foundation."[137] This emphasis on submission to God and individual responsibility underscores what I call the "mediated," rather than absolute, authority of the individual. Through this mediated individual authority, Muslims carry authority and responsibility in living out religious truth. Religion, as something in a continual state of renewal, gives and establishes the right of its own establishment to its believers.[138] For this reason, Düzgün sees Islam as fundamentally less prone to hegemony than Christianity. Recognizing the individual as the center of religion over any one institutional hierarchy helps put off the tendency for hegemony. It is in this sense that he urges individual Muslims to create their own modernities.[139] By realizing the power and responsibility they carry as living expressions of true religion, and by accepting religion as fundamentally modernizing regardless of place or time, pious individuals can realize their own responsibility in manifesting true religion on earth.

Notes

1. See his personal website: <http://www.sabanaliduzgun.com/> (last accessed September 17, 2018).
2. His doctoral thesis was entitled "Nesefi ve İslâm filozoflarına göre Allah-Alem ilişkisi" ["The God–World Relation according to Nasafi and Islamic Philosophers"] (1996) and was completed under the direction of Mustafa Sait Yazıcıoğlu.
3. His characterizations of religion are intentionally modern, but he sees positive value in deconstruction and postmodernity for their aid in challenging hegemony, or what he calls Western "truth monopolies." On "truth monopolies," see the present chapter's subsection entitled *Hegemony and Post-colonialism*.
4. Düzgün uses the term "*kelam*" to refer to classical Islamic theological thought, which he appropriates to include an even broader category than the English word "theology." He explains this in a footnote in *Allah, Tabiat ve Tarih: Teolijide Yöntem Sorunu ve Teolojinin Metaparadigmatik Temelleri* [*God, Nature, and History: The Question of Method in Theology and Theology's Metaparadigmatic Foundations*] (Ankara: Lotus Yayınevi, 2005; 2012), p. 19 fn.
5. It would be too cumbersome and not particularly illustrative to cite all references to the names discussed here. All figures mentioned in this section are cited variously and included in the bibliographies of the works of Düzgün discussed here: ATT, DBT, CDDD, ST, and SYEI (cited below). While these figures often come from very different contexts, the important thing to keep

in mind is that Düzgün's broader discussions, where names often appear in clusters or brief references, do not tend to focus on an individual scholar.
6. These figures appear throughout his work and so I have not cited individual pages. Admittedly, many of these figures serve merely as passing references; however, I would argue against the assumption that lack of sustained engagement makes them trivial references. More often than not, such references serve strategically, and others may simply be an accurate reflection of which sources he has spent more time investigating. That being said, it is often not clear from his references to these figures which ones he has spent more time with or who he is more influenced by.
7. Düzgün wrote his master's thesis on Syed Ahmad Khan (1992). His master's thesis was later published as the book *Seyyid Ahmed Han ve Entellektüel Modernizmi* [*Syed Ahmad Khan and His Intellectual Modernism*] (Ankara: Akçağ Yayınları, 1997).
8. The Islamic concept of *fiṭra*, or original disposition/nature, is a broad one. Düzgün's understanding of *fiṭra* will be treated in the section below on *fiṭra*. Arguably, the propensity to true religion is another aspect of *fiṭra*, but I separate it here for clarity and due to Düzgün's specific interpretation and emphasis of this aspect.
9. Philip C. Dorroll has remarked that "religious common sense" seems to be a shared assumption within Turkish theological discourse; his dissertation is an effort to trace this assumption and others back to thinkers of the early days of Turkish theology from the 1920s to the 1950s (communicated in email correspondence from November 18, 2015).
10. In *Sources of the Self: The Making of the Modern Identity* (Cambridge, MA: Harvard University Press, 1989), Charles Taylor argues that the modern self is a fundamentally decentered and fragmented one: "The original unity of the theistic horizon has been shattered [. . .]" (p. 496). This unity is shattered because, "[w]e are now in an age in which a publicly accessible cosmic order of meanings is an impossibility" (p. 512). By contrast, Düzgün's view of individual authority does not rest on such a view of the self (and Taylor does not espouse this sort of selfhood either, ultimately). Düzgün's view of the self rests on a firm grounding in *tawḥīd*, or the oneness of God, and *tawḥīd*'s implications for human beings. In Turkey, Charles Taylor's *Sources of the Self* has been translated into Turkish by the historian of religion Bilal Baş and his wife and fellow scholar of religion Selma Aygül Baş. See Charles Taylor, *Benliğin Kaynakları: Modern Kimliğin İnşası* (Istanbul: Küre Yayınları, 2012).

11. Şaban Ali Düzgün, *Çağdaş Dünyada Din ve Dindarlar* (Ankara: Lotus Yayınevi, 2012; 2014). Cited as CDDD.
12. CDDD, p. 15.
13. CDDD, p. 15.
14. CDDD, p. 16.
15. CDDD, p. 16.
16. CDDD, p. 17.
17. CDDD, pp. 17–18. Turkish: "Dolayısıyla dinlerin vahyedilmelerinin temel sebebi, toplumsal yapıyı adalet, özgürlük, haklarda eşitlik, karşılıklı saygı gibi temel evrensel değerler çerçevesinde yeniden inşa etmektir."
18. CDDD, p. 18.
19. CDDD, p. 18. In his preface, he cites Pope Urban II as a token example of religion and violence (p. 10). This is less a detailed historical analysis and more a hasty reference. Nonetheless, the effort to give Christian examples of violence and hegemony is sustained and dovetails with his own understanding of Islam.
20. CDDD, p. 18. Turkish: "Müminler eleştirel bilinç, yaratıcı imgelem, ütopik kurgular ve diyalektik düşünme biçimleriyle, yaşadıkları toplumda ilişkilerin temel insan hakları, adalet, özgürlük, güven gibi kavramlar ışığında yapılandırılıp yapılandırılmadığını test etmelidirler."
21. CDDD, pp. 28–30, 181–6, 288. Düzgün discusses dependency theory (*bağımlılık tezi*) and post-colonial theory, relying heavily on the work of Talal Asad. He stresses the need for multiple modernities no longer defined in terms of reaction to Western modernity.
22. CDDD, p. 182.
23. CDDD, p. 182.
24. CDDD, p. 186.
25. CDDD, p. 186. In this work, he does not offer a sustained engagement with these figures.
26. I am using the term "theological anthropology" to refer to his project. It is not his term, but I did ask him whether this term was appropriate at the May 2016 Building Bridges Conference held at Georgetown. At that time, he did not object to my use of the term to describe this aspect of his theology.
27. He uses the terms *'aql* and *qalb* nearly interchangeably in ATT, p. 125. The combining of both heart and mind into one term like *'aql* or *fu'ad* is not uncommon in the classical Arabic tradition. For instance, Farid Jabré's study of al-Ghazālī's terminology strongly emphasizes the functional interchangeability of the words *'aql* (mind) and *qalb* (heart)—see his *Essai sur le lexique de Ghazali*

(Beirut: Lebanese University Publications, 1970). The *'aql* is discussed further below.
28. These are in Turkish: *akıl, sağduyu, sezgi, vicdan*. *Vicdan*, though derived from an Arabic root, is not used in modern Arabic to denote conscience. The modern Arabic for conscience is *ḍamīr*. In the *Turkish Encyclopedia of Islam*, Osman Demir suggests that the current Turkish use and meaning of *vicdan* probably comes from its use by late nineteenth-century Ottoman authors, particularly Ahmed Cevdet Paşa. Osman Demir, "Vicdan," in *İslâm Ansiklopedisi* (Türkiye Diyanet Vakfı), <http://www.islamansiklopedisi.info/> (last accessed March 2, 2017).
29. Düzgün, *Din, Birey ve Toplum [Religion, Individual, and Society]* (Ankara: Akçağ Yayınları, 2013 [3rd printing]), p. 180. Cited as DBT.
30. CDDD, pp. 28, 182, 288.
31. He draws on Talal Asad's *Formations of the Secular: Christianity, Islam, Modernity* (Stanford: Stanford University Press, 2003), *Anthropology and the Colonial Encounter* (London: Ithaca Press, 1973), and *The Idea of an Anthropology of Islam* (Washington, DC: Center for Contemporary Arab Studies, 1986).
32. CDDD, p. 28. Dependency theory can also be taken to refer to the economic dependence and exploitation of non-Western states, but Düzgün does not stress this.
33. DBT, p. 37.
34. CDDD, p. 30. By positivism he means the reduction of philosophical explanations to material phenomena.
35. CDDD, p. 290.
36. CDDD, p. 181.
37. CDDD, p. 182.
38. CDDD, p. 182.
39. CDDD, p. 183. He also cites Talal Asad here.
40. CDDD, p. 184. He refers to Hegel's "Geist" but does not cite any specific passage. While he cites Hegel as an author of a system espousing a truth monopoly, I might argue that Hegel's famous rival Schleiermacher found ways of building a philosophical system that at least partly avoids this pitfall. Düzgün does reference Schleiermacher, but he does not engage the German theologian at length or as a philosopher. For a reading of Schleiermacher that highlights aspects of his thought which can be read to resist the colonial narrative, see Steven R. Jungkeit, *Spaces of Modern Theology: Geography and Power in Schleiermacher's World* (New York: Palgrave/Macmillan, 2012).

41. CDDD, p. 288.
42. CDDD, p. 184. Here he cites Q5:14, which addresses Christians, and Q5:64, which addresses Jews.
43. CDDD, p. 186.
44. DBT, p. 59. In support of this, he cites Q2:201.
45. CDDD, p. 16. Turkish: "Kurumsal bir dini yapının parçası olmadan önce de insanın sağduyu ve fıtratıyla hakikatı keşfetme kudretinde olduğu kabul edilmelidir." Note, Turkish pronouns are without gender, so I default to the feminine or "she" when translating "*o*."
46. CDDD, p. 21. Here he also points out that liberal theologians have spoken of a God of feeling and experience. While somewhat critical of liberal theology's emphasis of feeling and experience, his own approach does emphasize the individual, existential, and experiential elements of religious authority.
47. CDDD, p. 22.
48. *Allah, Tabiat ve Tarih: Teolojide Yöntem Sorunu ve Teolojinin Meta-Paradigmatik Temelleri* (Ankara: Lotus Yayınevi, 2005; 2012). Cited as ATT.
49. ATT, pp. 13–14.
50. Süleyman Uludağ, "Keşf," in *İslâm Ansiklopedisi*, vol. 25 (Türkiye Diyanet Vakfı, 2002), <http://www.islamansiklopedisi.info> (last accessed September 19, 2016). Turkish: "Aklın ve duyuların yetersiz kaldığı ilahiyyat konularında doğrudan bilgi edinme yolu anlamında bir tasavvuf terimi."
51. The status of Sufi piety and claims to authoritative knowing is in Turkish theology faculties, as it is elsewhere, a controversial matter. Some do not see it as a legitimate expression of Islam. Some see it as the lived heart of Islam. Düzgün, for his part, is not anti-Sufi. For an overview of Sufism's controversial relation to mainstream Sunni Islam, see Paul L. Heck, "Sufism—What Is It Exactly?", *Religion Compass* 1 (2007): pp. 148–64.
52. ATT, p. 23.
53. ATT, p. 194.
54. ATT, p. 195.
55. ATT, p. 95, cf. ATT, p. 192. In *Truth and Method*, Gadamer explains the fusion of horizons in the context of historical and linguistic interpretation. He cautions it is the height of naïveté to assume one can understand a text in categories purely derived from the text and its historical epoch, without respect to one's own historical situation and epoch. Interpretation is not simply about understanding the text; it is always understanding what the text can say "for us." It is this convergence between the world of the interpreter and of the text

which Gadamer terms "fusion of horizons." He writes: "In our analysis of the hermeneutical process we saw that to acquire a horizon of interpretation required a 'fusion of horizons'. This is now confirmed by the linguistic aspect of interpretation. The text is to be made to speak through interpretation. But no text and no book speaks if it does not speak the language that reaches the other person. Thus interpretation must find the right language if it really wants to make the text speak. There cannot, therefore, be any one interpretation that is correct 'in itself', precisely because every interpretation is concerned with the text itself. The historical life of a tradition depends on constantly new assimilation and interpretation. An interpretation that was correct 'in itself' would be a foolish ideal that failed to take account of the nature of tradition. Every interpretation has to adapt itself to the hermeneutical situation to which it belongs." Hans-Georg Gadamer, *Truth and Method* (New York: Crossroads, 1975), p. 358; original German publication dates to 1960.

56. ATT, p. 95. Turkish: "Metin sadece okunduğunda vardır."
57. This conflation has become a truism in the Christian hermeneutical literature. By directing authority to literal interpretation, traditional authority is easily undercut and discarded in favor of individual readings, which claim authority by virtue of their literalism—i.e., "I'm not interpreting, I'm just reading what the text says."
58. ATT, p. 97.
59. ATT, p. 98.
60. Düzgün, *Sarp Yokuşun Eteğinde İnsan* [*Humans Surrounded by a Precipitous Slope*] (Ankara: Otto, 2016), p. 18. Cited as SYEI.
61. CDDD, p. 116.
62. ATT, p. 94. Quranic commentary has also been considered a duty (*farḍ al-kifāya*) in the classical Islamic tradition—one not incumbent upon all individuals but on those in society qualified to do so. One might speculate that Düzgün cites Vanhoozer rather than Islamic tradition to emphasize the individual duty of interpretation rather than the general duty of interpretation traditionally assigned to those suitably qualified.
63. Kevin J. Vanhoozer, *Is There a Meaning in This Text? The Bible, The Reader, and the Morality of Literary Knowledge* (Grand Rapids, MI: Zondervan, 1998), p. 10.
64. Alpyağıl, by comparison, hones in on both the relational aspects of Gadamer's thesis and the question of what a correct or incorrect interpretation might look like within a Gadamerian framework.

65. CDDD, p. 131. Turkish: "İnsan her yerde, ama hiçbir yerde evinde değil. Bu güvensizlik hissi, insanı yeni bir anlam kaynağı bulma konusunda arayışa iten en büyük etkendir."
66. CDDD, p. 132. In this discussion, he also casts blame on socialism.
67. CDDD, p. 145.
68. CDDD, p. 146.
69. CDDD, p. 146.
70. CDDD, p. 318.
71. DBT, p. 186.
72. DBT, p. 186.
73. CDDD, p. 291.
74. CDDD, p. 291.
75. CDDD, p. 291.
76. English translation from M. A. S. Abdel Haleem.
77. CDDD, pp. 294–5. He also remarks on the need to avoid discourses that provoke Christians and stir racism. He aims for a peaceful discourse that does not demonize "them," i.e., those who are not with "us"—whether this be Muslims or Christians.
78. CDDD, p. 293.
79. CDDD, p. 294.
80. CDDD, p. 295.
81. CDDD, p. 294.
82. As stated above, at the May 2016 Building Bridges Conference at Georgetown University, I asked Prof. Düzgün if the term "theological anthropology" was a suitable label for his theological project. He acknowledged that the term, as I explained my intended use for it, reasonably reflected this central aspect of his work. To note, Düzgün has engaged more secular concepts of anthropology. For instance, at the beginning of *Religion, Individual, and Society* (DBT), he starts building what is essentially a case for a theological anthropology; however, he starts not with theology but with Western anthropology—citing Bronislaw Malinowski, Lucien Lévy-Bruhl (philosophy and ethnology), and Claude Lévi-Strauss (DBT, pp. 12–14). Düzgün seems to be telling the story of Western thought and spirituality, but he does so from a critically engaged perspective. In this respect, his endeavor is similar to Alpyağıl's quest for authenticity.
83. Ebrahim Moosa, *Ghazālī & the Poetics of Imagination* (Chapel Hill, NC and London: University of North Carolina Press, 2005), p. 175.

84. Moosa, *Ghazālī & the Poetics of Imagination*, p. 177.
85. Seyyed Hossein Nasr, *The Heart of Islam: Enduring Values for Humanity* (New York: HarperCollins, 2004), p. 6.
86. Şaban Ali Düzgün, "Değer Temelli Kişilik İnşası" ["The Construction of a Person on the Foundation of Value"] (given March 26, 2014, and organized by Hamamönü Kabakçı Konağında Mevlana Kültür ve Sanat Vakfı): <https://www.youtube.com/watch?v=3HyLYbIYuAs> (last accessed September 18, 2018). He recently re-delivered this talk on June 27, 2016. That link is: <https://www.youtube.com/watch?v=ut1nvvfKfsg> (last accessed September 18, 2018). Disposition is an English translation he offers in the talk, but he also admits there is no direct translation of the term.
87. *Vicdan* comes from an Arabic root but is used in Turkish to mean conscience. The modern standard Arabic word for conscience is *ḍamīr*. For a comparative etymology of the word conscience in Arabic and a history of the word in European languages, see the work of Leirvik. Oddbjørn Leirvik is a Scandinavian theologian highly engaged in interreligious dialogue and engages Egyptian authors of the mid-twentieth century. Leirvik traces "conscience" from biblical texts all the way up to its modern differentiation in various European languages from the notion of "consciousness." He then turns his analysis to Egyptian writers active in the 1950s. Oddbjørn Leirvik, *Human Conscience and Muslim–Christian Relations* (New York: Routledge, 2006).
88. In Q2:256 the Qur'ān explicitly states that there is no compulsion in religion.
89. The phrase is taken from his talk "Değer Temelli Kişilik İnşası" ["The Construction of a Person on the Foundation of Value"]. Turkish: "ikna edici bir kitap."
90. *Din Birey ve Toplum* (Ankara: Akçağ, 2014 [3rd printing]), original publication 1997. Cited as DBT.
91. DBT, pp. 11–12.
92. Philip C. Dorroll details the significance al-Māturīdī in the early days of the modern Turkish theology faculties in his thesis: "Modern by Tradition: Abu Mansur al-Maturidi and the New Turkish Theology" (doctoral dissertation, Emory University, 2013). For another extended discussion on *fiṭra* and al-Māturīdī in dialogue with European and Anglophone sources, see Hanifi Özcan, *Mâtüridî'de Bilgi Problemi* [*The Problem of Knowledge in Māturīdī*] (Istanbul: Marmara Üniversitesi İlâhiyat Fakültesi Vakfı Yayınları, 2015 [4th printing]), pp. 108–29.
93. Wilfred Madelung explains the connection between the earlier Seljuk Turks, Ḥanafī law, and Māturīdī theology: "As a result of the Turkish expansion,

eastern Ḥanafism and Māturīdī theological doctrine were spread throughout western Persia, 'Irāḳ, Anatolia, Syria and Egypt. Numerous Transoxanian and other eastern Ḥanafī scholars migrated to these regions and taught there from the late 5th/11th to the 8th/14th century. Māturīdī doctrine thus gradually came to prevail among the Ḥanafī communities everywhere." Wilfred Madelung, "Māturīdiyya," *EI2*. This being said, Ottoman madrasahs predominantly used Ash'arī "textbooks" in theology. Ömer Aydın, "*Kalam* between Tradition and Change: The Emphasis on Understanding Classical Islamic Theology in Relation to Western Intellectual Effects," in Sinasi Gunduz and Cafer S. Yaran (eds), *Change and Essence* (Washington, DC: The Council for Research in Values and Philosophy, 2005), pp. 104–5.

94. Düzgün uses an Arabic copy printed in Turkey: al-Māturīdī, *Ta'wīlāt al-Qur'ān*, ed. Ahmet Vanlıoğlu and Bekir Topaoğlu (Istanbul: Mizan Yayınevi, 2005).

95. Şaban Ali Düzgün, *Nesefî ve İslâm Filozoflarına Göre Allah-Alem İlişkisi* [*The God–World Relation according to Nasafī and Islamic Philosophers*] (Ankara: Akçağ Yayınları, 1998).

96. Other notable works of Abū al-Mu'īn al-Nasafī include his *Tamhīd fī Uṣūl al-Dīn* and *Kitāb Baḥr al-Kalām fī 'Ilm al-Tawḥīd*.

97. For more on this, see Madelung, "al-Māturīdī," in *EI2*. Blaming Ash'arī theology for not valuing human agency occurs in Turkish theology and in non-Turkish Muslim discourses.

98. As Düzgün remarks in his book *Social Theology*, Māturīdī theology and to a lesser extent Mu'tazilite theology, unlike Ash'arī theology, do not assume an inverse correlation between God's transcendence and human agency. In other words, God's transcendence and power does not depend on human lack of power or choice. Humans are not in competition with God. Düzgün, *Sosyal Teoloji: İnsanın Yeryüzü Serüveni* [*Social Theology: Humanity's Worldly Adventure*] (Ankara: Lotus Yayınevi, 2010; 2012), p. 11. Cited as ST.

99. DBT, p. 10.

100. DBT, p. 16.

101. At the outset of DBT, he discusses Bronislaw, Malinowski, Lucien Lévy-Bruhl, and Claude Lévi-Strauss especially with regards to the term "primitive" (*ilkel*). See DBT, pp. 12–15. The turning point of the discussion away from Western anthropology is when he uses *fiṭra* to redefine "primitive."

102. DBT, p. 16. For comparison, Catholic theologian Karl Rahner makes a similar remark in his *Foundations of Christian Faith*. However, rather looking back into human origins, Rahner speculates on humanity's future, deeming that the day

humans no longer have a concept of God is the day humans become a species other than human. In this same work, Rahner, similar to Düzgün, affirms that humans are moral beings by transcendental necessity and that humans as spiritual beings are necessarily free. Rahner's view of divine and human freedom as directly correlated rather than inversely correlated also strikes a parallel with Düzgün's Māturīdī-influenced positions. With regards to a theological anthropology, there are quite a few parallels between Düzgün and Rahner (including an emphasis on conscience), where the former ultimately stresses the finite–infinite relationship through *tawḥīd* and the latter through Christology. See Rahner, *Foundations of Christian Faith: An Introduction to the Idea of Christianity*, trans. William V. Dych (New York: Crossroads, 1993), original German published 1976.

103. CDDD, p. 111; DBT, p. 36.
104. The Arabic for this verse requires the reader to fill out the text from the preceding verses and context. The translation offered here is one made after consulting Düzgün's Turkish translation, M. A. S. Abdel Haleem's English translation, and the English Sahih International Translation. Abdel Haleem's translation looks significantly different, but the Sahih International more or less agrees with Düzgün's rendering. Düzgün's Turkish translation of the Arabic: "Allah insanın özüne neyin iyi neyin de kötü olduğunu bilme yetisi yerleştirmiştir." CDDD, p. 111.
105. CDDD, p. 111.
106. CDDD, p. 111.
107. CDDD, p. 112. To further support this reading, Düzgün cites the Muʿtazilite Shāfiʿī thinker al-Qāḍī Abduljabbār (935–1025), who held that humans know good and evil before coming to know God. He also notes that for the Mālikī school of Islamic jurisprudence something is inherently good or bad for humans while juridically (hükmen) good or bad in relation to God.
108. Düzgün does not explain why the will is less naturally endowed with orientation towards truth and reality than faculties such as conscience and reason. From a Christian perspective, the discrepancy could be explained by the effects of sin on the will, but Düzgün rejects the Christian doctrine of the fallen and inherently sinful state of humanity. This is not to say a Christian explanation is inherently better, but only to point out that the effects of sin on human faculties have been a long-standing conversation in Christian tradition due to the Christian doctrine of the Fall; and since Muslim theology does not build upon

a doctrine of original sin, it may be tricky to identify analogous discussions in Islamic tradition. One immediate parallel might be estrangement from *fiṭra*.

109. CDDD, p. 16. Turkish: "Varlıkla (*vücûd*) aynı kökten gelen vicdan ve insanın geldiği kaynağa kopmaz bir bağla (*akl*) bağlandığını imleyen akıl, insane doğru ve yanlış arasında ayrımı yapacak (*furkan* ve *basiret*) bir kudret verir. Bu vicdan be akıl ile insan, ilahi/doğal/evrensel değerleri keşfedebilir ve bunlar ışığında iyiye ve güzele doğru kodlanmış (*hidayet*) bir yaşam sürebilir."

110. DBT, p. 47.

111. Recall last chapter's discussion. Alpyağıl on Gadamer: KTHH, pp. 20, 67–8, 158, and FY, pp. 155–6.

112. DBT, p. 48. He differs slightly on the "reasonableness" of *īmān* from Alpyağıl— i.e., *īmān* is reasonable. For Düzgün, *īmān*, or faith, in Islam is something in harmony with an essentially reasonable and rational *fiṭra*. As we will see in chapter six, Alpyağıl does not see *īmān* as an entirely rational or unproblematic move (likening it to a passion and comparing it with the Christian idea of faith). This does not mean Alpyağıl discounts the necessity of sound *īmān*; rather, he simply investigates in a comparative philosophical setting how *īmān* can stand in tension with human rationality. On a comparative note, in the late eighteenth century in Europe, the concept of common sense was considered alongside reason and faith as a possible ground for human truth. On this see Frederick C. Beiser, *The Fate of Reason: German Philosophy from Kant to Fichte* (Cambridge, MA: Harvard University Press, 1987), for instance, pp. 111, 168, 173.

113. DBT, p. 49. Turkish: "Sağlam fıtrata dönüşüm adı, *tövbe*dir."

114. Some people translate *taqwā* as pious fear of God, but others argue for different primary shades of meaning than fear. Quranic scholar and linguist Toshihiko Izutsu translates *taqwā* as fear, in particular eschatological fear of final judgment. He argues that the Qur'ān uses *taqwā* in conjunction with several other words for fear (*khashya, khawf,* and *rahba*). Toshihiko Izutsu, *Ethico Religious Concepts in the Qur'ān* (Montreal and Kingston: McGill-Queen's University Press, 2002), pp. 195–200. Fazlur Rahman, widely read in Turkish theology faculties, translated *taqwā* as both fear and piety, explaining: "The unique balance of integrative moral action is what the Qur'ān terms *taqwā*, perhaps the most important single term in the Qur'ān." He remarks it is usually translated as fear of God and piety. For Rahman, *taqwā* designates a fear that comes from "an acute sense of responsibility, here and in the hereafter [. . .] *Taqwā*, then, in the context of our argument, means to be squarely anchored

within the moral tensions, the 'limits of God,' and not to 'transgress' or violate the balance of those tensions or limits. Human conduct then becomes endowed with that quality which renders it 'service to God [*'ibāda*].'" Fazlur Rahman, *Major Themes of the Qur'an* (Chicago: University of Chicago Press, 2009), pp. 28–9.
115. ATT, p. 45.
116. Deborah L. Black, "Psychology: Soul and Intellect," in P. Adamson and R. C. Taylor (eds), *The Cambridge Companion to Arabic Philosophy* (Cambridge: Cambridge University Press, 2005), p. 317. Additional stages of intellect Black refers to are: the agent intellect, the potential intellect, habitual/speculative intellect, and acquired intellect (pp. 317–18). These divisions have more to do with a theory of how the mind acquires knowledge; by contrast, this question does not play a major part in Düzgün's consideration. He is arguably more interested in the question of what sorts of mental and psychological states and activities bear intellectual authority.
117. Translations of this word (*'aql*) can vary, and even subtle differences will have significant effects on how one translates various texts.
118. ATT, p. 86.
119. ATT, p. 88. Turkish: "İnsanın 'bilme'sinin dini yahut teolojik bilme olarak adlandırılabilmesi başka bir ifadeyle teolojik bilginin kognitifliği için akıl, sezgi, vs. bilme yeteneklerini bir bütün olarak ve birbirini destekleyecek şekilde kullanılması gerekmektedir."
120. ATT, p. 190. Turkish: "Sufilerin sebep-sonuç zinciri dışına çıkmak için başvurduğu kavram ise '*sezgi*' idi. [. . .] bizim önerimiz 'akıl' ve 'sezgi' kavramlarını birbirine karşıt yapılandırmaktan vazgeçip, ikisinin birlikte iş gördüğü kognitif bir özne-nesne ilişkisi kurmaktır."
121. English translation by M. A. S. Abdel Haleem.
122. ATT, p. 150.
123. DBT, p. 26.
124. DBT, p. 57.
125. DBT, p. 58. See Q33:72 for the quranic trust offered to humankind.
126. ATT, p. 136.
127. This is reminiscent of Protestant theologian and philosopher F. D. E. Schleiermacher's view on human agency and passivity vis-à-vis the world.
128. DBT, p. 135.
129. English translation by M. A. S. Abdel Haleem.
130. CDDD, p. 174.

131. CDDD, p. 175.
132. CDDD, p. 176. Here he also harps on Catholic indulgences.
133. CDDD, p. 176. Turkish: "Liberal düşüncenin hatası insanı tanımamakta yatıyordu." His use of the term liberal is fairly broad. It seems to incorporate both early/mid-twentieth-century understandings of liberalism that stress free market capitalism alongside extreme individualism and early twenty-first-century associations of liberalism that focus on individualism in terms of identity rather than economics.
134. CDDD, p. 177.
135. CDDD, p. 178.
136. CDDD, p. 179. Turkish: "Allah'a kul olmakla gerçek hürriyeti elde etmiş bu birey [. . .]. O, toplumda var olan her harekette kendi üzerine düşen sorumluluğu omuzlayacak cesareti ve bilinci zihninde taşıyan bir ferttir."
137. CDDD, p. 179. Turkish: "İslam bireyi esas alır . . ."
138. CDDD, p. 196.
139. CDDD, p. 196.

6

Human Agency, Responsibility, and *Tawḥīd*

The previous chapter took up Düzgün's theological anthropology and its relationship to what I called his notion of "mediated" individual authority. As was seen, Düzgün's notion of authority and what it means to be human are not only interrelated concepts but also conscious responses to modernity. Not only that, Düzgün creatively used modern and traditional concepts together to construct a theologically coherent portrait of human responsibility and purpose. The present discussion will continue laying out major themes in Düzgün's thought to better illustrate the dialectical tendencies in Düzgün's conceptual vocabulary. For Düzgün does not simply mix Western, Christian, Turkish, or Islamic assumptions and concepts, he actively plays with them. I locate Düzgün's response to the challenges of modernity precisely in this dialectical playfulness. Attending to this dialectical use of concepts, the present discussion will take up several key themes: religion as a source of values, religion and civilization, religion and the individual, and what I will call a "tawḥīdic framework of plurality."

Religion as a Source of Meaning and Values

For Düzgün, religion is a source of meaning and values, and some of these values look decidedly modern. What is true religion for Düzgün? Düzgün speaks of religion in terms of an existential (*varoluşsal*) struggle.[1] Religion entails a struggle of meaning and value, where God is the ultimate source of values.² Religion is what produces and manifests values in creation.³ True religion also frees a human being.⁴ Further, religion is one, especially in the sense of morality. True religion, by definition, resists corruption and fossilization. Even though religion is one, real religion is not exclusivist.⁵ Düzgün highlights authentic Islam's superior capacity for inclusivism in contrast to a more exclusivist Christianity or Judaism.⁶ Even though he views an authentically lived Islam as less exclusivist than Christianity or Judaism, it is always clear that he holds Islam to offer the most solid foundations for living out true religion.⁷ According to the Qur'ān, as Düzgün reads it, living a virtuous life of doing good to others should be the basic aim of all religion.⁸

Since Düzgün stresses individual freedom, reform, and inclusivism as hallmarks of true religion, the question might arise as to whether Düzgün is a quranic deist like the popularly known Yaşar Nuri Öztürk.⁹ The answer to this question is no. Düzgün is adamantly not a deist, nor is he a pantheist. Düzgün's understanding of religion has a complex relationship to Islamic tradition. On one hand, Düzgün embraces traditional and classical Islamic resources and, on the other, he does not shy from challenging traditionally held opinions in the name of moral progress. He is, in short, a creative and critical theologian with significant grounding in the theological tradition he represents.

Düzgün maintains Islamic values are the same as universal human values.¹⁰ Instead of making Islam accountable to modern conceptions of universal human values, he argues that Islam has always upheld values which would be recognized today as universal ones. From an Islamic perspective, human beings are one family. Practicing brotherhood, mutual trust, and aid are what it means to be a slave of God.¹¹ In other words, religion is the essence of life: it informs all human bonds, duties, and relationships for the better.¹² Moral principles are common to all humans, but law alone does not exhaust morality—religion and individual conscience must also contribute.¹³ Piety (*taqwā*), as consciousness of one's finitude in relation to God, allows human beings to move past the tension and tragic limitations of their finitude and seek out loftier goals.¹⁴ This struggle for greater meaning is what helps a believer become a full individual. Yet this struggle does not reduce to mere individualism. Becoming a full individual is intensely relational and operates on a much broader plane than the value system of the material world.¹⁵

Düzgün puts a modern spin on the purpose of religion: ideally it functions to restore equal, just, and respectful relations. In this sense religion modernizes, renews, and reforms.[16] Religion functions to renew values and equality just as Islam did when it first appeared. Religion is "modernizing" (*modernleştirici*) in its very essence.[17] In its corrupted form, however, religion can be used as a tool of the state—and this, Düzgün repeatedly remarks, is one of Christianity's biggest sins.

Düzgün's standard for determining whether religion remains true to its essential function is modern, but it also remains grounded in an Islamic framework. The same applies to Düzgün's criterion for positively functioning religion, since honoring its essential function and having a positive impact on society go hand in hand. To evaluate whether religion stays true to its essential function, Düzgün proposes that one must ask whether or not its practitioners think critically, creatively, idealistically, and dialectically about basic human relations in human society, showing concern for "basic human rights, justice, freedom, and stability."[18]

Another fundamental criterion for evaluating the living truth of a religion according to Düzgün is the measure by which a religion addresses those who do not belong to it. In other words, how a religion treats non-believers and dissenters is an essential indicator of its health and vitality. How a religion treats non-believers is a standard applicable to other religions, not only Islam. He remarks that "exclusivism is likely a problem common to all religions."[19] Even if this problem is common among all religions, it is one that, as Düzgün affirms, still needs rethinking.[20]

One way of rethinking exclusivism is by looking at the internal resources a respective religion possesses to resist hegemony or monopolizing modes of thinking. Religions have within them currents of anti-hegemony; resources for fighting hegemony are found in critical consciousness, creative thinking, adherence to ideals, and dialectical thinking.[21] Thus, religions, even ones with plagued histories like Christianity, have resources to counteract harmful expression of exclusivism and hegemony.[22] When evaluating Düzgün's sense of what proves just and inclusive, it is clear that while striving for universality he remains positively situated within an Islamic perspective.

Another criterion for true religion which highlights Düzgün's integration of Islamic context and challenges common to all religions lies in his explanation of the real and ideal. One problem Düzgün observes when trying to determine religious values is confusing the real with the ideal.[23] For instance, when the Qur'ān was revealed, it addressed a specific audience on specific occasions. However, if those occasions of revelation (*asbāb al-nuzūl*) are made to serve as universal principles or general rules, the distinction between the real and ideal is overlooked. The historical realities of the original Muslim community might be negatively conflated with universal Muslim ideals. To mitigate this, Düzgün argues there should always be a dialectic between the real and the ideal (and this very dialectic is an essential part of religion).[24]

To give an example of the confusion of real and ideal in Islam, he treats the issue of slavery and polygamy in Islam. Düzgün does not think slavery is an ideal essential to Islam but instead sees slavery as an unfortunate social reality religion was meant to reform.[25] He remarks that the Meccan period started to abolish it, but this process was unsuccessful.[26] Nor does Düzgün think polygamy to be ideal.[27] While slavery and polygamy are real parts of Islamic history, that does not make them ideals to be sought after or upheld.[28] Religion is the driving force behind this real vs. ideal dialectic, where what is ideal eventually becomes real through reform and the development of human conscience.[29] For this dialectic to function, the individual must be at liberty to critically question the relationship between the real and ideal. This is an ongoing and continual dialectic, for which Düzgün refuses to offer an easy solution. In accordance with the divine purpose for humanity, each individual is embedded in her own age and the task is hers to develop her conscience by responding to the events of her age.[30]

The Relationship between Religion and Civilization

For Düzgün, the individual is both the foundation of an authentic lived religion and the one charged with ensuring a civilization that does not alienate humans from their *fiṭra*. In *Religion, Individual, and Society*, Düzgün speaks of humanity as one essential kind, with each individual representing the whole. In support of this view, he refers his reader to the important quranic verse Q5:32, which explains that to kill one person unjustly is tantamount to killing all of humankind.[31] He then accuses Western thought of not truly being able to face this truth—that one human individual is the microcosm of all humanity,[32] stating, "Islam has the individual as its foundation."[33] The individual is thus both the locus of religion and the microcosm of human civilization.

The view that human individuals are significant to the course of civilization stresses the value of free individual action. In a world ruled by statistical calculations that reduce people to passive, faceless figures on a page, Düzgün is pushing back as if to say that it does not matter how big our global world gets, an individual person's life and choices remain the foundation for everything we build as a race. While some read history as a blind play of forces beyond the scope of any one human life or meaning, Düzgün retorts it is ridiculous to assert that the individual plays no role in history.[34] He accepts that human society follows natural laws, but he also thinks society can be changed and guided by human choice.

Moreover, societal change is both natural and part of God's plan.[35] This perspective focuses less on the particular structures in society at a given time and more on their development and how that development expresses the values of true religion. He exclaims in *God, Nature, and History*, "For, what gives the world meaning is not its essence but the currents of events in it."[36] God is present in change. For instance, the de-Arabization of Islam is also the story of its universalization.[37] God provides a way for each age and country.[38] Throughout ages and places, religion, insofar as it is alive and well in the hearts of individual believers, keeps culture striving for universal standards. Therefore, it is important not to view religion as a force opposed to everything else around it.[39] Without religion and without a mission for higher values, society becomes destructive and real civilization is impossible.

Düzgün offers a rough historical narrative of human civilization. It starts before the birth of widespread urban environments and moves steadily towards our global, urbanized world. This trajectory is marked by two opposing currents: the corrupting aspects of urbanization and the positive, universalizing aspect of interconnected human civilization.

Düzgün takes the story of primitive versus civilized humanity and turns the categories around. His use of the term primitive (*ilkel*) in both a negative and a positive sense manifests creative resistance to a binary understanding of religion's relationship to modern values. Before Abrahamic religions, people believed in God as part of their *fıtra*, arguing that the person closest to their *fiṭra* is the primitive person.⁴⁰ For Düzgün, it is the primitive human being, understood positively, who is better suited to act as a true individual. By this logic, earlier peoples were not necessarily primitive, in the negative sense of the word, if they remained in touch with their inner God-given nature. In this vein of reasoning, Düzgün tells the tale of the urbanization and subsequent corruption of religion, blaming primarily urban environments for despotic trends in religion.⁴¹ At the same time, true religion (*din*) is fundamentally opposed to all forms of tribalism.⁴² With the rise of urbanized civilizations, humans were continually challenged to move beyond tribalist ways of expressing value. So while Düzgün criticizes urban civilization as a source of corruption, he also identifies it as a potential driving force towards universal values. Optimally religion should walk the fine balance line between respecting individual context and difference and pushing humans to more universal values.⁴³

Düzgün further looks to the Qur'ān for what it means to be a functional civilization.⁴⁴ Real civilization is civilization that helps individuals be better people, that is, be peaceful people.⁴⁵ According to his reading, quranic civilization is a civilization with "*kitāb*," an Arabic word commonly translated as "book,"⁴⁶ but here Düzgün takes it to mean law, revelation, and a sense of common good.⁴⁷ "False civilization" (*sahte medeniyetler*) lacks "*kitāb*" (Turkish: *kitap*) and is based on misuse and exploitation.⁴⁸ In this manner, Islamic civilization is a "civilization of agreement" or a "civilization of convention" (*uzlaşı medeniyeti*), that is, one governed justly by fair standards, laws, and a sense of the common good amid a plurality of ways of life. A "civilization of agreement" also values the quality of being flexible and inclusive rather than exclusive. Within this context, he interprets Q49:13 to mean that homogenization of human civilization actually prevents this process of divinely intended human knowledge production.⁴⁹ Q49:13, a verse commonly cited in the context of interfaith dialogue,⁵⁰ reads: "People, We created you all from a single man and a single woman, and made you into races and tribes so that you should come to know one another."⁵¹ In this verse, the diversity of human peoples is depicted as part of the divine plan for human growth and development. Düzgün cautions against understanding this quranic verse as calling human beings to know one another in a superficial sense; instead, Düzgün reads this verse to refer to an ongoing process of inter-civilizational knowledge production from which all humanity is called to benefit.[52] In other words, Düzgün takes Q49:13 to mean that all human nations and peoples will benefit when civilizations dialogue and learn together.[53] Yet, since Düzgün identifies as a universalist, is it fitting to speak of civiliziations in the plural in this context? Important to keep in mind, he stresses plurality within unity, envisioning one humanity with many civilizational expressions. This vision of a unified, diverse humanity is shaped by both his convinctions as a Muslim and by his identity as a scholar who writes and thinks about religion in the modern era.

The Relationship between Religion and Individual

This section consolidates previous discussions to contend that the relationship between religion and individual is arguably one of Düzgün's most fundamental concerns. For Düzgün, religion is not something to be forced on the individual. Religion, in its true form, is life-giving. This life-giving relation between religion and the individual can only exist in a relationship of genuine freedom. On this point, Düzgün consistently stresses that human freedom should not be understood as in competition with divine freedom.[54] This freedom is non-trivial and embraces the free use of human faculties—faith is not merely the freedom to assent blindly. Since faith, or *īmān*, is founded on reason and common sense, it is not tantamount to blind following.[55]

Further, while Islam does not reject human difference, it also does not take human differences as fundamental to our human character. In a nutshell, this is Düzgün's universalist understanding of Islam. He writes, "While Islam does not deny all these [various human] realities, it accepts none of these qualities as its basic character."[56] What then is Islam's basic character for Düzgün? Arguably, Islam's character is founded on an affirmation of God's oneness, which does not reduce human agency to nothing, but rather empowers individuals to take on responsibility in the created world. Significantly, he equates this responsibility with the Islamic idea of *khalīfa* or successorship. The Arabic root *kh-l-f* forms the word meaning successor (and is also the origin of the word "caliphate"); Düzgün employs this word to indicate human responsibility. Interestingly, the same root also forms the verb to differ—both meanings occur in the Qur'ān. While Düzgün does not stress the second meaning of the root, it may be helpful to use the duality of meaning in the root *kh-l-f* to illustrate his position of unity in diversity—on the one hand God gave humans a shared responsibility and hence authority in creation (*khalīfa*), on the other God also gave humans diversity and the richness of differing with one another (*ikhtilāf*).[57] Or, as Düzgün affirms, with divine successorship given to humans, humanity marks a new page in creation.[58] True religion is the locus of this responsibility, and as such it does not reduce human existence to nothing before God.[59] Humans, especially individuals and individual pious efforts, fundamentally matter in the human struggle to live up to the responsibility of divine successorship.

Düzgün views true religion as a perennial and indispensable resource in rising to the challenges of the modern world. For Düzgün, Ancient Greece, humanism, and existentialism all claim that religion alienates humans from themselves.[60] With some irony, he implies at many turns that true religion (*din*) is in this sense more human than humanism.[61] This is because true religion, by definition, does not alienate an individual from herself, quite the contrary. While this opposition may oversimplify the issue, it reflects Western culture and Westernized religion's perceived failure to attribute meaning and value to the individual's role in an increasingly impersonal and overwhelming modern world. Yet, Düzgün does not simply stop with a critique. Instead, he offers a solution grounded in the Islamic idea of human nature and the divine purpose for humanity. His solution proposes a self that is not alienated, disjointed, or driven by market value. For him, true religion (*din*) manifests the very opposite of alienation from an individual's true self.

When Düzgün speaks of an individual (*birey*) he means an individual both in touch with her true religious nature and responsible for facing the world she is born into, an individual in touch with her true identity and purpose. Yet, what does this individual do in the world? What does a truly free and pious individual look like in action? Certainly, it is possible for an individual to fail to achieve true freedom and authentic piety. He admits to the dangers of an individual being made into a passive object of social forces—often with negative effect.[62] These negative effects express themselves in spiritual poverty, such as blind following and materialism but also in outright violence, strife, and war. By contrast, God's gift of *khalīfa*, or the divine trust of responsibility, is not a license for human beings to kill each other but a call to human beings to write their own history.[63] God's gift of responsibility to humanity is also a sign that change is part of God's plan for humanity. The possibility of change secures the basic freedom of movement for humans to grow, develop, and have real responsibility. In this way, religion has always been "modernizing."

Theology, Düzgün admits, is necessarily tied up with society, culture, and history. He remarks, "Theological development's particularity, that is its being tied to a particular social and cultural framework, is an inescapable fact of history."[64] This does not mean he cedes all theological value to historicism or a material view of history. He simply acknowledges that theology is a living and developing human process, which necessarily unfolds within particular historical and social contexts. As we saw with Alpyağıl in the previous chapter, Düzgün does not think theology, insofar as it represents a human endeavor, can ever be neutral or claim an objectivity that is not also inflected by its historical and socio-political context. Yet, in order to foster dimensions which transcend material context, more is needed. An individual must employ a "critical consciousness" (*eleştirel bilinçlilik*) and "dialectical thinking" (*diyalektik düşünme*). These tools help the individual connect to both her place in society and history as well as to her divine purpose, expressed in the transcendent recognition of God's unity and purpose for humanity. The infinite is always in the finite, or the universal is always manifest in the local, the particular.[65] And since religion is always localized, a counter force is needed to push it always in the direction of the universal.[66] It is the critical and dialectical process internal to each individual that provides the locus for this counter force.

Accordingly, a religious individual mediates her relation to society and zeitgeist with a faith that transcends her era. The religious individual must have recourse to a "higher doctrine" (*üst doktrin*) in order to transcend the currents of societal thought that shape her.[67] This is how she realizes herself as more than a mere object of societal and material forces and, moreover, how she expresses her God-given freedom.

Düzgün grounds this critical and mediating process through several epistemological assumptions, proposing a general method for vetting theological knowledge. His proposed method is that believers start from a foundation of 1) *a priori* knowledge, 2) experience, and 3) trustworthy reports.[68] While still highly general, the criteria mix Islamic and Western epistemological terms, where the term *a priori* lends connotations of Enlightenment discussions of reason and where the idea of trustworthy reports harkens back to Islamic prophetic reports or hadith. Although the category of *a priori* connotes Western philosophical discussions, Düzgün does not differ greatly from common Islamic (or even Aristotelian) views of what constitutes the basis of sound knowledge.[69] Still, within the category of experience he also leaves some room for intuition and direct religious insight (*kashf*), without overly detailing this process.[70] Since God is both Creator and sender of revelation, this means humans can also have knowledge of God by logic and inference.[71] At the heart of this process stands the *fiṭra*, which allows humans to accurately seek God-knowledge.

In sum, true religion (*din*) positively affects society through the individual person.[72] Although many thinkers and individuals in the West have thought negatively of Islam,[73] Düzgün's understanding of Islam is one that actively contributes to the health of any society through the conscientious and free contributions of Muslims. This vision of individual contribution is paired with a view of religion that refuses to idolize any one human particularity over another and refuses to falsely proclaim one religious status quo as a universal category free from change. He exclaims, "Humanity is the source of change."[74] For this reason, it is wrong to see religion as a source of the status quo.[75] Rather, religion should be seen as a positive instrument for change and agency. It is not helpful to overgeneralize tradition and then force this oversimplified and overgeneralized ideal onto religion. God positively transforms humanity insofar as humans, as a society, change themselves.

Tawḥīdic Framework of Plurality

Düzgün stresses the value of divinely willed plurality as essential to humanity and creation's flourishing. In this section, I will show how *tawḥīd*, or the affirmation of divine unity, provides the foundation for this divinely willed plurality. Not only is *tawḥīd* foundational for the flourishing of pluralism, this "tawḥīdic" framework also provides the grounds for the affirmation of individual agency. Düzgün's understanding of the role of *tawḥīd* regarding questions of pluralism and individual agency is yet another theological instance of how his thought integrates long-standing Islamic concerns with humanistic values and contemporary issues. I argue that *tawḥīd* plays a vital role in this integration.

Tawḥīd is an Arabic term indicating the affirmation of God's oneness. The term has a long history and can indicate anything from simply affirming verbally that "God is one" to a metaphysical or mystical view on reality's most fundamental fabric. In Düzgün's case, *tawḥīd* means affirming that God's power and goodness are one.[76] Seyyed Hossein Nasr, many of whose works have been translated into Turkish and are cited by Turkish theologians, offers an explanation of *tawḥīd* closely in line with Düzgün's understanding:

> In an ordinary sense [the affirmation of *tawḥīd*] means the surrender of ourselves to God, and in the highest sense it means the awareness of our nothingness before Him, for, as the Quran says, "All that dwells in the heavens and earth perishes, yet there abideth the Face of thy Lord, Majestic, Splendid" (55:26–27). The very name of the religion, Islam, comes from this reality, for the Arabic word *al-islām* means "surrender" as well as the peace that issues from our surrender to God.[77]

For Nasr and for Düzgün *tawḥīd* lies at the heart of a believer's orientation to truth. And although Islam affirms God's oneness, this does not mean it rejects the plurality of creation or the plurality of human existence. For Düzgün, Islam does not reject human difference, but neither does it take our differences as fundamental to our human character.[78] *Tawḥīd* is a central concept in making unified sense of human difference. Affirming God's unity goes hand in hand with affirming human plurality. As mentioned above, Düzgün refers to Q49:13 to stress God's plan for human plurality.[79] Once again, this verse reads:

> People, We created you all from a single man and a single woman, and made you into races and tribes so that you should come to know one another. In God's eyes, the most honored of you are the ones most mindful of Him: God is all knowing, all aware.[80]

This verse indicates that behind the obvious fact of human plurality lies a unified divine purpose. *Tawḥīd* is not just about unity, it is also about the plurality of finite reality.[81] And as a guarantor of human freedom, *tawḥīd* is also the guarantor of human morality—affirming God's oneness and affirming God as the sole true source of one's being frees the individual from the claims of the world upon her person. By recognizing God as the ultimate authority, the pious individual at the same time refuses to recognize the unquestioned authority of any being other than God.[82] In affirming *tawḥīd*, all earthly sources of authority are recognized as finite and relative.[83] God alone is the ultimate source of authority. As Düzgün reminds his reader, the first Muslims distinguished themselves by acting with a God-centered sense of authority.[84] Even the *'ulemā'* of later ages would end statements with the recognition that "God knows best."[85]

For Düzgün, Islam's most pointed universality lies in its dual affirmations of *tawḥīd* and human morality—after all, morality is recognized even by secular thinkers as something common to humanity. On this, he refers to Rawls' *Theory of Justice*, remarking that even liberals still believe in morality.[86] This universal Islam is "islam" with a lowercase "i."[87] Düzgün explains that "[i]slam means voluntary submission [to God]. This submission is valid for all things whether living or inanimate."[88] In this sense, all of creation is Muslim. Even natural laws, which are divinely ordained, constitute a form of submission.[89]

Düzgün offers another reason for pairing *tawḥīd* and morality together as central to Islam's universality. *Tawḥīd* is not only the affirmation of God's oneness, it also entails the affirmation of God as wholly other. Theologically speaking, when God is wholly other, the believer's connection to God is moral, not ontological or anthropological, or so goes his argument.[90] Another way of speaking about God's otherness is through the finite/infinite relation, where humans are relatively finite beings and God is absolutely infinite. As Düzgün explains, this finite/infinite relation is both symmetrical and asymmetrical, and the subtle implications of this are not lost on Düzgün.[91] As he puts it, theological language reflects the complex finite/infinite relation. Revelation should not be reduced to a subject–object relation, because the subject–object relation is too reductive to express the intricate dialectic of the finite/infinite relation. Moreover, the finite/infinite relation actively resists this reductive use of language. Theological language is in fact deeply indebted to this order of affairs:

> Our basic connection with God is moral rather than ontological or anthropological. [. . .] The relationship between God and humans, infinite and finite beings, is both symmetrical and asymmetrical. Theological language owes its existence to this distinction. [. . .] It is necessary not to reduce revelation to a subject–object relation. For, the quality of the finite/infinite relation prevents

"language," which is used to bridge these two spheres, from being reduced to a subject–object relation.[92]

More concretely, *tawḥīd* is a way of putting the pieces back together after recovering from modernity's unhealthy need for a false unity of human experience.[93] Yet, how should individuals resist the human tendencies towards monopoly and homogenization? His answer is to reject a single history, a single type of human being, and a single type of modernity. Q5:48, a verse that both affirms the finality of Islam but also reminds believers that God willed human heterogeneity even in matters of faith, Düzgün holds as a divine command to honor heterogeny.[94] Q5:48 reads:

> We sent to you the Scripture with the truth, confirming the Scriptures that came before it, and with final authority over them: so judge between them according to what God has sent down. Do not follow their whims, which deviate from the truth that has come to you. We have assigned a law and a path to each of you. If God had so willed, He would have made you one community, but He wanted to test you through that which He has given you, so race to do good: you will all return to God and He will make clear to you the matters you differed about.[95]

Düzgün reads this verse as a divine injunction to foster tolerance and honor plurality. When Düzgün speaks of plurality in this manner, he is not speaking of a do-whatever pluralism that admits of no shared human values but rather he means a concrete ethnic and religious plurality that expresses core human values in infinite variation.[96] Plurality does not mean a plurality of goods and commodities for purchase and sale; he does not advocate a market pluralism but instead a real plurality for human ways of life.[97] Even in the sphere of sacred text and textual commentary—plurality of opinion and a healthy diversity in readings keep believers open to the transcendent speaking through the text. What brings all of this plurality together is divine unity. Humans require a healthy *tawḥīd* for a real plurality.[98]

In light of this, various civilizations need to develop an ethic not just of recognizing the other but also of seeing the other as a living source of value and human civilization.[99] Further, he calls specifically on European culture to rediscover its own heterogeny. He advocates for a "dialogue of life" (*hayat diyaloğu*).¹⁰⁰ Such a dialogue is not abstract, nor does it pretend to mete out universal standards. What Düzgün envisions is more particular and local, advocating for the development of discourses in various local cultural codes, especially among non-Western cultures; he writes, "it is necessary to accept the possibility for Non-Western societies, whatever their cultural context, to develop a modernity with their own cultural codes."¹⁰¹

Finally, Düzgün stresses that Muslims in particular have the potential to create new forms of religious expression, and this process means they develop their own forms of civilization.¹⁰² For a Muslim individual who takes on this responsibility, religion becomes something truly living and not merely a status quo to maintain, a lost ideal to be retrieved, or a fossilized tradition to be handed down. Further, Muslims and non-Muslims alike need to let go of the temptation to see all Muslims as a homogenous group.¹⁰³ This message is accompanied by calls for Muslims in the West to recognize the polar dangers of radicalization and assimilation. Instead of allowing themselves to be homogenized by reductive discourses, he urges Muslims to engage in intellectual or social activity.¹⁰⁴

Conclusion

To summarize, the following elements are fundamental to Düzgün's understanding of individual authority: 1) He holds a universalist position on human morality. 2) He argues for an Islamic affirmation of the plurality of human life. 3) Religion is constructive *and* deconstructive. 4) True religion is fundamentally modernizing—and there is not merely one modernity but a plurality of modernities. As a corollary to this, Muslims must take their own agency seriously and take charge of their civilization in such a way that is no longer a reaction to Western modernity. 5) Human agency is not in competition with divine agency (for this he draws on al-Māturīdī). Further, change is an inescapable part of God's plan. In a changing world, as humans we have responsibility, *khalīfa*, from God, which allows our agency and authority, when true to true religion and our commonly shared *fiṭra*, to share in God's agency. 6) The individual *fiṭra* is equipped with the authority of *'aql* (the combination of heart and various aspects of cognition), common sense, human intuition, and conscience.[105] With the aid of these faculties, the individual can know right and wrong intuitively, in a way consistent with Ḥanafī views on human knowledge of good and evil.

The individual plays a central role in Düzgün's theological project, which integrates discussions from Muslim and Christian, religious and non-religious sources. In order to argue for the theological value of taking responsibility as individual believer, Düzgün champions individual authority. Again, this authority is not absolute. It is in constant dialectical interaction and dialogue with tradition, society at large, and even non-believers. Most importantly, Düzgün's case for individual authority is also a case of individual responsibility.

Moreover, it is not merely reason which carries weight but a broader understanding of human cognition that leaves room both for the heart and for the conscience.[106] Düzgün's idea of conscience is not a radically individualized conscience. Instead, human conscience is grounded in a shared human community and is developed in specific social contexts, whose variation and change is a divinely willed aspect of human destiny. Düzgün's understanding of conscience may well converge with the following description by scholar of Islam Paul Heck: "Conscience is not a principle or authority on its own but is assumed to act in a dynamic relation with the moral standards of society even when one is in good conscience dissenting from them."[107] Moreover, conscience stands out as an internal authority for Düzgün—an internal authority paramount for exercising moral responsibility in society.[108] In this sense, to stress individual authority does not mean the individual possesses authority in an unqualified sense. For Düzgün, it is the divinely planned human constitution and the divinely willed social and historical varieties of universal human nature which vest the individual with authority to discern. Individual authority does not come by coercion but from conviction in true religion.

As with Alpyağıl, Düzgün uses sources from various traditions and discourses to present the case to the reader that it is ultimately the believer who must stand up, engage, and negotiate her place and role in the modern world. The case for mediated individual authority, for Alpyağıl as well as Düzgün, is equally a case for individual responsibility.

Finally, Düzgün's case for mediated individual authority involves an integration of modern and traditional values as well as an integration of (non-Muslim) Western and Islamic sources. One way to frame this integration is to view his theological efforts as successful integration of a real binary that remains intact, like that of tradition and modernity. Another way to frame this integration is to view it as evidence that binaries, such as tradition and modernity, are not absolute and, accordingly, that Düzgün's reference to values defined in both modern and traditional terms indicates these values should not be expressed or understood in terms of binaries. In other words, rather than remain in dichotomies like Islam vs. West or religion vs. tradition, Düzgün's case for the centrality of individual authority points beyond these dichotomies, legitimately drawing on Arab-Islamic, Turkish, and Western intellectual resources.

Notes

1. In the Christian tradition, two seminal figures who cast faith in terms of existential struggle are Søren Kierkegaard (1813–55) and Paul Tillich (1886–1965). While these two figures are well known in Turkish theology faculties, Düzgün does not extensively engage either thinker in the works cited here.
2. To note, Düzgün does not generally identify with the philosophical school of existentialism. Generally, he refers to philosophical existentialism in a negative, positivist context.
3. CDDD, p. 195.
4. DBT, p. 21.
5. DBT, p. 23.
6. DBT, p. 23.
7. In discussions of exclusivist vs. inclusivist religion in the Euro-American academy, there is a recognition that inclusivism is itself a kind of exclusivism. In this case, Düzgün's inclusivism assumes that authentic Islam is superior and ultimately in a privileged relationship to truth, but other religions like Judaism and Christianity share in this truth to a lesser degree insofar as they are misguided expressions of true monotheism. In the Turkish academy, theologian and historian of religion Şinasi Gündüz, himself abreast of the Euro-American discussions on the debate, also remarks on the exclusive aspects of both inclusivist and pluralist paradigms. Gündüz, *Küresel Sorunlar ve Din* (Ankara: Ankara Okulu Yayınları, 2010), pp. 90–4.
8. DBT, p. 24.
9. See Yaşar Nuri Öztürk, *Tanrı, Akıl ve Ahlaktan Başka Kutsal Tanımayan İnanç Deizm* (Istanbul: Yeni Boyut, 2015). This title translates to *Deism: Belief that*

Recognizes Nothing Sacred except God, Reason, and Morals. In this book, the late Öztürk argued the Qur'ān, while not espousing deism, offers resources for the deist position. As a proponent of laicity and a supporter of Turkish Republican values, Öztürk's work is more overtly political than any of the theologians the present study focuses on. His book joins the discussion in chapter seven.

10. DBT, p. 110.
11. DBT, p. 164.
12. DBT, p. 115.
13. DBT, p. 122.
14. ATT, p. 151.
15. CDDD, p. 19.
16. CDDD, p. 17–18.
17. CDDD, p. 18. This is an interesting turnabout on using the term modernity, but not too far from Muhammad Abduh. Adbuh, in his writings on *tawḥīd* (divine unity), argues that it is the Qur'ān and Islamic culture which is originally modern (i.e., inherently reasonable) and thus already in harmony with modern science. See Muhammad Abduh, *The Theology of Unity*, trans. Kenneth Cragg (Selangor: Islamic Book Trust, 2003).
18. CDDD, p. 18. Turkish: "temel insan hakları, adalet, özgürlük, güven[.]"
19. CDDD, p. 20. Turkish: "bütün dinlerin başına gelmesi muhtemel bir dışlayıcılık belasıdır."
20. CDDD, p. 20. Though he urges for rethinking on this matter, Düzgün sees Islam as more likely to be inclusive, starting with the divinely ordained protections for non-Muslims like "people of the book" (Jews and Christians) and further warns his readers not to expect inclusivism from (presumably non-Muslim) "monopolists" of religion (p. 21).
21. CDDD, p. 130.
22. CDDD, pp. 129–30. Düzgün mentions both Christianity and Islam in this discussion. While he is not his most critical of Christianity here, he consistently tends to portray Christian history as more monopolizing, destructive, and hegemonic than Islamic history.
23. CDDD, pp. 113–17.
24. CDDD, p. 114.
25. CDDD, p. 114.
26. CDDD, p. 114 fn.
27. CDDD, p. 114.

28. CDDD, p. 114.
29. CDDD, p. 115.
30. CDDD, p. 115.
31. DBT, p. 66.
32. DBT, p. 67. Whether or not his accusation stands up to scrutiny, affirming the individual human being as microcosm of the whole exists both in the classical Islamic tradition of *adab* and in European humanist writings of the Renaissance. Arguably, Christian tradition has never had a problem affirming that *some* human individuals represent all of humanity in important respects, particularly Adam and Christ or Eve and the Virgin Mary.
33. DBT, p. 69. Turkish: "İslâm ferdi esas alır."
34. CDDD, p. 43.
35. DBT, p. 90.
36. ATT, p. 234. Turkish: "Zira dünyaya anlam katan şey, tözsel/cevhersel olarak dünyanın ne olup olmadığı değil, onda cereyan eden olaylardır."
37. CDDD, p. 127.
38. DBT, p. 112.
39. CDDD, p. 15. Perhaps this is where he distinguishes his position slightly from that of Ali Shariati, who pits opposing societal currents against one another under the shared category of religion; however, he shares with Shariati an understanding of positive religion as progressive and dedicated to social flourishing. Düzgün's position also stands in contrast to Salafist trends, where taking on the habit, dress, and attitudes of a specific cultural moment in the past (that of the first generations of Muslims) is considered necessary to express a truly authentic Islam.
40. DBT, p. 27.
41. CDDD, p. 71.
42. CDDD, p. 76.
43. CDDD, p. 84. Here he speaks against religions being used for destroying customs. For example, he claims Indonesian expressions of Islam avoided this.
44. In this context he prefers the quranic word "*ümran*" (in Turkish) rather than the usual Turkish word "*medeniyet*" for civilization. Both words derive from Arabic.
45. CDDD, p. 204.
46. On the question of how to translate "book," see Daniel Madigan, *The Qur'an's Self-Image* (Princeton: Princeton University Press, 2000). In this work, Madigan questions the conventional translation of *kitāb* as "book" and argues for the importance of an oral and recited understanding of quranic scripture.

47. CDDD, pp. 205–6.
48. CDDD, p. 206.
49. CDDD, p. 207. In support of his claims of Islamic civilization, the work of the following two scholars might aid his case: Walid Saleh has argued that Sunni tradition is marked by its tolerance for diversity, and tendency for inclusivity, like a large umbrella. See Walid Saleh, *The Formation of the Classical Tafsīr Tradition: The Qur'ān Commentary of Al-Tha'labī (d. 427/1035)* (Leiden: Brill, 2004). Also, the late Shahab Ahmed's posthumous work details theoretical and historical considerations which highlight the broad and inclusive aspects of Islamic civilization. See *What is Islam? The Importance of Being Islamic* (Princeton, NJ: Princeton University Press, 2016).
50. For an example of the use of this verse to exhort interfaith dialogue, see Reza Shah-Kazemi, *The Other in the Light of the One: The Universality of the Qur'ān and Interfaith Dialogue* (Cambridge: The Islamic Texts Society, 2006), p. 113. Shah-Kazemi's book argues for the value of *tawḥīd* (divine unity) in Muslim efforts of interfaith dialogue.
51. This is a slight modification of the M. A. S. Abdel Haleem translation, where "recognize" is substituted with "come to know."
52. CDDD, p. 208.
53. CDDD, p. 208.
54. CDDD, pp. 44, 178–9; DBT, p. 21. The truly free individual, he explains here, is one that is truly God's servant. Elsewhere he attributes the error of conceiving of human freedom in conflict with divine freedom to many Western religious and secular strands of thought—for instance, ATT, p. 91. It may be useful to note that Karl Rahner makes a similar case about the relationship between human and divine freedom. Rahner argues in *Hearer of the Word* that God's freedom and human freedom do not correlate inversely but directly.

    God's free act is intelligible, and that free action is luminous in itself and is only dark for one standing outside. Thus, being, truth, and revelation can become intelligible to another by co-enactment in love. The human being freely takes part in the performing or re-enacting and thereby understands God's free act. See Rahner, *Hearer of the Word*, trans. Joseph Donceel (New York: Continuum, 1994).
55. DBT, p. 38.
56. DBT, p. 38. Turkish: "Bütün bu gerçeklikleri inkâr etmemekle birlikte İslâm bu niteliklerden hiçbirini temel karakter olarak kabul etmez."

57. He does not stress the meaning "difference" associated with the root kh-l-f at least in the works covered here.
58. DBT, p. 51.
59. DBT, p. 75.
60. DBT, p. 76.
61. DBT, p. 77.
62. CDDD, p. 48.
63. ATT, p. 233.
64. ATT, p. 216. Turkish: "Teolojinin bağlamsal olması yani belli bir sosyal ve kültürel yapıyla bağlantılı gelişmesi, tarih içinde yer tutmanın getirdiği kaçınılmaz bir durumdur."
65. CDDD, p. 110.
66. CDDD, p. 113.
67. ATT, p. 217.
68. ATT, p. 126.
69. Aristotle names "credible opinions," or "*endoxa*," as a valid source of knowledge. Aristotelian credible opinions and Islamic trustworthy reports, though not precisely the same concept, have much in common: both acknowledge the social aspect of knowing and both recognize the validity, even necessity, of second-hand knowledge. In the *Organon*, a collection of works devoted to logic, Aristotle writes, "[*Endoxa*] are those opinions accepted by everyone, or by the majority, or by the philosophers—i.e., by all, by all or the majority, or by those who are the most notable and illustrious of them" (*Top.* i 1, 100b21–23). *The Basic Works of Aristotle*, ed. Richard McKeon (New York: The Modern Library, 2001), p. 188. On the translation of *endoxa* as "credible opinions," see Christopher Shields, "Aristotle," *The Stanford Encyclopedia of Philosophy* (Winter 2016 Edition), <https://plato.stanford.edu/archives/win2016/entries/aristotle/> (last accessed March 27, 2018).
70. Though, as discussed above, Düzgün does critique "modern" theology for not recognizing the legitimate contribution *kashf* and intuition make in the individual's efforts to orient themselves to reality and truth.
71. ATT, p. 129.
72. CDDD, p. 180.
73. CDDD, p. 180.
74. CDDD, p. 55. Turkish: "değişimin kaynağı ınsandır."
75. CDDD, p. 55.

76. ATT, p. 141.
77. Seyyed Hossein Nasr, *The Heart of Islam: Enduring Values for Humanity* (New York: HarperCollins, 2004), pp. 7–8. Nasr goes on to explain that "Islam considers all authentic religions to be based on this surrender, so that *al-islām* means not only the religion revealed through the Quran to the prophet Muḥammad, but all authentic religions as such" (p. 8). While Düzgün's focus is less the authenticity of other religions, he does espouse the idea of "islam" with a lowercase "i" in a similar sense.
78. DBT, p. 38.
79. DBT, p. 117; CDDD, pp. 207–8.
80. English translation is a modification of the M. A. S. Abdel Haleem translation.
81. To compare, Muslim scholar Jerusha T. Lamptey's work *Never Wholly Other: A Muslima Theology of Religious Pluralism* (Oxford: Oxford University Press, 2014) also emphasizes the significance of this quranic passage and takes up the category of difference in the context of religious pluralism.
82. DBT, p. 123.
83. While I here use the word "relative," Düzgün does not espouse relati*vism* (Turkish: *görecilik*). He is a universalist who also recognizes the social embeddedness of human knowledge. On the social character of knowledge, see, for instance, ATT, p. 99.
84. DBT, p.123.
85. DBT, p. 123. The quranic verse he uses to support this is (Yūsuf) Q12:76.
86. DBT, p. 121.
87. DBT, p. 105. Daniel Madigan, in lectures, has spoken of "islam" in this universal sense. Madigan briefly explains the term "islam" with a lowercase "i" as "entrusting oneself to God alone," i.e., the natural human response to *tawḥīd*, in Madigan, "Sacred Texts: Koran," in M. C. Horowitz (ed.), *New Dictionary of the History of Ideas Vol. 5* (Detroit: Charles Scribner's Sons, 2005), p. 2165. Also, for a short summary of what Madigan proposes Christians can learn from Islam see David Marshall, "Muhammad in Contemporary Christian Theological Reflection," *Islam and Christian–Muslim Relations* 24:2 (2013): pp. 161–72.
88. DBT, p. 105. Turkish: "İslâm, gönüllü teslimiyeti ifade eder. Bu teslimiyet, canlı cansız herkes ve her şey için geçerlidir."
89. DBT, p. 106.
90. ATT, p. 63.
91. ATT, p. 63.

92. ATT, p. 63. Turkish: "Tanrı ile iletişimimizin temel zemini ontolojik ve antropolojik olmanın ötesinde ahlakidir. [. . .] Tanrı ile insanlar, sonsuz ile sonlular arasındaki ilişki hem simetrik hem de asimetriktir. Teolojik dil varlığını, bu farklılığa borçludur. [. . .] vahyi bir özne-nesne ilişkisine indirgememek gerekir. Zira sonlu ve sonsuz arasındaki ilişkinin niteliği, bu iki alan arasındaki ilişkide kullanılan 'dil'i özne-nesne ilişkisine indirgemeyi engellemektedir."
93. CDDD, p. 188.
94. CDDD, p. 189.
95. M. A. S. Abdel Haleem translation.
96. CDDD, p. 197.
97. CDDD, p. 197. Düzgün's critique of the marketization of an otherwise divinely willed blessing is a similar motion to that of Fatma Barbarosoğlu and her critique of Islamic "fashion" as a contradiction in terms at odds with Islamic values of modesty, humility, and frugality. Barbarosoğlu, though not a theologian, is a sociologist by training and a popular writer in Turkey.
98. CDDD, p. 198. He writes here that where the concept of *tawḥīd* is compromised, pluralism cannot be fruitful.
99. CDDD, p. 201.
100. CDDD, p. 289.
101. CDDD, p. 289. Turkish: "hangi kültür ortamında olurlarsa olsunlar Batı dışı toplumların kendi kültür kodlarıyla bir çağdaşlık geliştirmelerinin imkânını kabul etmek gerekecektir."
102. CDDD, p. 289.
103. CDDD, p. 295.
104. CDDD, p. 295.
105. These are in Turkish: *akıl, sağduyu, sezgi, vicdan*.
106. I do not wish to argue that freedom in religion, individual authority, the weight of reason, and conscience are new phenomena to the Turkish theology faculty. Notably, Yusuf Ziya Yörükân, in his work *Muslim-ness*—first published in 1957 and 1961 and meant to be a standard teaching book for instructing the basics of Islam outside the academy—strongly asserted that human reason and choice are conditions for proper religion and that the exercise of reason and freedom of conscience (*vicdan*) are pillars of religion. Yusuf Ziya Yörükân, *Müslümanlık ve Kur'an-ı Kerim'den Âyetlerle İslâm Esasları* [*Muslim-ness and the Foundations of Islam with Verses from the Holy Qur'an*], ed. Turhan Yörükân (Istanbul: Ötüken, 2006), p. 246. To note, the Turkish nominalization of "Muslim" used in the title (*Müsümanlık*) is often simply translated as "Islam."

107. Paul Heck, "Conscience across Cultures: The Case of Islam," *The Journal of Religion* 94:3 (2014): p. 292. Heck argues that conscience can function as a shared human mechanism across cultures and religions, even if agreement is lacking on the details of its functioning. Düzgün would most likely agree. Düzgün has cited Heck, but to my knowledge has not commented on Heck's definition of conscience. CDDD, p. 276: Paul Heck, "Jihad Revisited," *Journal of Religious Ethics* 32 (2004): pp. 95–128.
108. Heck, "Conscience across Cultures," p. 295. Heck's characterization of an idea of conscience potentially held in common between Christianity and Islam may easily apply to Düzgün's understanding of conscience. Heck further writes, "conscience serves as a necessary foregrounding for engaging in the moral good in society by conviction rather than by coercion." With Heck and with Düzgün, a sense of internal authority is permitted to transcend external authority.

IV
CONCLUSIONS

7

From Dialectics to Direct Address: Turkish Theologians on Atheism and Other Religions

Questions of skepticism, atheism, and the value of competing religious claims to truth are an unavoidable hallmark of the present global age. While these topics are often treated alongside one another in other contexts, when it comes to Turkish theology, these subjects are especially interconnected. This is because Christianity is viewed by many Turkish theologians as the standard bearer for all three categories.[1] Skepticism and atheism are viewed primarily as products of Christianity. The same holds for religious pluralism. The contemporary trend towards religious pluralism, far from being viewed as a neutral term connoting the truth claims of various religions, signifies for many Turkish theologians an especially Christian theological venture. Given the strong association between Christianity and these three challenges, this chapter looks at what might be Turkish theology's most obvious instance of its characteristic threefold engagement.

This chapter will move between closer case examples and more broad-brush surveys of relatively recent publications. The aim is to give the reader both concrete examples and a rich context in which to process these examples. My claim throughout is that skepticism, atheism, and pluralism are related topics in Turkish theology largely due to the common association of Christianity with all three terms. As the chapter unfolds, I address wider assumptions in Turkish theology along with counterexamples to said assumptions, dividing the discussion into three sections: the first on atheism and related concepts, the second on skepticism in dialogue with Christian sources, and the third on religious pluralism.

Atheism, Deism, and Unbelief

Materialism and positivism are heavily associated with the theological questions of skepticism and atheism. Turkish works outside the theology faculties include Murtaza Korlaelçi's *The Arrival of Positivism in Turkey*,[2] Mehmet Akgün's *The Arrival of Materialism in Turkey*,[3] and Ahmet Yaşar Ocak's more recent *Atheists and Heretics in Ottoman Society of the 15th to 17th Centuries*.[4] Unlike the first two, Ocak's work looks at the question of deviance with little reference to categories like "modernity" or the "West," portraying different sects and groups as integral parts of Ottoman society.[5] Turkish theologian Mehmet S. Aydın's *Philosophy of Religion* is still heavily referenced in theology faculties.[6] Additionally, theologian Mustafa Açıköz's three volumes on skepticism give a broad overview of skepticism in various religions, times, and places.[7] As Şinasi Gündüz has remarked, between 1950 and 1990, Turkish theology faculties saw a lack of specialized works on the history of religions, those that proliferated being encyclopedic, over-general, apologetic, and polemical.[8]

In Turkish theology faculties, skepticism and deism are heavily associated with Western trends in philosophy and religion. Many of the theological crises in the West are seen primarily as Christian problems. For instance, the Western rejection of the God of ontotheology is not a foregone conclusion in Muslim frameworks. Ontotheology is generally seen as indefensible on Christian rather than Muslim terms, and it is still common for scholars in Turkey to devote works to subjects of being, necessary being, and knowledge—insofar as all acts of knowing are dependent on God's necessary being—through the lens of classical and some Ottoman Islamic scholars.

Tawḥīd and the God of Ontotheology

> Which god is dead? We may answer: the God of metaphysics—and also of theology, inasmuch as theology relies on the metaphysics of a first cause, of a necessary being, of a prime mover which is absolute goodness and the origin of values. Let us say that it is the God of ontotheology, to use the word coined by Heidegger.
>
> —Paul Ricoeur[9]

For Turkish theologians, many of whom cite Paul Ricoeur, Sigmund Freud, and Friedrich Nietzsche, the statement above simply does not hold. The God of theology—one described in the metaphysics of first cause, of necessary being, and of the originator of values—is very much alive. In Turkish theology, the God of ontotheology lives and thrives. This does not mean everyone takes this route. Still, when it comes to the question of skepticism, it is not uncommon to view unbelief in terms of an improper ontological grounding. That is, Turkish theologians are more likely to attribute the death of ontotheology in the West to the corrupting influence of Christian doctrine on said ontotheology rather than to the project of ontotheology itself.

In fact, a cursory glance at recent publication titles suggests the widespread role of ontotheology in Turkish theology and sometimes philosophy. Düzgün, whose work we have already encountered, wrote *The God–World Relation according to Nasafī* [d. 1142] *and Islamic Philosophers* (1998).[10] Yaşar Türkmen has recently edited a volume on al-Ghazālī and causality, making leading Anglophone Islamic studies scholarship available to Turkish theologians.[11] Sema Özdemir has written a work on an Anatolian figure of particular significance to Turkish scholars: *Being, Knowledge, and Humanity in Davūd al-Qayṣarī* [d. c. 1350] (2014).[12] The Avicennist İlhan Kutluer has authored *Necessary Being in the Ontology of Ibn Sīnā* (2013).[13] Fatma Zehra Pattabanoğlu has written *Ibn Kammūna* [d. 1284] *and His Philosophy* (2014).[14] İsmail Hanoğlu has penned *Theological Anthropology in the Philosophy of Fakhr al-Dīn al-Rāzī* (2014).[15] Ömer Türker, another Avicenna scholar, has written *The Problem of Possibility in Metaphysical Knowledge in the Philosophy of Ibn Sīnā* (2010).[16] Ankara theologian Fehrullah Terkan, who completed his PhD at Chicago University on the subject of al-Ghazālī and Ibn Rushd, has written extensively on Muslim philosophy, including treatments of Ibn Ṭufayl and al-Fārābī.[17] Finally, fellow Avicennist Ömer Mahir Alper, Professor of Islamic Philosophy at the Theology Faculty of Istanbul, has authored *Being and Humanity: The Recreation of an Idea in the Context of Kemalpaşazâde* (2010).[18]

Atheism as a Product of Christianity

If ontotheology is not defunct, nor are philosophical attempts to articulate God's relationship to the world problematic. Generous scholarly output continues to tackle such ontological themes in Turkey. Nevertheless, Turkish theologians are aware of the crisis of ontotheology in Christian theology. İbrahim Coşkun and Şaban Ali Düzgün offer two examples of how Turkish theologians attribute the crisis of ontotheology to flawed Christian beliefs.

Turkish theologian İbrahim Coşkun argues in *Atheism and Islam: A Kalām Critique of Atheism in the Modern Era*[19] that atheism's primary cause is Western Christianity. When he treats the causes and trends in atheism, focus lies squarely on Western intellectual history and corrupted Christianity.[20] Specifically, in sections devoted to the causes of atheism, he delves straight into Christian beliefs and history of the Western church.[21] In addition to tying atheism to Muslim–Christian polemics, Coşkun cautions his reader to distinguish between types of atheism—theoretical and practical, further warning that many people are falsely labeled atheists for criticizing the religious belief of their community. And like Açıköz above, Coşkun denies the possibility of "absolute" atheism—arguing it is impossible to be an atheist without in some way affirming God's existence. Unlike his evaluation of Christianity, Coşkun does not fault any mainstream trends in Islam for directly causing or encouraging atheism. In his estimation, Islam is more immune to atheism than Christianity.

For Coşkun, several things went wrong in Western Christian history that sowed the seeds for widespread atheism.[22] First, he holds that Christianity was corrupted from the outset—especially with the preaching of St. Paul, offering a standard position in Muslim–Christian polemics that traces back as far as the Middle Ages.[23] Second, he offers the more contemporary thesis that Europe does not represent authentic Christianity.[24] For Coşkun, Christianity in its corrupted form requires human beings to believe irrational things without any certainty. Rationally indefensible doctrines like original sin, the Trinity, the Eucharist, and baptism are the reason faith and reason clashed in the West. Further errors include the restriction of religion to the fortress of the human conscience,[25] Western Christianity's history of oppression,[26] and the failure of pious Christians to live up to their own standards.[27] Coşkun also assures his reader that monotheistic religions, while necessarily containing some suprarational elements, will never ask a believer to accept something irrational—unless corruption has taken place.[28]

In addition to Christianity serving as the primary cause of atheism, there may also be a positive factor that legitimates an Islamic case for the continued validity of ontotheology. In Coşkun's explanation of *tawḥīd* (divine unity), he not only affirms that God is the greatest being to exist, he also affirms God is the only being to exist.[29] In this way, Coşkun asserts Islam to be simultaneously monotheistic and monistic. This double affirmation inherent in many scholars' understanding of *tawḥīd* may contribute to the view that, from a Muslim perspective, ontotheology has not ceded to the winds of doubt and secular modernity. Coşkun's reference to *tawḥīd* in questions of unbelief is one shared with Açıköz above and will also come up in our discussion of Düzgün.

Düzgün: A Tawḥīdic Counter to Unbelief

Şaban Ali Düzgün tackles contemporary Christian theologians' responses to unbelief and skepticism. Sympathetic at times, Düzgün nonetheless looks for what went wrong in the intellectual history of Western Christianity to account for a perceived explosion of atheism. Unlike Coşkun, he targets not Christianity as a whole but a toxic Western appropriation of Christianity.[30] In particular, Düzgün sees deformed/secularized Protestantism as a threat to all religions.[31]

Düzgün, like Coşkun, claims that the opposition between revelation and reason was never as direct in Islamic societies as it was in Western Christianity.[32] Nor does he think science and religion necessarily come into conflict, sharing the opinion of other Turkish theologians on the matter.[33] Science and religion answer different questions, and in his view, science does not fully answer humanity's basic questions.[34] Religion is not irrational but super-rational, so there need not be a strict dichotomy of faith vs. reason.[35] Yet, in the Christian West, Düzgün claims that Aquinas' synthesis of Aristotelian thought and Christian doctrine made the criticisms applicable to Aristotle also applicable to Christianity. Namely, the integration of Aristotle into Christianity caused undue polarization of religion and science, which came to a head in the eighteenth and nineteenth centuries.[36] Galileo's *Dialogues* and Newton's *Principia* are also at fault.[37] The problem, he claims, occurred when Newton's method morphed into unquestioned metaphysic.[38] For Düzgün, rationality is a question of method rather than of content.[39] Although Aristotle started as a positive influence on Western Christianity, this had reversed by the eighteenth and nineteenth centuries. Science acquired the authority to judge all other forms of knowledge with the prevailing attitude that "something is only meaningful insofar as it can be proved."[40] Düzgün does not claim that the trajectory of science and religion in the West was *necessarily* doomed to fall out of balance, only that it eventually *did* fall out of balance.[41] And while some blame theology for the modern epistemological crisis,[42] Düzgün, for his part, blames the specific trajectory of not only Christian theology but also the wider culture it helped create. Finally, he does not think that the answers of contemporary Anglophone theology are adequate to address this crisis.

For instance, Düzgün does not view the linguistic turn in theology as a definitive one. Düzgün accepts without objection that theology is grounded in a culturally specific grammar and language and, so, accepts that theological language also differs from other discourses.[43] Yet, he dismisses Wittgenstein and Lindbeck as insufficient theological answers to the epistemological crisis in theology.[44] He also looks at the efforts of theologians David Tracy and Janet Soskice in addressing the challenge of positivism, yet is not entirely satisfied.[45] He takes up subjective and experiential aspects of knowing, even if he is not always satisfied with Christian theological arguments from religious experience.[46] He formulates the matter as follows: moral and religious claims have to do with the process of forming an individual and, as such, these claims have little to do with proving something about an object.[47] Thus he does not advocate unrestrained subjectivity as an epistemological position; rather, he argues that religious and moral claims exist to form the subject.

Düzgün does not build his argument on ontology but rather on shared human morality, yet all of this is grounded in an understanding of *tawḥīd*. His basic ontological claim is that when God is wholly other, our connection to God is moral, not ontological or anthropological.[48] At other moments, he seems to elaborate both anthropological and ontological aspects of humanity's connection to God. God as creator and sender of revelation entails the human ability to have knowledge of God by logic and inference, and it is the *fiṭra* that allows individuals to seek God-knowledge with accuracy.[49] Seeking God beyond the causal chain of events is something done with the *'aql*, or mind, according to classical *kalām* and is something done through love (*sevgi*) for Sufis.[50] Humanity's ontological connection with God transcends physical and even metaphysical considerations, and this connection is a locus of existential meaning.[51] The fundamental tie between a human being and God is a matter of the heart and not of the head. Perhaps this is what Düzgün means by a moral connection to God, since the heart more than the head stands for moral agency. Using traditional Muslim understandings of the heart, he lists six layers of the heart that go beyond the *'aql*: (in Turkish) *sadr, kalb, fuad, lübb, nühâ*, and *hicr*.[52] Only at the fourth level of the heart, the *lübb*, does one achieve full realization of *tawḥid* or divine unity. Thus, monotheism is not simply a matter of logic and propositions but also a much deeper journey of knowledge, self-knowledge, and self-actualization. It is the act of seeking and trying to understand God which sustains humans. God is not an object of thought but an essential part of our thought process.[53] Presumably, it is this morally significant process that falls by the wayside when science and rationality are seen in stark opposition to religion.

Düzgün's overall evaluation of Christianity's role in atheism does not significantly diverge from common polemical readings; however, it does distinguish itself by direct, if at times passing, engagements with contemporary Christian theologians. In tackling the matter of belief and unbelief, Düzgün dialectically navigates his Turkish context, classical Islamic sources, and a range of Western sources.

An Exception in Attitudes towards Deism: Öztürk

Deism can often get thrown into the mix of terms such as materialism, positivism, skepticism, and atheism. For many, deism is a step on the way to atheism, but the late Yaşar Nuri Öztürk used the term positively as an antidote for the atheism caused by the unchecked abuse of religion—not only in Christian contexts but also in Muslim ones.

Yaşar Nuri Öztürk (1945–2016) was a public figure, politician, and professor of theology at Istanbul University. His position on religion in Turkey was redolent of Kemalist laicism,[54] and his work engaged the Western deist tradition. Famously, he prepared a simplified Qur'ān commentary based on the Qur'ān commentary by the late Ottoman figure Elmalılı Muhammed Hamdi Yazır, entitled *Hak Dini Kur'ân Dili* (*The Religion of Truth [is the] Language of the Qur'ān*)—a work of undisputed popularity in Turkey. While familiar to non-specialists, his work is controversial. Perhaps for both reasons, he has received more scholarly attention outside of Turkey than most of the other Turkish theological figures mentioned or treated in the present inquiry.[55]

In his book *Deism: Belief that Recognizes Nothing as Sacred Except God, Reason, and Ethics (A Theo-philosophical Analysis)*,[56] Öztürk calls upon the authority of his conscience, of his identity as a scholar, and of one who has spent his life in study of the Qurʾān to claim that the Qurʾān leaves the door open for a deist position.⁵⁷ Even though the Qurʾān does not explicitly call for a deist position, he identifies quranic resources that leave open the possibility for an Islamically acceptable deism.⁵⁸ For Öztürk, one of deism's central insights is that religion itself, revelation itself, and places of worship are not sacred; instead, reason, knowledge, and ethics are sacred.⁵⁹ He further identifies two early tenth-century Islamic thinkers Ibn al-Rāwandī (d. 913) and Abū Bakr al-Rāzī (d. 925) as authentic resources for systematizing an Islamically acceptable deism. As an Ottoman example of deist-friendly thought, he cites Şehbenderzade Filibeli Ahmet Hilmi's (d. 1914) *History of Islam*.⁶⁰

Öztürk invites his audience to understand why some raised as Muslims or Christians might be fed up with organized religion. Christians may be disillusioned with the church and its attempts at "inquisition;" while Muslims may be fed up with individuals (in particular Sufis) who claim special spiritual authority and then abuse it.⁶¹ Pointing out how the Old Testament illustrated the sins and depravity of biblical prophets, he departs from traditional Muslim interpretations of biblical prophets, which stress their blamelessness.⁶² For Öztürk, the prophets, as the Old Testament describes them, justify the reaction of deists who rejected religion as harmful religiosity and a corruption of values through the authority of corrupt human beings. Unlike the Old Testament, the Qurʾān does not depict prophets in this manner—stressing rather their moral excellence and freedom from worldly corruption, and specifically the temptations of political power.⁶³ He thinks this is how the Qurʾān hints at deistic values across theistic traditions.

Öztürk writes, "Religiosity is a deception and an ideology of power that turns the religion of *tawḥīd* into a religion of *shirk* [i.e., unbelief]."⁶⁴ Unlike many theologians, he does not see deism or atheism as the fundamental threat to religion. In fact, he remarks that those who are sincerely religious, deists, and even atheists who still practice respect towards other humans have a common enemy: "falsely religious irreligion" (*dinci dinsizlik*).⁶⁵ To elucidate, Öztürk begins with the word "*ikrāh*" (Turkish: *ikrah*) or "compulsion," recalling the quranic verse "There is no compulsion in religion" (Q2:256). Religiosity— in the false sense—breeds compulsion, and this compulsion leads to both violence and hypocrisy.⁶⁶ Öztürk associates compulsion with false pharaonic religion. Compulsion has wreaked havoc in the histories of various religions, including cultures affected by those religions. Just as in the Islamic world injustices were at times committed in the name of countering "*fitna*" (Turkish: *fitne*), so too does the buzzword "democracy" often serve to justify compulsion.[67]

Öztürk thinks deism is particularly necessary in the Muslim world today. Since secularism (*laiklik*) is already rooted in European culture, that cultural nexus does not have to make such a conscious turn to deism to save itself from the negative effects of religiosity and radicalism. By contrast, he holds that in the Islamic world there is no getting around the challenge of destructive religiosity. For this reason, he claims deism should be the shelter and resource of choice.[68] If deism is not seen as a quranically sanctioned option, people who are fed up with religiosity will simply turn to atheism and away from human values.[69] Moreover, not only is deism a solution for responding to the negative impact of religiosity today, deism is also at the heart of religious dialogue. Rather than pandering to what he sees as less-than-helpful Christian calls for dialogue on Christian terms, Öztürk asserts that behind the jargon of any honest attempt of religious dialogue among theists, it is deism that provides common ground.[70]

Öztürk's views on Deism represent a minority opinion among Turkish theologians, and his engagement with Islamic and Western sources is, arguably, less a product of dialectical interplay of traditions and more a Kemalist reading of religion. Nonetheless, he still engages the Western tradition alongside traditional Islamic sources.

Christianity and Skepticism

Christians have long viewed Islam as a kind of heresy. John of Damascus (d. 749) set the tone when he treated Islam as a type of Arian heresy. According to John of Damascus, Muhammad—whose prophetic calling John denied—chanced upon the Old and New Testaments and spoke with an Arian monk. The result is John's approximation of the Muslim creed, and I quote from his "On the Heresy of the Ishmaelites":

> there is one God, creator of all things, who has neither been begotten nor has begotten . . . Christ is the Word of God and His Spirit, but a creature and a servant, and that He was begotten without seed of Mary the sister of Moses

and Aaron . . . the Word and God and the Spirit entered into Mary and she brought forth Jesus, who was a prophet and a servant of God . . . the Jews wanted to crucify Him in violation of the law, and that they seized His shadow and crucified this. But the Christ himself was not crucified . . . for God out of his love for Him took Him into heaven . . .[71]

John was a well-educated Syrian with likely broad exposure to Muslim power and culture. Beyond polemical jabs, his words reflect some of the actual Muslim beliefs. Polemics from both sides and beyond have continued down the ages. Muslims have, for instance, asked: if the Christian Gospels are not the Gospel given to Jesus, then why does the Qur'ān call Christians people of the book? Did they not take a message of *tawḥīd* (divine unity), like that given to all prophets, and corrupt it with superstitious and irrational tales of Incarnation, divine sonship, and above all the Trinity? Are Christians not gravely misled in insisting faith transcends rationality?

With the rise of missionary and colonial activity in the nineteenth century, Muslim responses to Christian doctrine took on new dimensions, as responses to politics and power. Ottomans, for instance, saw a great rise in Christian missionary activity, especially with the arrival of Protestant groups. As Turkish scholar of religion İsmail Taşpınar notes in his *Hacı Abdullah Petrici's Critique of Christianity*,[72] Ottoman intellectuals penned many *rediyye* works at this time—sometimes diverging from the established genre of refutations by directly taking into account contemporary Western Christian sources. In that same century, Ottomans witnessed the arrival of Darwinism and materialism through the works of Louis Büchner.[73] Ottoman and Turkish religious thinkers have been engaging contemporary Western Christian sources of all variety for about two hundred years.

I suggest there are common moves contemporary Turkish theologians can and have made vis-à-vis Christian concepts and beliefs—recall Turkish theologians do not always strictly distinguish between secular concepts from Western Christian civilization and religious doctrines from Christian theology. After looking at some of these broader trends, this section will go into more concrete detail with a limited survey of Turkish theological evaluations of Christianity and skepticism, with dual focus on Mehmet Bayrakdar of the Ankara Theology Faculty and Recep Alpyağıl of the Istanbul Theology Faculty.

One move Turkish scholars make is to reappropriate a concept. For instance, many scholars say "yes" to the stress on local identity and the necessity for embracing pluralism, but simultaneously claim that Christianity and Western culture actually export the opposite reality under the banner of pluralism. This same pattern of reappropriation was also seen in the previous chapters on Şaban Ali Düzgün, including his use of the concept "primitive."[74]

Another approach is to critically apply a concept or a particular theological discourse endemic to Christian or Western tradition. In the realm of religious hermeneutics, the well-established Zeki Özcan, for instance, is heavily versed in Western hermeneutic theory and responds to debates on authorial intent in sacred text with the clear statement, "God is not an author."[75] Recep Alpyağıl, whom we discussed previously and will discuss again below, argues for a critical application of narrative in the reading of sacred texts—drawing heavily on Paul Ricoeur as well as faulting Arab thinkers like Abu Zayd for not going far enough.

Another critical tactic is to deconstruct a monolithic view of Christianity through appeals to its diverse history. For instance, Şinasi Gündüz and Hakan Olgun use historical inquiry and church history, including the opinions of Christians theologians on church history, to deconstruct Christianity *qua* monolith.[76] Scholars like Gündüz and Olgun analyze the historical research on Christianity, even that done by Christian scholars, to stress its plurality, potential contradictions, and admitted self-criticisms.

A fourth approach—and this is by no means an exhaustive list—is to do philosophical comparisons between Western and classical Arab thinkers.[77] Such a comparison might ultimately champion the insight of the Muslim thinker and apply that insight to the interpretation of the Christian thinker in question—as, I will argue, is the case with Mehmet Bayrakdar's comparison of al-Ghazālī and Pascal on skepticism.

Bayrakdar: Dispersing the Specter of Skepticism

Returning to the topic of skepticism,[78] we will now take a more in-depth look at Mehmet Bayrakdar's *Pascal's Wager: Rolling Dice on the Afterlife According to Ali, al-Ghazālī, and Pascal.*[79] Mehmet Bayrakdar (b. 1952), a retired professor at the Ankara Theology Faculty, studied at the Theology Faculty of Ankara University and then went to the Sorbonne for his doctorate. While interested in European and Islamic intellectual history, he has a special research interest in mathematics and technology.[80]

In his book *Pascal's Wager* (2013), Bayrakdar argues that Islamic intellectual tradition significantly influenced Pascal's formulation of his famous wager, situating Pascal's wager within the context of an earlier, Islamic precedent—centered on the line of reasoning developed by al-Ghazālī (d. 1111). Al-Ghazālī's position on the afterlife is straightforward but not trivial.[81] For al-Ghazālī and for Pascal the crucial consideration lies in the difference between finite goods and infinite consequences. For al-Ghazālī, finite happiness cannot compare with infinite happiness; and given any doubt that there might be an eternal afterlife, it is safer to hedge one's bets and avoid eternal damnation. Pascal too follows along these lines.

Bayrakdar then draws attention to a potential textual parallel between Pascal and al-Ghazālī,[82] tracing a specific trajectory of influence from Raymond Martin to Pascal. And while fascinating, his case would benefit from more supporting details. Regardless, to trace direct lines of influence from Islamic thought not only to medieval Western sources but onward into the beginnings of the Enlightenment could be significant to Muslim as well as modern self-understanding, marking a shift in who defines authority vis-à-vis Western intellectual canon.[83]

Finally, Bayrakdar asks why al-Ghazālī's formulation of what became known as Pascal's wager underwent no significant criticism in the Islamic world, not even from one of al-Ghazālī's biggest critics, Ibn Taymiyya,[84] while Western intellectual tradition has subjected Pascal's wager to significant criticism. Bayrakdar surmises that neither al-Ghazālī nor Pascal actually doubted the existence of God in formulating the wager, and Pascal's formulation was misunderstood as an exercise in skepticism.[85] For Bayrakdar, rather than formulating an expression of real doubt, the Pascal's formulation of the wager is a call to Christian morals and faith, just as the *Ihyā'* was a call to renew the faith of al-Ghazālī's fellow Muslim scholars.[86] To suspect either al-Ghazālī or Pascal of entertaining real doubts about the existence of God or the afterlife fails to give either positive credit. Pascal's wager represents an invitation to believe. This invitation is not merely to believe with one's heart but to believe also with the mind. In his argument, Bayrakdar points to al-Ghazālī as an Islamic example of what in the Christian tradition is known as "faith seeking understanding." Drawing on al-Ghazālī's *Mishkāt al-Anwār* (*Niche of Lights*), *al-Munqidh min al-Ḍalāl* (*Deliverer from Error*), and his theological work *al-Iqtiṣād fī'l-I'tiqād* (*Moderation in Belief*), Bayrakdar argues that for al-Ghazālī faith (*īmān*) is not merely the work of the heart but also the mind.[87] Even though skepticism provides intellectual stimulus for faith, Bayrakdar in no way admits that skepticism poses an actual intellectual challenge. Like other Turkish literature on skepticism, Bayrakdar largely denies that skepticism poses any real intellectual challenge to sound faith. In the case of Alpyağıl, however, we will encounter an exception to this attitude.

Alpyağıl on Faith and Reason

In contrast to the work of Coşkun, Düzgün, and Bayrakdar, Alpyağıl takes up the question of skepticism as a serious challenge to faith. For Alpyağıl, himself not a skeptic, skepticism is not something to be philosophically dismissed as irrelevant or simply as a Christian problem. This intellectually curious attitude towards the problem of doubt stands out in his critical dialogue with Kierkegaard and Western representatives of philosophy of language, where Alpyağıl treats Christian arguments for fideism—both radical and moderate. This treatment can be found in Alpyağıl's *Doing Philosophy of Religion with Wittgenstein and Kierkegaard as Points of Departure* (2002).[88] In this work, Alpyağıl engages Christian debates on fideism to carve a fresh perspective for Muslim discussions on the question of faith vs. reason.

First, he looks at the radical fideism represented in Kierkegaard's pseudonymous works, *Concluding Unscientific Postscript* (1846) and *Fear and Trembling* (1843). Søren Kierkegaard (1813–55) has long been a controversial figure for Protestant Christianity; theologically trained, he never took up a position in the Danish church.[89] Mocked by many philosophers and theologians for possibly advocating a teleological suspension of the ethical,[90] or in crasser terms "divine command theory" (i.e., God told me to do this, so I do it without question), Kierkegaard brings into sharp focus Christian doubts on the compatibility of faith and reason. Particularly, in *Fear and Trembling*, his pseudonym Johannes de Silentio claims that the essence of faith is paradox, and to believe means to believe in the absurd.

Alpyağıl does not label Kierkegaard as irrational but instead describes him primarily as ironic and anti-intellectual.[91] He appreciates Kierkegaard's understanding of faith as a passion but warns his reader not to take the idea too far. He cedes that Kierkegaard is justified in his criticism of those who try to ground faith in reason alone, claiming grounding faith in reason is just as problematic for Muslims as it clearly already is for Christians.[92] Alpyağıl nevertheless does not think it acceptable for Muslims to believe *quia absurdum* as Kierkegaard's pseudonym advises.[93]

In his analysis of *Fear and Trembling* (Turkish: *Korku ve Titreme*), Alpyağıl picks out an especially fruitful double angle: existence as a divine test and whether the logic of divine trial stands up to scrutiny.[94] *Fear and Trembling* depicts the biblical account of Abraham's faith when he was told to sacrifice his son Isaac. Kierkegaard problematizes faith and ethical responsibility in pointing out that by obeying God's command, Abraham was essentially preparing to murder his own son. So why is Abraham a man of faith, when reason tells us that Abraham was ready to murder his own son? Many understand Kierkegaard to be claiming that there is a religious sphere of action which goes beyond the ethical sphere ruled by universal reason. And, in Alpyağıl's reading, Kierkegaard denies there can by any synthesis between faith and reason.[95] By looking at *Fear and Trembling* through the lens of a divine test, Alpyağıl disparagingly remarks that Kierkegaard manages to transform positive faith into blind obedience to a senseless, strange, and amoral God.[96] Still, Alpyağıl does not merely dismiss Kierkegaard—he takes a closer look, criticizing Kierkegaard for portraying God solely under the aspect of power:

> Whether from a Christian perspective or some other religious perspective, to think of God entirely in terms of God's power proves a misguided approach.[97]

Alpyağıl further rejects that the religious sphere goes beyond the ethical, because it is not clear what Kierkegaard means by "going beyond." Things get murky once a person starts going "beyond" rationality.[98] For, once a person denies rationality, what objective standard can be taken up to measure validity?[99] In this sense, Alpyağıl accepts the value of *Fear and Trembling* as a philosophical work, that is, a criticism of overconfidence in reason, but rejects the work as a definitive statement on faith in the true theological sense,[100] referencing the quranic story of Abraham. The Qur'ān, too, presents the tale as a test of faith, acknowledging that even from a quranic perspective some of the same questions of faith arise. Not having found a satisfactory answer with Christian formulations of radical fideism, Alpyağıl turns to more moderate formulations of fideism, such as those influenced by Wittgenstein.

Wittgenstein, in his second period, argued that beliefs and religious statements are language games and, as such, cannot be evaluated by terms and rules from other language games. Wittgenstein, as Alpyağıl notes, stresses the intricate relation between belief and life.[101] For Wittgenstein, faith statements only make sense in religious language games.[102] However, this leaves open the question of how people offer rational validity for their religious convictions. Alpyağıl's theologian of focus is here not actually Wittgenstein but D. Z. Phillips (1934–2006)—again a thinker whose contributions he openly appreciates but still finds inadequate.

For D. Z. Phillips, a believer's beliefs form her entire life into a picture that allows her to make sense of her life. For this reason, Phillips does not look at beliefs as things to be proved.[103] Others have criticized Phillips for being a theological non-realist—that is, "I do not claim my religious beliefs correspond to reality." Within this treatment of theological realism vs. non-realism, Alpyağıl develops a serious discussion of the merits and drawbacks of theological non-realism (*teolojik nonrealism*).[104] As Alpyağıl appreciates to a certain degree, Phillips would say the question of realism vs. non-realism misses the point about beliefs. Alpyağıl then brings in several atheists as points of engagement, one of whom being K. Nielsen. Nielsen raises the case of those who start out believers and then reject the religious picture that gave their life religious meaning.[105] Phillips, for his part, explains this phenomenon by saying changing pictures is not the same as saying one picture is better than the other. For Phillips this sort of situation ultimately boils down to a trading of a religious picture for a secular picture. In other words, changing one's worldview does not necessarily negate the old one or entail that the old view is false.[106] Unsatisfied, Nielsen retorts that if Christianity is just a language game among others, then it cannot claim to be better or more correct than any other language game. This brings us to the point Alpyağıl sees as the fundamental weakness of even moderate fideism: if you understand religion/faith as a language game, what is there to distinguish it from any other hobby or activity?[107] In short, while Alpyağıl appreciates the sort of criticisms of rationality which fideism can bring to the table, he thinks even a moderate fideist like D. Z. Phillips cannot successfully convince the rational skeptic.[108]

In Alpyağıl's conclusion, he sums up with the following evaluations:[109] 1) Though fideist epistemology gets many things right, separating faith from reason is not a viable solution—and among Christian fideists such as Augustine, Kierkegaard, and D. Z. Phillips Alpyağıl has also included the Muslim al-Ghazālī. 2) Any theoretical synthesis of faith and reason will always be open to criticism, because people cannot agree on a shared objective criterion for measuring authority. 3) He appreciates here and elsewhere Kierkegaard's notion of faith as a passion, but warns that if taken too far, faith becomes an empty concept and degrades into a senseless, blind passion. In this context, he points out that asking questions about faith and reason does not necessarily amount to attacking religion. 4) Alpyağıl objects to the practice of not trying to ground beliefs. He positively objects to simply giving up, though acknowledges that the task of grounding beliefs is a messy business. 5) He accepts to a degree that faith and reason run on their own language games but contends that real believers in today's world generally cannot avoid asking about the rationality of their beliefs. A faith without facts is not enough.[110] Alpyağıl predicts that people will not get over the desire to reconcile reason with beliefs, but neither will people within and across religions come to a clean consensus.[111] His position on fideism may be compatible with fellow philosopher of religion Cafer S. Yaran, who distinguishes "hard fideism" (*katı imancılık*) from "verified fideism" (*tahkiki imancılık*), where the latter is not incompatible with critical reasoning,[112] even if Alpyağıl rejects Christian iterations of soft fideism.

Alpyağıl offers further insights into how philosophy of religion might respond to the task of faith vs. doubt in *From Derrida to Caputo: Deconstruction and Religion* (2007),[113] where he endeavors to navigate the respective Charbdys and Scylla of modernity and postmodernity.[114] He affirms the necessity of engaging both analytic and continental philosophies of the West and endeavors to take deconstruction seriously as a philosophical concept.[115] Assuaging the fears of those who view deconstruction as something essentially pessimistic, he assures his reader that a "philosophy of hope" is indeed always within reach.[116] For those afraid of losing religious identity through dialogue with deconstruction, he reminds his reader that learning a foreign language does not require one to forget her mother tongue; in fact, it often strengthens a person's grasp over her native language.[117] In short, his assessment of deconstruction's value for Turkish theological discussions is hopeful and looks towards the future. Alpyağıl is less concerned with having all the answers and more interested in the philosophical journey that accompanies human change, acknowledging that since humanity is always developing, so too are human conceptions of God.[118] Alpyağıl's sentiments seem to parallel those of Ricoeur, who writes:

> Atheism opens a new path to faith, though a path full of uncertainties and dangers. We might be tempted not to follow this path but to leap instead directly to its destination. A philosopher, however, cannot go so far so quickly.[119]

Though Alpyağıl does not advocate doubt or skepticism, he takes the challenge very seriously and recognizes the importance of this challenge for believers everywhere. While the intellectual challenges to belief encountered in modern philosophy and elsewhere can still serve the journey of faith, Alpyağıl nevertheless resists facile resolutions of such challenges. This new path toward faith cannot be so easily or quickly navigated as scholars like Açıköz may wish to claim—at least not from Alpyağıl's philosophical perspective.

Pluralism—Fuel for Faith or Skepticism?

Turkish discussions of religious pluralism strongly associate the concept with Christian stances towards other religions. Recently, these discussions of religious pluralism tend to reflect attitudes of inclusivism as espoused by John Hick and Muslim Perennialists,[120] but the first well-known discussion of this kind in Turkish theology dealt with matters of exclusivism and inclusivism without reference to non-Turkish debates.[121] Whereas, in the late 1980s, debates on the status of other religions were grounded in Islamic categories and were initially done without reference to Alan Race's typology of exclusivism, inclusivism, pluralism and without reference to John Hick, for over the last two decades the discussion has been replete with non-Islamic terms, non-Turkish figures, and appropriations of Race's paradigm.[122]

Mahmut Aydın

Mahmut Aydın's *From Monologue to Dialogue: Christian–Muslim Dialogue in Contemporary Christian Thought* (2001) addresses the Christian history of pluralism.[123] He began his studies in theology but finished his masters on aspects of the Christian church in the social sciences—a move not uncommon among those who begin their studies in a Turkish theological faculty. He then completed his doctorate at Birmingham University in England with the thesis entitled, "Modern Western Christian Theological Understandings of Muslims Since the Second Vatican Council" (1998). After his studies abroad, he returned to his alma mater, Ondokuz Mayıs University, to take up teaching in the faculty of theology. He publishes in English as well as Turkish and engages in academic interreligious dialogue. M. Aydın thinks it possible to be a Muslim pluralist, and his understanding of pluralism is that "those who attain God's grace are saved by their own religious traditions independently from others," or in other words he allows for multiple possible salvations.[124] For M. Aydın, who draws heavily on Rumi, religious diversity is divinely willed by God.[125] Muslim knowledge of God is not complete knowledge of God, for God is always "more," and this "more" means truth spills over into multiple religions.[126]

From Monologue to Dialogue provides a history of Christian views of Islam, progressing, with some exceptions, from negative and exclusive attitudes towards Islam towards more positive and dialogical attitudes. The work divides into four sections: 1) A history of Christian views of Islam prior to Vatican II, 2) a treatment of Vatican II and its stance on dialogue, 3) a survey of dialogue in the wake of Vatican II, and finally 4) a treatment of non-Catholic Christian views on dialogue in light of the World Council of Churches (*Dünya Kiliseler Birliği*). Significantly, M. Aydın announces the profound change in interreligious relations starting in the 1970s, calling this shift the onset of an "age of dialogue."[127]

Aydın views Christian efforts to take up constructive dialogue with non-Christian religions as a natural result of the Enlightenment and globalization.[128] This has allowed for Christians to correct older, incorrect views of other religions, but—perhaps even more importantly—this turn to dialogue has opened the doors for greater interreligious cooperation on issues such as better stewardship of planetary resources and other global crises.[129] Even though there are still many obstacles to dialogue, neither Muslims nor Christians can afford to avoid it any longer.[130] Dialogue is not merely a medium for finding reasons to respect the "other"—such an approach is one-way; dialogue also requires us to grapple with the religious "other" in ways that they (the "other") themselves recognize and self-describe.[131] For M. Aydın, dialogue is not simply a way of perfecting or describing those different from us; it is also a profound journey in self-development and growth.[132] On this point, he approvingly points to opportunities for Christians to review their own Christologies in light of what the Qur'ān has to say about Jesus, as well as the benefits open to Muslims who make use of Christian scriptural understandings to engage the Qur'ān more deeply.[133] As a constructive warning, M. Aydın also states it is necessary for Christians to move beyond notions of mission in order to enter into genuine dialogues that do not reduce to polemics.[134] Finally, he stresses the quranic call to turn to God rather than to obsess about one's own creed.[135] On this point, he reminds the reader that the present age of dialogue is not guaranteed a future unless the faithful of non-Christian religions rise up to claim their place in said dialogue.[136] He calls for Muslims to come together in concert on the question of dialogue, together with non-Muslims, after the model of Vatican II or the World Council of Churches, and precisely this is where he envisions a positive role for Turkish theological faculties in providing research to better facilitate and enrich official religious dialogue.[137] In a similar spirit, M. Aydın has also edited, translated, and written in a volume dedicated to the question of truth claims and religious pluralism, entitled *Religious Pluralism and Absolute [Truth] Claims from Christian, Jewish, and Muslim Perspectives* (2005).[138] Thanks to his efforts, primary source excerpts from John Hick, Dan Cohn-Sherbok, Langdon Gilkey, Paul Knitter, and Gavin D'Costa are now available to Turkish students of theology.

Adnan Aslan

Adnan Aslan (b. 1963)[139] studied theology first at the Erciyes University Faculty of Theology, acquired his masters at the University of London, and achieved his doctorate at Lancaster University on the subject of religious pluralism (1995).[140] Aslan's Turkish-language *Religious Pluralism, Atheism, and the Perennial School: A Critical Approach* (2010)[141] treats several non-Turkish positions on pluralism as well as atheism; second, in dialogue with the Muslim

Perennial School, he makes a case for Turkish theologians to construct their own Muslim responses to such issues. Starting with the common paradigm of exclusivism, inclusivism, and pluralism, Aslan meticulously presents various non-Turkish views on pluralism, opening the discussion in the spirit of Q11:118, "If your Lord had pleased, He would have made all people a single community, but they continue to have differences."[142]

Aslan understands pluralism to be a Western framework for dealing with competing truth claims of various religious traditions.[143] Aslan acknowledges the recent history of Christian debates on pluralism, bringing up Vatican II, and deftly engaging well-known figures like Karl Rahner, Paul Tillich, John Cobb Jr., Wilfred Cantwell Smith, Ninian Smart, Gavin D'Costa, and John Hick.

Aslan then constructively dialogues with John Hick and the Muslim Perennialist School. While Aslan appreciates his interlocutors' positions, he identifies with neither and says his views on pluralism are closest to those of al-Ghazālī.[144] Although Aslan does not want to say that all religions are correct, he recognizes the tension inherent in affirming both a just God and an exclusive religious claim to salvation. In other words, Aslan neither wishes to condemn non-Muslims nor does he wish to say all religions are true. He finds an echo of his concerns in the work of al-Ghazālī, drawing from the medieval thinker's *Fayṣal al-Tafriqa bayn al-Islām wa'l-Zandaka (The Criterion of Distinction between Islam and Unbelief)*. In this work, al-Ghazālī begins by hoping God's mercy is extended to those Turks and Christians outside the Islamic Empire who die without having received the call to faith. Al-Ghazālī then considers three possibilities for those living outside the Islamic faith: 1) those who have not heard anything of the Prophet or his message, 2) those who have both heard of the Prophet and his miracles, and 3) those who have heard both good and bad reports of the Prophet and are seeking the truth.[145] Those in the first group are excused of accountability and receive God's mercy. Those in the second are accountable and do not receive God's mercy. For those in the third group, things prove more complicated. If they err in their final judgment of the matter, they are held responsible. Yet, for al-Ghazālī, those who die without having come to a final judgment may still receive God's mercy.

Aslan, though he affirms that Islam stands as the most complete religion, recognizes it is normal for believers in other religions to continue in their faith, despite the quranic warning; and that God already foresaw this in God's plan for the salvation of humanity. People who have not heard the quranic address are not capable of seeing the limitations of their own faith. Thus, he does not hold those who have not heard the quranic address accountable for their corrupt religion, nor does he believe God will hold them accountable.[146] This is his modern application of al-Ghazālī's position in *Fayṣal*.[147] Further, Aslan is willing to recognize that a non-Muslim could be a Muslim in terms of the beliefs of her heart. Thus, in his final stance towards other religions, he is arguably an inclusivist, similar to the Catholic theologian Karl Rahner.[148] Şinasi Gündüz defines an inclusivist as one who posits one view of salvation as normative (while still recognizing truth in other religious views),[149] and by this definition Aslan can be called a Muslim inclusivist.

Nevertheless, for Aslan, it does not seem logical to bind one's personal salvation to the prospect of having a perfect religion, since perfection is not a quality of average human beings. Underpinning this is a view of God whose justice is fundamentally characterized by mercy towards finite creatures. There remains an unresolved tension. Aslan continues to hold non-Muslim faiths are corrupted, yet he wants to acknowledge the workings of God's mercy even in these corrupted faiths.[150] His position belies the characteristic tension underlying all inclusivist positions, whether Christian, Hindu, Muslim, and so on. He also diverges from al-Ghazālī in positively holding non-Muslims responsible for maintaining their own religions—that is, he encourages those who have not come to the point of conversion to Islam, at the very least, to maintain their own faiths with care and sincerity.

Having dealt with the question of other religions, Aslan turns to atheism as a related discussion. Meticulously engaging various atheist positions, Aslan is not quick to throw all atheists into one pot. On the contrary, he makes a point to say that just as there are many ways to believe in God, there are also many ways to not believe in God.[151] Aslan's treatment stands out in two distinct ways. First, he recognizes and explores the intellectual coherence of atheist objections to theism. Second, Aslan does not defend monotheism by claiming reason and faith must ultimately agree, as Muhammad Abduh did in his *Risālat al-Tawḥīd* (*Theology of Unity*) over a hundred years before him. Aslan's response to the challenges of modernity are subtler. For Aslan, to reduce faith to logical arguments misses the point. It is not a solution to equate the most perfect faith with the most reasonable. Aslan instead contends that "faith is a psychological condition" that cannot be destroyed by logic alone.[152] This does not mean faith is illogical. Faith simply has more dimensions to consider. In this, Aslan tips his hat to the objections of fideism. This is not to say he abandons reason. On the contrary, his argument is very reasonable: coming to faith or losing faith is an incredibly complex process that cannot be reduced to a few logical arguments. His position moves the discussion on faith, reason, atheism, and pluralism beyond narrow, well-rehearsed arguments.

Aslan concludes his book with a case for building Turkish Muslim responses to the challenges of modernity. He takes up the Perennialist School as a model of what has been done before. He neither wishes Turkish theologians to copy what scholars like Muslim representative of the Perennialist schoool S. H. Nasr have done nor does he think it would be wise for Turkish theologians to ignore the challenges, limitations, and successes of the Perennialist School. For him, the Perennialist School represents a way for Islam to exist in a pluralistic world without losing its identity, even spreading its message to a broader audience. Aslan calls for a new Muslim approach to modernity. He does not simply use al-Ghazālī as a symbol of orthodoxy by which to measure the religious "other." Rather, Aslan uses al-Ghazālī as an anchor in sailing out onto the sea of pluralism, while the boat is entirely his own, moving beyond al-Ghazālī to ask what a modern Turkish Islamic perspective would look like—an extremely relevant question.

Others on Pluralism

Other Turkish theologians have made efforts to tackle the question of pluralism as well. While John Hick and Seyyed Hossein Nasr tend to come up most frequently in this body of literature, those like Karl Rahner, Hans Küng, and Paul Knitter also make sustained appearances in discussions.

Two works that focus especially on John Hick are Ruhattin Yazoğlu's *The Problem of Religious Pluralism: A Study of John Hick* (2007)[153] and Mustafa Eren's *Religious Pluralism in John Hick* (2016).[154] Hick's pluralism is famous for his articulation of the Real and his notion of religiosity as a move from self-centeredness to Reality-centeredness.¹⁵⁵ Hick argued that no one religion can fully express the Real, so all religions err partially and are partially correct. Hick goes on to distinguish between first- and second-order approaches to the Real. The first-order distinction entails one's particular belief system, which allows a believer to connect with the Real in an authentic way. The second-order distinction is philosophical consideration, which maintains the impossibility of fully defining or exhausting the infinite Real.¹⁵⁶ While Hick's philosophical understanding of the Real's relation to concrete religions, insofar as it implies *all* religions are incorrect at some level, is less well-received in Turkey; the Hickean emphasis on shifting consciousness towards the Real finds greater appreciation.

Yazoğlu's study on Hick draws on the work of other Turkish scholars, such as Adnan Aslan, Mahmut Aydın, Mustafa Köylü, Şinasi Gündüz, Hanifi Özcan, Recep Kılıç, and Cafer S. Yaran. As Yazoğlu understands the term pluralism, it signifies the philosophical question of a plurality of expressions and claims made about the singular truth of reality, rather than the question of multiple or conflicting ultimate truths.¹⁵⁷ As he interprets Hick, the question of pluralism is not about religion, but about God, who is essentially unknowable.¹⁵⁸ Further describing Hick, Yazoğlu notes that due to this ontological gap between human understanding and God, ethical and existential approaches to God prove the most fruitful; however, such a reduction of religion excludes the role of revelation, an unacceptable position for Abrahamic religions.¹⁵⁹ Implicit in Hick's assessment of religions is the claim that all religions err partially in their truth claims. And while some may try to read Hick as espousing one global religion, Yazoğlu recognizes this does not accurately reflect Hick's philosophical position—there may be one reality, but the paths are many. Nevertheless, Hick's philosophical interpretation of religions threatens their sacredness and, moreover, comes off in a remarkably Christian color—that is, Hick tries to describe all religions in terms of salvation.¹⁶⁰

Mustafa Eren offers a more positive appraisal of Hick. Eren began his theological studies at the theology faculty of Dokuz Eylül University and went on to complete a doctorate in philosophy of religion at Johann Wolfgang Goethe University in Frankfurt, writing a comparative thesis on Hans Küng and the medieval Muslim Brethren of Purity.¹⁶¹ In his *Religious Pluralism in John Hick* (2016) he provides a Muslim commentary on John Hick and accepts without much objection that human beings necessarily access one Absolute Truth through a plurality of human experience. One acceptable way of viewing the human journey towards Absolute Truth is a Hickean move from self-centered existence to Truth-centered existence.[162] Relying heavily on Mahmut Aydın, Hanifi Özcan, and Adnan Aslan, Eren speaks approvingly of fellow Turkish scholar Hanifi Özcan's work on al-Māturīdī's religious inclusivism (*kapsayıcı tutum*) and partial pluralism.[163] Eren ultimately affirms that, given a sound Islamic grounding for a limited religious plurality, the discussion does not devolve into a meaningless, relativistic pluralism.[164] Like Şaban Ali Düzgün, he views human beings as essentially religious, regardless of particular form, and he embraces the diversity of human religious experience within this overarching sense of unified human identity.[165]

Turkish theologians also sometimes bring in a classical Islamic scholar into their discussion of religious pluralism. Two examples of this are Hidayet Işık's *Islam and Other Religions according to al-Āmirī* (2006)[166] and Hanifi Özcan's frequently cited *Religious Pluralism in Māturidī*.[167] This latter and more influential work affirms the importance of religious pluralism as a philosophical problem.[168]

Lastly, Düzgün, whom we discussed in part three, conducted an interview during his time in Washington, DC, with controversial Catholic theologian Roger Haight. He published the initial English interview in the *Ankara University Theology Faculty Journal* in 2006 and then offered a translation of the interview in his book *Religion and Religious [People] in the Modern World* (2012). In the interview, Düzgün asks Haight:

> The postmodern situation in its emphasis on historicity and religious pluralism poses new questions and puts severe pressure on the traditional absolutistic claims. In your understanding is a new theocentrism something necessary, one which refrains from traditional totalizing metanarratives? Is pluralism an indispensable consequence of the necessity to interpret religious texts? How is it possible to decide whether a text admits a pluralism of different interpretations?[169]

In response, Haight distinguishes between a religious metanarrative and a theory of religions, the former being more problematic than the latter. Religious metanarrative tries to assign a place and role for the religious other that does not fit that other's self-understanding. In this way, a religious metanarrative boldly makes claims about the whole of reality.[170] While I am not entirely certain how a metanarrative and a theory of religions can remain distinct in practice, Turkish discussions of religious pluralism (and even skepticism) remain in the space of religious metanarrative—one that is shaped by an underlying embrace of *tawḥīd* or divine unity.[171] At the same time, with figures like Recep Alpyağıl and Adnan Aslan, there has been a conscious effort to limit evaluations of those practicing other religions, thereby opening up spaces for new engagements with the religious other. In view of such conscientious acts of limited evaluation on the part of Turkish theologians, the practical distinction between metanarrative and theory may be moot.

Conclusion

In this chapter, we looked at how Turkish discussions of skepticism, atheism, and the question of other religions tend to be treated in connection. The causes of skepticism and atheism were often attributed to Christianity—either as a rejection of a corrupt and irrational Christianity (Coşkun) or as a result of secular worldviews informed by toxic expressions of Christianity (Düzgün). We also saw that Turkish theologians still find the God of ontotheology robust and fruitful—their confidence in the connection between sound metaphysical claims and lived faith is expressed in literature devoted to *kalām*[172] and Islamic philosophy as well as in reflections on the profound significance of *tawḥīd* or divine unity.

While Turkish theologians often fault Christianity for corrupt hierarchies, corrupt beliefs, and for its resulting susceptibility to skepticism and atheism, the work of Yaşar Nuri Öztürk and the work of Recep Alpyağıl offered exceptions to this pattern. Öztürk does not single out Christianity as the cause of atheism but instead targets false religiosity—he faults Islamic practices with false religiosity and does not reserve his criticisms for Christianity. For Öztürk, it is this false religiosity, rather than atheism, that proves the most harmful to society and the spiritual life of true believers. In the case of Recep Alpyağıl, while he accepts that Christian history and belief may be more problematic than Islamic history and belief, he nevertheless views the question of skepticism and doubt as a real challenge to both religions. He refuses to relegate the modern clash of faith and reason to Christian discussions alone.

On the question of other religions, Turkish scholars associate religious pluralism with Christianity. While critical of some aspects of pluralism, many Turkish scholars develop their own versions of inclusivism (Aslan) or even go so far as to call themselves pluralists (M. Aydın), and these positions are frequently marked by an understanding of *tawḥīd*.[173] As echoed in Düzgün's words to Haight, Turkish theologians interested in engaging Christian theologians on the question of pluralism stress Islamically grounded "theocentrism." Lastly, a number of Turkish scholars see the value of religious dialogue and encourage Muslims, especially Turkish Muslims, to do their part in taking up a voice in a conversation which has heretofore been dominated by Christian discourses.

Even though Christianity is a prominent theme in Turkish discussions of atheism, skepticism, and religious pluralism, the more nuanced discussions cannot be reduced to a simple dichotomy of reaction against Christianity or Western philosophical trends. There is serious engagement, and such engagement also draws on Islamic sources, both classical and modern. Once again, Turkish theologians dialectically navigate multiple intellectual traditions, and this navigation cannot be reduced to oversimple dualities. Certainly, there are oversimplified treatments of atheism, skepticism, Christianity, and pluralism. But there are also sustained theological engagements which move beyond reductive assumptions and deserve to be taken as original theological contributions.

Notes

1. As a comparison, the Ottoman intellectual Abdullatif Harputi (1842–1916) took pains to distinguish between Judaism and Christianity, on the one hand, and more classical forms of materialism, on the other, by pointing out that Jews and Christians believe in the limits of human reason and this belief is a property of religion. Abdullatif Harputi, *Kelâm Tarihi* [*A History of Kalām*], ed. Muammer Esen (Ankara: Ankara Okulu Yayınları, 2014), p. 89.

2. Murtaza Korlaelçi, *Pozitivizmin Türkiye'ye Girişi* (Ankara, 2000) and (Ankara: Kadim Yayınları, 2014). This work came out earlier than 2000—the original preface is dated to 1980. However, I was unable to find the original publishing information. Intellectual historian Korlaelçi looks at Ottoman responses to Enlightenment ideas including Beşir Fuad, Ahmet Rıza, Salih Zeki, Rıza Tevfik, Hüseyin Cahit Yalçın, Ahmed Şuayb, and Ziya Gökalp.

3. Mehmet Akgün, *Materyalizmin Türkiye'ye Girişi* (Ankara: Elis Yayınları, 2005). First printing 1988.
4. Ahmet Yaşar Ocak, *Osmanlı Toplumunda Zındıklar ve Mülhidler 15–17. Yüzyıllar* (Istanbul: Tarih Vakfı Yurt Yayınları, 1998). The word "*zındık*" means atheist in modern Turkish, even though Turkish speakers also use the word "*ateist*." The word "*mülhid*" comes across as more archaic in modern Turkish and signifies someone who is faithless or who does not believe correctly. On these definitions in modern Turkish see, for instance, *Türkçe Sözlük* (Ankara: Türk Dil Kurumu Yayınları, 2011). Both terms come from Arabic. Yet they connote slightly different things in modern Turkish than those who primarily work with Arabic texts of classical Islam may initially suppose, where the Arabic term *zindiq* (*Turkish: zındık*) has even been translated as "freethinker." See, for instance, Sarah Stroumsa, *Freethinkers of Medieval Islam: Ibn al-Rawandi, Abu Bakr al-Razi, and their Impact on Islamic Thought* (Leiden and Boston: Brill, 1999).
5. Scholar of Sufism Ahmet T. Karamustafa has also published in the Anglophone scholarly world in this vein. Karamustafa has stressed, contra M. F. Köprülü, the Islamic nature of Turkish sects, personality, and groups. This includes groups otherwise seen as deviants from orthodox Islamic practice. See, for instance, Ahmet T. Karamustafa, "Kaygusuz Abdal: A Medieval Turkish Saint and the Formation of Vernacular Islam in Anatolia," in Orkhan Mir-Kasimov (ed.), *Unity in Diversity: Mysticism, Messianism and the Construction of Religious Authority in Islam* (Leiden and Boston: Brill, 2014), pp. 329–42.
6. Mehmet S. Aydın, *Din Felsefesi* (Izmir: İzmir İlâhiyat Vakfı Yayınları, 2014), 14th printing. The original preface dates to 1987. Two indications of the influence of a Turkish work is the number of reprintings as well as the length of time over which the reprintings occur. Successive reprintings over time point to a sustained interest and demand for a work. This work, cited extensively in most of the theologians' works discussed here, enjoys a remarkable number of reprintings.
7. The three volumes are: *Tevhidi Kozmik Holizm, Şüphe ve Eski Uygarlıklar* [*Tawḥīdic Cosmic Holism, Doubt, and Ancient Civilizations*] (Ankara: Elis Yayınları, 2006); *Skeptikus Şüphe ve Bilgi* [*Skepticism, Doubt, and Knowledge*] (Ankara: Elis Yayınları, 2006); *Sextus Empirikus ve Şüphe* [*Sextus Empiricus and Doubt*] (Ankara: Elis Yayınları, 2006). Açıköz's treatment expresses little interest in the intellectual value of skepticism, affirming its value only insofar as it unwittingly affirms *tawḥīd*, i.e., God's unity.
8. Sinasi Gunduz, "From Apology to Phenomenology: The Current State of the Studies of the History of Religions in Turkey," in Sinasi Gunduz and Cafer S.

Yaran (eds), *Change and Essence* (Washington, DC: The Council for Research in Values and Philosophy, 2005), p. 38.

9. Paul Ricoeur, "Religion, Atheism, and Faith" in Alasdair MacIntyre and Paul Ricoeur (eds), *The Religious Significance of Atheism* (New York and London: Columbia University Press, 1969; 1970), pp. 65–6.

10. Şaban Ali Düzgün, *Nesefî ve İslâm Filozoflarına Göre Allah-Âlem İlişkisi* (Ankara: Akçağ Yayınları, 1998).

11. Yaşar Türkmen (ed.), *Gazâlî ve Nedensellik [al-Ghazālī and Causality]* (Ankara: Elis Yayınları, 2012).

12. Sema Özdemir, *Dâvûd Kayserî'de Varlık Bilgi ve İnsan* (Istanbul: Nefes Yayınları, 2014).

13. İlhan Kutluer, *İbn Sina Ontolojisinde Zorunlu Varlık* (Istanbul: İz Yayınları, 2013).

14. Fatma Zehra Pattabanoğlu, *İbn Kemmûne ve Felsefesi* (Ankara: Elis Yayınlar, 2014).

15. İsmail Hanoğlu, *Fahruddîn er-Râzî'de Felsefî-Teolojik Antropoloji* (Ankara: Araştırma Yayınları, 2014). In the second chapter of this book, Hanoğlu takes up the categories of relativism and pluralism within the context of human nature. For these categories, he draws primarily on Matthew J. Moore, "Pluralism, Relativism, and Liberalism," *Political Research Quarterly* 62:2 (2009): pp. 244–56.

16. Ömer Türker, *İbn Sînâ Felsefesinde Metafizik Bilginin İmkânı Sorunu* (Istanbul: İSAM Yayınları, 2010).

17. See bibliography for details. Fehrullah Terkan is also an instrumental figure in the Ankara Theology Faculty's English theology program, which offers courses in English in addition to Turkish instruction. He kindly let me speak with one of his undergraduate classes on the subject of Western modernity when I visited in Ankara, fall 2015.

18. Ömer Mahir Alper, *Varlık ve İnsan: Kemalpaşazâde Bağlamında Bir Tasavvurun Yeniden İnşası* (Istanbul: Klasik, 2010; 2013).

19. İbrahim Coşkun, *Ateizm ve İslam: Kelamî Açıdan Modern Çağ Ateizminin Eleştirisi* (Ankara: Ankara Okulu, 2014). Throughout this work, he cites heavily from Mehmet Aydın's *Din Felsefesi* (2014) in addition to another of Aydın's works *İslam'ın Evrenselliği [The Universality of Islam]* (2000). He also frequently cites Şaban Ali Düzgün.

20. Unlike Düzgün's work as discussed in the previous chapter, Coşkun does not tend to offer at least a few positive evaluations of Christianity alongside his criticisms. Recall that Düzgün positively evaluated Protestantism's focus on

the individual but chided it for taking individualism too far and that he also saw in postmodernity resources for Western epistemological humility.
21. Coşkun, *Ateizm ve İslam*, pp. 113–70. This section entitled "Causes of Atheism in the Modern Age" is more or less a doctrinal and philosophical critique of Christianity.
22. While Christian theologians may first wish to object to broad-brush characterizations of Church history and doctrine; rather than trying to "correct" the academic myths about Christianity, I find it more useful to give voice to them. It seems to be an inevitable reality that, in any academic circle, some assumptions will accrue enough authority by common consensus as to become monolithic myths, slow to change and resistant to data that does not fit into the reigning schema. While arguably applicable to many Turkish views of the West and Christianity, this is *also* applicable to numerous Anglophone and European views of Turkey, the Muslim world, and Islam. As such, I will try, in my own analysis, to minimize instances of the pot calling the kettle black and direct critical efforts at engagement towards more constructive ends. For a brief overview of the variety of European, Christian, and Anglophone positions on Islam, see William Dalrymple, "The Truth about Muslims," *New York Review of Books* 51.17 (November 1, 2004): pp. 31–4. This is a review and critical assessment of the positions on Islam of three authors who treat Islam's relation to Christian and European culture: historians Bernard Lewis, Richard Fletcher, and Nabil Matar.
23. For an earlier example, take Ibn Ḥazm's (d. 1064) critique of Jewish and Christian scriptures in his larger work on the doctrines of other sects and religions, *A Treatise on Religions, Heresies, and Sects*. For more on this work and the genre of Muslim critiques of the Bible, see Abdelilah Ljamai, *Ibn Ḥazm et la polémique islamo-chrétienne dans l'histoire de l'islam* (Leiden and Boston: Brill, 2003). See also Theodore Pulcini, *Exegesis as Polemical Discourse: Ibn Ḥazm on Jewish and Christian Scriptures* (Atlanta, GA: Scholars Press, 1998). For a printing of the original source see Ibn Ḥazm, *al-Fiṣal fī al-Milal wa-al-Ahwā' wa-al-Niḥal* (Beirut: Dar al-Jil, 1985). For an overview of medieval and modern Muslim–Christian polemics, see also Georges C. Anawati, "Polémique, apologie et dialogue islamo-chrétiens: Positions classiques médiévales et positions contemporaines," *Euntes Docete* 22 (1969): pp. 375–451.
24. Coşkun, *Ateizm*, p. 114.
25. Coşkun, *Ateizm*, p. 140.
26. Coşkun, *Ateizm*, p. 132.
27. Coşkun, *Ateizm*, p. 134.

28. Coşkun, *Ateizm*, p. 117.
29. Coşkun, *Ateizm*, p. 186.
30. CDDD, p. 156.
31. CDDD, p. 146. Even if his main criticism is of a certain form of Protestantism, he also entertains negative views of Catholic hierarchy and Catholic medieval history.
32. CDDD, p. 24.
33. Another influential theologian Cafer S. Yaran also thinks religion and science need not come into conflict and that philosophy of religion has a lot to say on this matter. Yaran, *Bilgelik Peşinde: Din Felsefesi Yazıları* [In Pursuit of Wisdom: Essays on Philosophy of Religion] (Istanbul: Ensar Neşriyat, 2011), p. 112.
34. DBT, p. 41.
35. DBT, p. 42.
36. ATT, p. 19. By contrast, Louis Dupré lays more blame on the nominalism that developed after Aquinas, viewing neither Neo-Platonic nor Aristotelian worldviews as insufficient forces in themselves to produce the rupture that led to the challenge of modernity (citing the alternate course of Eastern Christianity to support his thesis). Dupré does however cite the combination of Judeo-Christian theology with Greek cosmology as part of the story of the Western "double breakup" of God and Cosmos, Person and Cosmos. See Louis Dupré, *Passage to Modernity: An Essay in the Hermeneutics of Nature and Culture* (New Haven and London: Yale University Press, 1993).
37. ATT, p. 27.
38. ATT, p. 34.
39. ATT, p. 46. On this point, he cites Karl Popper's *Objective Knowledge* and Ingolf Dalferth.
40. ATT, p. 20. Turkish: "Bir şey ancak delillendirilebiliyor ise anlamlıdır."
41. ATT, p. 35.
42. ATT, p. 53.
43. ATT, p. 62. For instance, he also brings in Ian Ramsey and the *sui generis* logic of religious language (p. 80).
44. ATT, p. 58.
45. ATT, p. 66.
46. He, for instance, accuses Schleiermacher of missing the moral piece of the religious puzzle. ATT, p. 91. Whether this is a valid criticism is another matter for a different discussion.

47. ATT, p. 106.
48. ATT, p. 63. This sort of position is criticized by a theologian below, but the critique is directed at Christian religious pluralism. See the discussion below on Ruhattin Yazoğlu. In any case, Düzgün's is an interesting answer. For instance, someone like Dupré views the Western ontological crisis as a breakup between the Divine and the World, locating much of the issue in the way Western Christianity made the Divine something wholly other through trends like nominalism and the Reformation. The idea of God as wholly other does not seem to be an issue for Düzgün, as God's alterity does not threaten the individual's moral relation to God.
49. ATT, p. 131.
50. ATT, p. 134.
51. ATT, p. 152.
52. ATT, p. 208.
53. ATT, p. 153. For instance, Karl Rahner has famously made a similar argument in his *Hearer of the Word*, published first in German in 1941.
54. See, for instance, his work on Laicism: *Kur'an Verileri Açısından Laiklik* [*Laicism from the Perspective of Quranic Data*] (Istanbul: Yeni Boyut, 2003).
55. For example, Ayşe Öncü, "Becoming 'Secular Muslims': Yaşar Nuri Öztürk as a Super-Subject on Turkish Television," in B. Meyer and A. Moors (eds), *Religion, media, and the Public Sphere* (Bloomington, IN: Indiana University Press, 2006), pp. 227–50.
56. Yaşar Nuri Öztürk, *Deizm: Tanrı, Akıl ve Ahlaktan Başka Kutsal Tanımayan İnanç (Teofilozofik Bir Tahlil)* (Istanbul: Yeni Boyut, 2015)—henceforth cited as *Deizm*.
57. Öztürk, *Deizm*, p. 9.
58. Öztürk, *Deizm*, p. 9.
59. Öztürk, *Deizm*, p. 10.
60. Sadly, footnotes are scant. The work he refers to can be found in a modern edition: Şehbenderzade Filibeli Ahmet Hilmi, *İslam Tarihi* (Istanbul: Huzur Yayınevi, 2011).
61. Öztürk, *Deizm*, p. 18.
62. For a study on how the Islamic concept of prophethood moved away from biblical views of prophethood, stressing infallibility over guidance out of error, see Uri Rubin, *The Eye of the Beholder: The Life of Muhammad as Viewed by the Early Muslims* (Princeton: The Darwin Press Inc, 1995).

63. Öztürk cites, for instance, Erich Fromm's description of the virtue of prophets as an unintentional description not of Old Testament prophets but quranic prophets (pp. 22–3).
64. Öztürk, *Deizm*, p. 24. Turkish: "Dincilik, tevhit dinini şirk dinine dönüştüren bir aldatma ve saltanat ideolojisidir."
65. Öztürk, *Deizm*, p. 24.
66. Öztürk, *Deizm*, p. 25.
67. Öztürk, *Deizm*, p. 26.
68. Öztürk, *Deizm*, p. 31.
69. Öztürk, *Deizm*, p. 32.
70. Öztürk, *Deizm*, p. 35.
71. From *Saint John of Damascus Writings: The Fount of Knowledge—The Philosophical Chapters, on Heresies, the Orthodox Faith (The Fathers of the Church, Vol. 37)* (South Bend, IN: Ex Fontibus, 2015), pp. 153–60.
72. İsmail Taşpınar, *Hacı Abdullah Petrici'nin Hıristiyanlık Eleştirisi* (İstanbul: Marmara Üniversitesi İlâhiyat Fakültesi Vakfı Yayınları, 2014), p. 20.
73. On this, see, for instance, Mehmet Akgün's *Materyalizmin Türkiye'ye Giriş* (Ankara: Elis Yayınları, 2005). Akgün is not a theologian but held a position in the literature department at Pamukkale University until his retirement in 2018. His work has been mentioned above.
74. Düzgün took "primitive" out of its anthropological connotations and redefined it in terms of estrangment to *fiṭra*, or original monotheistic nature.
75. Zeki Özcan, *Teolojik Hermenötik* [*Theological Hermeneutics*] (Istanbul: ALFA Yayınları, 1998; 2000), p. 254. Although he criticizes some Christian assumptions regarding theological hermeneutics, he generally argues for the positive value of hermeneutics in protecting textual continuity and ensuring proper engagement with the text.
76. See Şinasi Gündüz, *Pavlus Hıristiyanlığı Mimarı* [*Paul the Architect of Christianity*] (Ankara: Ankara Okulu, 2001; 2004; 2011; 2014) and Hakan Olgun, *Protestanlık: Sekülerliğin Teolojik Kurgusu* [*Protestantism: The Theological Foundation of Secularism*] (Istanbul: İz Yayıncılık, 2006). Gündüz even uses the work of modern theologians like Bultmann, Fitzmyer, and Küng in such a way as to stress that none of them claim Paul is Christianity's founder. Olgu, for his part, makes the case for why secularism is an essentially Christian phenomenon—an argument also sometimes made in Anglophone literature.
77. Two examples of comparisons by Turkish theologians not treated here are Metin Yasa, *İbn Arabî ve Spinoza'da Varlık* [*Being in Ibn 'Arabī and Spinoza*] (Istanbul:

Elis Yayınları, 2003; 2014) and H. Ömer Özden, *İbn Sînâ-Descartes Metafiziği* [*The Metaphysics of Ibn Sīnā and Descartes*] (Istanbul: Dergâh Yayınları, 1996; 2015).

78. This section draws on Taraneh Wilkinson, "Moderation and al-Ghazali in Turkey: Responses to Skepticism, Modernity and Pluralism," *The American Journal of Islamic Social Sciences* 32:3 (2015): pp. 29–43.

79. Mehmet Bayrakdar, *Pascal Oyunu: Hz. Ali, Gazzâlî ve Pascal'a Göre Âhirete Zar Atmak* (Istanbul : İnsan Yayınları, 2013). The translation of the title is my own, as well as all subsequent translations from Turkish. Henceforth referred to as *Pascal's Wager*.

80. Mathematics plays a large role in his work on Pascal. Bayrakdar also published *İslâm'da Bilim ve Teknoloji Tarihi* [*History of Science and Technology in Islam*] (Ankara: TDVY, 2012).

81. Bayrakdar refers mainly to the *Iḥyā'* (vol. 3) for al-Ghazālī's version of Pascal's wager. But al-Ghazālī also discusses it elsewhere in his *Mīzān al-'Amal*, where the argument for preparing for the afterlife is more or less the same; he even uses a common analogy of the report of poisoned food. One of al-Ghazālī's arguments runs as follows: if someone told you your food was poisoned, would you take a chance and eat it? This is like hearing a report of the threat of eternal hellfire, and al-Ghazālī also uses it in his *Mīzān*. While the afterlife is a recurrent and omnipresent feature in much of al-Ghazālī's work, his views on the afterlife are not simple or undisputed. For instance, Egyptian Qur'ān exegete and literary critic Nasr Hamid Abu Zayd severely berated al-Ghazālī for his obsession with the afterlife; see his "Al-Ghazālī's Theory of Interpretation," *Journal of Osaka University of Foreign. Studies* 72 (1986): pp. 1–24 (I am grateful to Hume scholar Ryu Susato for access to this obscure article).

82. In this, Bayrakdar refers to Bousquet's "Un Mot de Pascal dans l'Ihyâ de Ghazâlî," *Studia Islamica* 30 (1954): p. 104.

83. And if at any point, a more direct line can be traced from Islamic responses to skepticism, linking such issues clearly with Enlightenment debates, this would open the way for a rethinking of Western Enlightenment (and hence modern) intellectual heritage. As it stands, there remains a stereotype of medieval Europe as fundamentally superstitious and backward, so it is no surprise to some that Islamic civilization offered many advances to European philosophy and technology. However, to say that Islamic thought directly fed into debates on skepticism which raged throughout the Enlightenment, and even beyond, would require many to rethink the Islamic contribution to Western thought and

modernity. Mark Sedgwick's recent book, *Western Sufism: From the Abbasids to the New Age* (New York: Oxford University Press, 2017), fills in some of these potential gaps in intellectual history, showing instances of intellectual influence moving from Ottoman Islamic culture to European spirituality in the pre-modern and modern eras.

84. Bayrakdar, *Pascal's Wager*, p. 75. Notably, Bayrakdar unhesitatingly designates Ibn Taymiyya as a *kalām* theologian.
85. Bayrakdar, *Pascal's Wager*, p. 77.
86. The fact that he interprets Pascal's motives in light of what are generally seen to be al-Ghazālī's is not a point he dwells on, but rests implicit in his treatment.
87. Bayrakdar, *Pascal's Wager*, p. 88. Al-Ghazālī tends to use terms like heart (*qalb*) and mind (*'aql*) to refer to a similar or identical faculty in the human being—an issue that Bayrakdar does not go into.
88. Alpyağıl, *Wittgenstein ve Kierkegaard'dan Hareketle Din Felsefesi Yapmak* (Istanbul: İz Yayıncılık, 2002, 2013). Henceforth referred to as WK.
89. The Folkschurch of Denmark is Evangelical Lutheran.
90. WK, pp. 116–17. The Turkish for "teleological suspension of the ethical" is "etik olanın ereksel askıya alınması."
91. WK, p. 106. While this position is not an uncommon one in Kierkegaard's scholarship, this position is uncommon with respect to Turkish treatments of Christianity and skepticism, which still tend to be less charitable and to emphasize the irrationality of Christian faith.
92. WK, p. 106.
93. WK, p. 107.
94. WK, p. 107.
95. WK, p. 122.
96. WK, p. 123.
97. WK, p. 126. Turkish: "Gerek Hıristiyanlık açısından gerekse diğer dinler açısından tanrıyı bütünüyle kudreti bağlamında tanımlamak hatalı bir yaklaşım olsa gerekir."
98. WK, p. 127.
99. Alpyağıl is very sensitive to the issue of objectivity, from a Kierkegaardian as well as a Gadamerian perspective. He does not throw the term around carelessly and often qualifies it.
100. WK, p. 128.
101. WK, p. 149.
102. WK, p. 151.

103. WK, p. 220.
104. WK, p. 231.
105. WK, p. 232.
106. WK, p. 233.
107. WK, p. 234.
108. This attitude contrasts strongly with Açıköz's attitudes towards skepticism. For the latter, skepticism cannot help but affirm in some way God's unity and absolute existence. As such, it is skepticism which proves intellectually lacking, never faith insofar as it remains uncorrupted.
109. WK, pp. 246–9.
110. Again, Alpyağıl does not throw around the world *olgu* (event or fact). He has a fairly nuanced understanding of the philosophical challenges of historical knowledge. As such, he does not throw this criticism at Phillips simplistically.
111. WK, pp. 250–1.
112. Yaran, *Bilgelik Peşinde*, p. 89. Yaran objects to understanding faith as something opposite to reason.
113. Alpyağıl, *Derrida'dan Caputo'ya Dekonstrüksiyon ve Din* (Istanbul: İz Yayıncılık, 2007; 2010). Henceforth DCDD.
114. DCDD, p. 18.
115. DCDD, p. 18.
116. DCDD, p. 19.
117. DCDD, p. 20.
118. DCDD, p. 281.
119. Ricoeur, "Religion, Atheism, and Faith," p. 69.
120. In the Arab world, John Hick's *The Myth of God Incarnate* (1977) was quickly received and translated into Arabic, as it seemed to support the Muslim rejection of Jesus as God incarnate. Hugh Goddard, *Christians & Muslims: From Double Standards to Mutual Understanding* (Surrey: Curzon Press, 1995), p. 7.
121. Cafer S. Yaran notes a major debate on who had a "heaven monopoly" took place in the late 1980s and early 1990s between Suleyman Ateş and Talat Koçyiğit. Ateş argued against the case for a heavenly monopoly and Koçyiğit argued for it. See Yaran's "Non-exclusivist Attitudes towards Other Religions," in *Change and Essence*.
122. Yaran, "Non-exclusivist Attitudes towards Other Religions," p. 16.
123. Mahmut Aydın, *Monologdan Diyaloğa: Çağdaş Hıristiyan Düşüncesinde Hıristiya-Müslüman Diyaloğu* (Ankara: Ankara Okulu, 2001). Henceforth: *From Monologue to Dialogue*.

124. Mahmut Aydin [sic.], "Religious Pluralism: A Challenge for Muslims—A Theological Evaluation," *Journal of Ecumenical Studies* 38 (2001): p. 336.
125. Mahmut Aydın, "A Muslim Pluralist: Jalaluddin Rûmi," in Paul F. Knitter (ed.), *The Myth of Religious Superiority: A Multifaith Exploration* (New York: Orbis Books, 2005), p. 220.
126. Aydın, "A Muslim Pluralist: Jalaluddin Rûmi," pp. 228, 234.
127. Aydın, *From Monologue to Dialogue*, p. 9.
128. Aydın, *From Monologue to Dialogue*, p. 247. On this point, he would find many European and Anglophone Christian theologians at his side in relative agreement. For a critical and non-theological account of the Enlightenment and imperialist roots of religious pluralism, see Tomoko Masuzawa, *The Invention of World Religions, or, How European Universalism was Preserved in the Language of Pluralism* (Chicago: University of Chicago Press, 2005).
129. Aydın, *From Monologue to Dialogue*, p. 278. He explicitly speaks of ecological and nuclear threats and affirms the need of religions to cooperate in fostering attitudes and practices to respond effectively to this.
130. Aydın, *From Monologue to Dialogue*, p. 256.
131. Aydın, *From Monologue to Dialogue*, p. 256.
132. Aydın, *From Monologue to Dialogue*, p. 256.
133. Aydın, *From Monologue to Dialogue*, p. 256.
134. Aydın, *From Monologue to Dialogue*, p. 257. On this point, Roger Haight has suggested that mission not be reduced to the old goal of exclusionary conversion but rather broadened to embrace a wider mission of dialogue. Gerard Mannion, "Constructive Comparative Ecclesiology: The Pioneering Work of Roger Haight," *Ecclesiology* 5 (2009): p. 188. While Aydın speaks in terms of abandoning mission, some Christian theologians are active in promulgating a fundamental change in the understanding of mission which accepts and seeks to break from the historical reality of imperialism. Haight writes, "The Christian conception of salvation is rooted in a historical narrative of God's entering into dialogue with human freedom. If the church is to represent this initiative of God to the world as it has been revealed in Jesus Christ, it must do this in a way that has the deepest respect for human freedom." This dialogue is modeled after human conversation, "a project of mutual discovery of something new for each party and affirmed together from different perspectives." Roger Haight, *Ecclesial Existence*, vol. 3 of *Christian Community in History* (London: Bloomsbury, 2004; 2014), pp. 251–2. For a discussion of agency in dialogue, modeled on conversations between two friends, see Taraneh Wilkinson, "On

Drawing and Being Drawn: On Applying Friendship to Comparative Theology," *Journal of Ecumenical Studies 48* (2013): pp. 307–16.
135. Aydın, *From Monologue to Dialogue*, p. 258.
136. Aydın, *From Monologue to Dialogue*, p. 259.
137. Aydın, *From Monologue to Dialogue*, p. 265.
138. Mahmut Aydın (ed.), *Hıristiyan, Yahudi ve Müslüman Perspektifinden Dinsel Çoğulculuk ve Mutlaklık İddiaları* (Ankara: Ankara Okulu, 2005). I acquired my copy of this book at the Ankara Theology Faculty bookstore.
139. My treatment of Adnan Aslan's view of pluralism is largely based on Wilkinson, "Moderation and al-Ghazali in Turkey."
140. Adnan Aslan was affiliated with İSAM's Center for Islamic Studies, 29 Mayıs University, and the now defunct Süleyman Şah University.
141. Adnan Aslan, *Dinî Çoğulculuk, Ateizm, ve Geleksel Ekol: Eleştirel Bir Yaklaşım* (Istanbul: İSAM Yayınları, 2010). This title is referred to below as "*Pluralism*." Aslan also published an English version of the work: *Religious Pluralism in Christian and Islamic Philosophy: The Thought of John Hick and Seyyed Hossein Nasr* (Abingdon: RoutledgeCurzon, 2004)—published in 1998 and based on his 1995 dissertation. I refer to the Turkish, as it was intended for Turkish readers. A more recent general work, which will not be commented upon here, is Adnan Aslan's *Din Felsefesine Giriş* [*Introduction to Philosophy of Religion*] (Istanbul: Ufuk Yayınları, 2015).
142. English translation from M. A. S. Abdel Haleem. See Aslan, *Pluralism*, p. 13.
143. Aslan, *Pluralism*, p. 14.
144. Aslan, *Pluralism*, p. 10.
145. Aslan, *Pluralism*, pp. 43–4.
146. Aslan, *Pluralism*, p. 49. One might ask what then happens for believers in other faiths who read the Qur'ān and study Islam and yet do not convert. I suppose in this case the same paradigm applies—such people are part of al-Ghazālī's third group and may or may not receive God's mercy, provided they are still spiritually seeking truth.
147. Aslan is by no means the only reader of al-Ghazālī to interpret this text as assuring salvation for many non-Muslims. See, for example, Ahmed El Shamsy's chapter "The Social Construction of Orthodoxy," in Tim Winter (ed.), *The Cambridge Companion to Classical Islamic Theology* (Cambridge: Cambridge University Press, 2008).
148. Aslan, *Pluralism*, p. 50. Rahner is a famous Catholic inclusivist and coined the controversial term "anonymous Christian" for believers in other religions who

nevertheless could be seen as living lives in the spirit of Christ. Although Aslan treats Rahner, he does not identify his position with Rahner's. That identification is my own. One non-academic Turkish evaluation of Rahner's anonymous Christianity can be found in Ramazan Yazçiçek, *Anonim Din Arayışı ve Dinsel Çoğulculuk* [*The Search for Anonymous Religion and Religious Pluralism*] (Istanbul: Ekin Yayınları, 2008; 2014).

149. Şinasi Gündüz, *Küresel Sorunlar ve Din* (Ankara: Ankara Okulu Yayınları, 2010), p. 83.

150. This tension is in no way unique to Aslan's case or Islam more generally. *Nostra Aetate*'s "Declaration on the Relation of the Church to Non-Christian Relations" issued by Paul VI on October 28, 1965, has set the tone for Catholics to view other religions both as vehicles of God's truth and mercy whilst still inevitably corrupted reflections of truth.

151. His words are, "Just as there are infinite ways to bind a man to God, there are also infinite ways to obstruct a man from God." (Turkish: "İnsan Tanrı'ya bağlayan sonsuz sayıda yollar olduğu gibi, insanı Tanrı'dan ayıran sonsuz sayıda engeller de olabilir.") Aslan, *Pluralism*, p. 61.

152. Aslan, *Pluralism*, p. 80.

153. Ruhattin Yazoğlu, *Dinî Çoğulculuk Sorunu: John Hick Üzerine Bir Araştırma* (Istanbul: İz Yayıncılık, 2007). Henceforth: *The Problem of Religious Pluralism*.

154. Mustafa Eren, *John Hick'te Dini Çoğulculuk* (Istanbul: Otorite Kitab, 2016). Henceforth: *Pluralism in Hick*. Another earlier work worth noting is Mustafa Köylü's *Dialogue between Religions* (2001). Mustafa Köylü began his studies in the Turkish theology faculty system at the Ondokuz Mayıs University and went on to complete his doctorate at the United Theological Seminary in Dayton, OH. Taking up both Muslim and Christian perspectives on dialogue, he treats John Hick; discusses Hans Küng, and Paul Knitter, and then takes up Muslim scholars like Shi'ite scholar Mahmoud Ayoub, Tunisian historian Mohamed Talbi, and finally Seyyed Hossein Nasr. Köylü documents and appreciates the mutual efforts made by both Christians and Muslims and interprets the Qur'ān to all Muslims into dialogue with those of other faiths (p. 164). Mustafa Köylü, *Dinler Arası Diyalog* (Istanbul: İnsan Yayınları, 2001; 2007).

155. John Hick, *Problems of Religious Pluralism* (New York: St. Martin's Press, 1985), p. 29.

156. Hick writes of the Real: "It is infinite, eternal, limitlessly rich beyond the scope of our finite conceiving or experiencing. Let us then both avoid the particular names used within the particular traditions and yet use a term which is

consonant with the faith of each of them—Ultimate Reality, or the Real." Hick, *Problems of Religious Pluralism*, p. 39.
157. Yazoğlu, *The Problem of Religious Pluralism*, p. 97.
158. Yazoğlu, *The Problem of Religious Pluralism*, p. 100.
159. Yazoğlu, *The Problem of Religious Pluralism*, p. 100.
160. Yazoğlu, *The Problem of Religious Pluralism*, p. 102. I would rate this as a fair assessment, in that Hick does speak of religions in terms of their soteriological value, effectively arguing for a plurality of paths to salvation.
161. Eren's thesis title: "Die Diskussion über die zeitgenössische Globalethik im Kontext von Hans Küng und Iḫwān aṣ-ṣafā'" (2013).
162. Eren, *Pluralism in Hick*, pp. 118–19.
163. Eren, *Pluralism in Hick*, p. 96.
164. Eren, *Pluralism in Hick*, p. 96.
165. Eren, *Pluralism in Hick*, p. 117.
166. Hidayet Işık, *Âmirî'ye Göre İslâm ve Öteki Dinler* (Istanbul: İz Yayıncılık, 2006).
167. Hanifi Özcan, *Mâtüridî'de Dînî Çoğulculuk*, 3rd printing (Istanbul: Marmara Üniversitesi İlâhiyat Fakültesi Vakfı Yayınları, 2013). Henceforth: *Religious Pluralism in Māturidī*.
168. Özcan, *Religious Pluralism in Māturidī*, p. 7.
169. Düzgün, "Pluralism and Christianity in a Postmodern Age: An Interview with Roger Haight," *Ankara Üniversitesi İlahiyat Fakültesi Dergisi* 47 (2006): p. 46. This part of the article (i.e., the interview) is in English.
170. As far as I understand, a theory of religions is not exempt from this pitfall either. On an abstract level, a theory might be more limited in what it tries to explain, but theories themselves operate within the broader contexts of paradigms and metanarratives.
171. The distinction between religious theory and metanarrative is problematic, and it would be hard not to judge a great many Christian or post-Christian theologians as remaining in the space of metanarrative.
172. There is a movement called "New *Kalām*" (Turkish: *Yeni Kelam*). It has some precedent in late Ottoman thinkers—for instance, Abdüllatif Harpûtî, İzmirli İsmail Hakkı, Filibeli Ahmed Hilmi, Ömer Nasuhi Bilmen, Mehmet Ali Ayni, and Ferit Kam. Modern Turkish figures include Bekir Topaloğlu and M. Sait Özervarlı. See Yusuf Şefki Yavuz, "Kelâm," in *İslam Ansiklopedisi* (Türkiye Diyanet Vakfı), <https://islamansiklopedisi.org.tr/kelam—ilim> (last accessed October 1, 2018). Coşkun also brings up the subject under the title *Yeni İlm-i Kelam*, describing these theologians as those who have taken up the task of

defending divinity in the face of a barrage of Western atheistic trends. See Coşkun, *Ateizm ve İslam*, p. 223.

173. Some of these inclusivisms, even for those not specifically engaging Anglophone literature on pluralism, are built on a framework of *tawḥīd* or divine unity. This arguably allows Turkish theologians to affirm one truth, while still embracing various levels of plurality. This said, the distinction between inclusivism and pluralism is not always definite in Turkish theology, which is in part due to the limitation of the typology itself.

8

Conclusion: Reflections on Turkish Islam, Modernity, and Dialogue

The former one-way street has become open to two-way traffic, and the one-sided monologues have been supplemented with a readiness to listen and understand.

—Mahmut Aydın[1]

From the start of this examination I have argued that Turkish theology is marked by engagement with Western intellectual tradition, alongside Turkish and broader Islamic sources, in such a way as cannot be characterized by strict dichotomies. Turkish theologians examine and incorporate voices from the Western intellectual tradition, including academic Christian theology. The work of Turkish theologians does not reduce to a simple, polarized reaction to the West or Western Christianity. The responses vary and include negative, positive, and constructive elements; they include clichés, generalizations, critical insights, and points of active dialogue. This engagement with Western sources may be conceptual or it may be played out in footnotes. It can be indirect or direct. At its most creative it is dialectical, navigating Western sources with the help of Turkish and Arabic ones and at times navigating Turkish or Arabic discussions with the aid of Western sources. And since many of these dialectical moments are directed at the Muslim Turkish reader, they form, inform, and generate Muslim Turkish self-understanding.

Turkish theology cannot be read through the lens of reductive dualities; it must be understood in terms of its complex dialectical relations between intellectual traditions, hence the title "Dialectical Encounters" for this book. These complex dialectical relations I have characterized by a threefold schema, which includes Turkish/Ottoman, Arab-Islamic, and Western sources. While this threefold characterization suggests broad patterns, the dialectical dynamics present in Turkish theology manifest, at times most strikingly, in individual discussions and in critical re-narrations of Turkish and Muslim identity today. After a brief recapitulation, I will turn to the implications of these Turkish dialectics for academic dialogue between Turkish theologians and Western Christian theologians.

Summary

Part one of this study looked at the context and history of Turkish theology faculties. I proposed that Turkish theology faculties are both expressions of Ottoman-Turkish continuity as well as products of modernity, arguing that Turkish theology has an ongoing history of complex intellectual tributaries. Due to this complexity, I held that Turkish theology needs to be studied in non-binary frameworks, which do not reduce it to politics or debates on secularism. Instead of limiting analysis to reductive dualities, I argued that it is necessary to look at the theological value of the arguments presented by Turkish theologians—particularly in their responses to Western Christianity. To better evaluate Turkish theological contributions, I proposed a roughly threefold schema of engagement, suggesting that Turkish theology involves a dynamic interplay of Turkish, wider Islamic, and Western sources.

Part two took up the case of philosophical theologian Recep Alpyağıl and the importance of individual authority, especially in forging dialectical continuity between a Muslim individual's Islamic past, present, and integrated vision for the future. Alpyağıl advocates for the integration of European and Anglophone voices alongside figures from the Arabic and Ottoman traditions as necessary for an authentic Turkish canon of philosophical theology. For Alpyağıl, the wide spectrum of voices claiming authority—from classical Islamic sources, Ottoman and modern Turkish sources, to Christian and Western sources—necessitate the mediating, creative, and self-conscious execution of individual authority. Since there are no easy answers, according to Alpyağıl, the burden to ask better questions and to navigate claims of authenticity and authority lies largely on the informed efforts of the believer.

In part three, I argued that individual authority also lies at the heart of Özgün's theological anthropology. It is the internal, though not absolute, authority of the individual which both ties the believing individual to God and to her own tradition and thereby allows her to face the challenges of a global world. Düzgün stresses that God created human beings to be free and that the most authentic form of authority is internal—as opposed to external. The freedom underpinning individual authority is not a freedom that necessarily contradicts tradition or society. Insofar as tradition or society may be considered corrupted, the individual who pursues true religion may at times find herself in conflict with said tradition or society. Yet, individuals are meant to mediate their place in society. As a human being, the individual believer is deeply connected to the rest of humanity. For Düzgün, who cites Ḥanafī tradition, all human beings are equipped with cognitive faculties, common sense, intuition, and conscience. He further draws from his reading of Māturīdī theology to argue that human diversity is divinely willed and that human agency—when properly put to use—shares in divine agency. Thus, I read Düzgün's case for individual authority to simultaneously be a case for individual responsibility. The responsible believer is willing and able to critically approach her own tradition as well as authentically engage other individuals who do not share in her faith tradition or way of viewing the world.

The two examples of Alpyağıl and Düzgün give detailed and concrete illustrations of the extensive engagement of Turkish theologians with various facets of the Western intellectual tradition. This engagement incorporates explicitly Christian, secular philosophical, and even atheist voices. In the cases of both Alpyağıl and Düzgün this engagement involved criticism, positive appraisal, and a call to redefine the terms of this engagement. Neither figure held that engagement with non-Muslim and non-Turkish thought should or could be avoided. Instead, Alpyağıl and Düzgün respectively espoused philosophical and theological approaches for individual engagement with non-Muslim and non-Turkish thought—with Alpyağıl arguing for the common ground of philosophical theology and Düzgün arguing for a universal theological anthropology that recognizes diversity and mutual engagement as part of humanity's divinely willed responsibility and journey. Neither thinker saw their own use of Western sources as un-Islamic, and Alpyağıl actively argued for intellectual synthesis as part of an authentic Turkish Muslim intellectual canon. Their creative use of concepts from multiple traditions re-designated and re-narrated how the label "modern" was applied, weakening the strong association of "Western" with "modern" and challenging the binaries that pit "modern" and "Western" against "traditional," "Islamic," or "Turkish."

Part four began with another aspect of Turkish navigation of multiple authoritative traditions, offering a survey of Turkish treatments of skepticism, atheism, and religious pluralism, all with the common thread of Christianity. Many Turkish theologians strongly associate skepticism, atheism, and religious pluralism with Christianity—sometimes with negative connotations. Turkish theologians tend to view Christianity as both a cause of skepticism and of atheism. In addition, Turkish theologians tend to view Christianity to be more vulnerable to the forces of skepticism and atheism than Islam. Further, for some Turkish theologians, religious pluralism functions nearly as synonym for Christian theological responses to other religions or is at the very least heavily defined by Christian concepts. Against these widely held assumptions, I also examined counterexamples. For instance, Yaşar Nuri Öztürk did not claim that Christian theology or even the European deist heritage were major causes of atheism; instead, he claimed false religiosity fueled unbelief. Alpyağıl, in another example, claims that skepticism is not merely a Christian problem but that it also poses intellectual challenges for Muslims. Adnan Aslan also seriously engages atheism within the discussion of religious pluralism. And while pluralism, even for Aslan, represents a strongly Christian project, Turkish theologians, including Aslan, have developed their own variations of inclusivism and, in the case of Mahmut Aydın, even pluralism. This Muslim and Turkish inclusivism/pluralism tends to embrace *tawḥīd*, or divine unity, as a keystone for inclusivism, a fulcrum around which diversity can be properly celebrated without the possibility of universal truth falling into question.[2]

Taking a step back to reflect, Turkish theologians are very much products of modernity; but they are not *passive* products of modernity. Turkish theologians engage, respond to, and reshape the discussion of modernity, claiming the authority to pronounce judgment on it. They are definers and shapers of modernity. And while Turkish theology faculties are institutions of the state and not immune to political visions of religion, be it Kemalist or AK Party visions of Islam, their dialectical identity means that their self-understanding, and by extension their intellectual contributions, cannot be reduced to the dichotomies still present in political discussions of religion in Turkey. After all, humans are simultaneously passive products of the world that shapes them and active agents shaping the world,[3] and so it is possible to be a product of modernity and still respond critically to it. If this were not the case, then the considerable body of Anglophone and European literature on the concept of modernity would be unthinkable. In the Turkish context, the question of how Turkish theology reflects and responds to modernity is largely a function of how modernity is defined. And as I have tried to argue, in Turkish theology, the terms of discussion along with their definitions are often a function of the proposed threefold dynamic of Turkish/Ottoman, Western, and Arabic intellectual traditions.

I would now like to turn to a modest reflection on the category of modernity in light of Turkish theology.

Reflection: Back to the Topic of Modernity

If Turkish theologians are also active shapers of modernity, what can dialogue with Turkish theology add to the discussion of modernity? This section draws on contributions of Christian theologian Roger Haight, Islamic historian Thomas Bauer, scholar of Islam Shahab Ahmed, and philosopher Louis Dupré to further reflect on the question of modernity in Turkish theology, arguing that valuing Turkish theology as a resource for creative responses to modernity can enrich academic dialogue between Turkish and Christian theologians.

Globalization and Dialogue: Roger Haight

> Globalization, the process by which the world is shrinking and nations and cultures become ever more interdependent, forces specific groups of people to take note of other nations and cultures. The international rubbing of shoulders across great distances has a universalizing and a particularizing effect. The common international standards of communication and commerce that are being constructed threaten local cultural values and encourage them to become more entrenched. Because Western nations hold such power, globalization carries a Western bias. For example, though the majority of Christians now live in the developing world, the church still remains associated with Western culture and is often resisted on those grounds alone.
>
> —Roger Haight[4]

I begin with Haight's statement above as an opening mirror, point of contrast, and theological challenge for the present discussion on Turkish theology.

Haight, who was in contact with Şaban Ali Düzgün,[5] suggests that globalization, and by extension modernity, carries a Western bias, backed not only by ideas but by more practical histories of power, economy, and influence. Like some of his Turkish theologian counterparts, Haight also recognizes the potential threat globalization can pose to local cultures and systems of value. Globalization and Western cultural bias are interconnected. While this bias cannot be eliminated, I suggest that Turkish theological portrayals of and responses to Western and Christian modernity are valuable contributions in coming to terms with and gaining new perspective on this bias. In learning from Turkish theological portrayals of Western modernity and Christianity, Christian theologians have an opportunity to engage Turkish theologians in dialogue.

Haight, in his own work, distinguishes between pragmatism when dealing with difference of historical consciousness and the positive appreciation of difference in "pluralist consciousness." The former does not positively value diversity, while the latter does. In Haight's view, the historical consciousness now common to many within and outside of academia "looks more like pragmatic negotiation than an effort at agreement in a shared internalized truth."[6] In other words, people in and outside academia worry more about practical measures of mutual tolerance than valuing diversity as part of a collective journey towards truth. By contrast, Haight explains, "pluralist consciousness" does not see different perspectives as a neutral or even negative obstacle to negotiate but rather views them as opportunities for greater mutual enrichment. He writes:

> Dialogue provides a way of taking the pluralistic character of the present situation with utmost seriousness while at the same time not surrendering commitment to a common truth that makes claims on all. But dialogue is not a simple concept. It contains an implicit ethic, a set of rules that governs its authenticity.[7]

Haight cautions that dialogue, when lacking an ethic of mutual respect, can easily devolve into manipulation.[8] Taking Haight's advice, with the help of an ethic of mutual respect, theologians both inside and outside of Turkey might successfully develop fruitful discussions. Yet to have successful and mutually respectful inter-academic dialogue on modernity and dialogue, it is necessary to acknowledge the relevant material power dynamics and Western bias present in the project of globalization.

Haight further remarks that, unlike an individual given over to the compulsion of seeking pleasure after pleasure, "distinctively human freedom begins with constancy and commitment to stable values."[9] I suggest this discussion of values may be richer and more complete if continued through increasing efforts of academic dialogue across theological traditions, especially since human freedom, ethical values, and dialogue with the modern world are already topics treated by Turkish theologians.[10]

Lastly, when engaging Turkish theology, the category of West/Western should not be dismissed. Turkish theologians use it intentionally, challenge it, discuss it in engagement with post-colonial literature, and associate it strongly with Christianity. In this way, using the terms "West" and "Western" may serve to help theologians move away from thinking of the world in terms of West and other. For instance, Recep Alpyağıl's engagement with Western philosophy of religion is a very successful example of this turnabout, and it allows him to redraw the lines of intellectual canon to include Western voices within an authentic Turkish intellectual heritage. It is important to recognize that Turkish theological references to the Western intellectual tradition do not inevitably result in polarization, but sometimes produce active integration, as in the case with Alpyağıl. This category of West/Western, though at times deceptively monolithic, is used by Turkish theologians; and how they use it both matters and merits attention.

Ambiguity and Authenticity: Thomas Bauer and Shahab Ahmed

Some might object: can Turkish theologians who strongly engage Western intellectual tradition and Christianity represent authentically Muslim voices? Opinions will differ. Turkish theologians have their fans and their critics. Drawing on the work of Thomas Bauer and Shahab Ahmed, I want to suggest, with all due humility, that Turkish theological voices in dialogue with Western intellectual tradition can and do represent authentically Muslim voices.

As discussed in chapter two, the work of Islamic historian Thomas Bauer studies the intolerance of ambiguity symptomatic of modernity, tracing this intolerance through the changes in Islamic self-understanding prior to and after interactions with Western modernity. Bauer cautions that normative Islamic claims which seem reactionary or traditional may also be manifestations of Western influence. This is because reactionary or traditional voices reflect modernity's intolerance of ambiguity and plurality of meaning—they too are products of modernity. Contrary to the traditional image of Islam that reactionary voices paint, ambiguity and polysemy are historically part of Islamic intellectual culture prior to modernity. As we have seen, Turkish theologians in dialogue with Christian and Western sources exhibit a significant tolerance for ambiguity and plurality.[11] To view this tolerance as a deficit in Islamic authenticity is not a reaction *against* modern values but rather an instance *of* modern intolerance.

The late scholar of Islam Shahab Ahmed, like Bauer, also addresses the question of Islamic authenticity. In his work *What is Islam? The Importance of Being Islamic*, he argues for a more inclusive view of what counts as authentically Islamic culture. In his discussion on various ways to categorize and conceptualize Islam, he writes:

> We need to resist our conceptual predisposition to conceptualize and categorize by elimination of difference, and conceptualize and categorize, instead, *in terms of inclusion of difference*. As such, the goal and touchstone of a successful conceptualization of Islam as theoretical object and analytical category must be to *locate and explain*, to the fullest degree possible, the *logic of internal contradiction that allows contradictory statements and actions to cohere meaningfully to their putative object* . . .[12]

Ahmed's position is similar to Bauer's in arguing for an inclusion of difference when categorizing cultural and intellectual products as "Islamic." When evaluating Islamic authenticity, the question should not be limited to an either/or discussion but rather set amid an analysis of the complex both/and's and contradictions present in any one manifestation of Islam.

Many of the Turkish theologians treated above were consciously explorative and creative in their theological projects. Critics may question their religious authority on these grounds: the theologians examined here are not figures who issue fatwas, but scholars who open up discussions. Are these then true representatives of Islam? I would like to respond to this question with Ahmed's remarks on the question of what is and is not Islam:

Symptomatic of the marginalization of exploration, ambiguity, ambivalence, relativism and contradiction in the conceptualization of Islam is the fact that a unique feature of the study of societies of Muslims, as compared to other societies, is that so much *value* is given and *meaning* ascribed to the prescriptive and restrictive discourses of Muslims, such as law and creed, and so little *value* is given and *meaning* ascribed to *explorative* and *creative* discourses such as fictional literature, art and music. Simply, when Muslims act and speak *exploratively*—as opposed to *prescriptively*—as they seem to have spent a very great deal of their historical time doing, they are somehow not seen to be acting and speaking in a manner and register that is representative, expressive and constitutive of Islam.[13]

Ahmed stresses that stopping at the prescriptive elements of Islamic thought and culture does not do justice to more creative and exploratory expressions. Even though the present discussion is not about art or music (though Turkish theology faculties *do* have subdepartments for Islamic art and music), it is still worthwhile to heed Ahmed's observation. Is a creative or explorative venture in Muslim thought inherently less Islamic than Muslim discourse on jurisprudence or ritual practice? Is it not possible to act and speak *exploratively* in the name of authentic Turkish Islam? I would argue that at least some Turkish theologians think that it is possible—the exploratory and dialogical aspects of both Alpyağıl and Düzgün's projects depend on this assumption. And though Alpyağıl and Düzgün feature as primary cases in this study, these two figures are not the only instances of *explorative* discourses in Turkish theology. In chapter seven's discussion of skepticism, atheism, and other religions, figures arose willing to either explore grounds for new Islamic positions or to explore non-Muslim positions. Öztürk argued for a quranically grounded deism. Alpyağıl considered Christian fideist responses and the challenges of skepticism. Adnan and others explored different possibilities for Muslim inclusivism, even pluralism. There are no doubt further examples of this exploratory practice not considered in the present study awaiting treatment.

Turkish theologians range in a continuum from taking on more prescriptive roles to more explorative roles. The present study has given pride of place to projects that dialogue with Western sources and has highlighted more exploratory theological projects. Admittedly, not all Muslims in Turkey recognize these more exploratory (or even some of these prescriptive) attempts as authoritative.[14] For instance, there are critics of the Ankara Paradigm today.[15] The Ankara Paradigm is one that takes up Enlightenment values and assumes religion and reform are compatible, and its influence is still notable among Turkish theologians today. One notable critic of the Ankara Paradigm is Hayreddin Karaman.[16] As a fiqh scholar, his work is more focused on prescriptive values in Islam than exploratory ventures.[17] Those like Karaman who see prescriptive Islam as inherently more authentic may, as Ahmed notes, consider more exploratory and progressive theological ventures as inherently less authentic. Nonetheless, some Turkish theologians *do* undertake exploratory ventures and they do so from an explicitly Muslim perspective. The present analysis has endeavored to highlight these more creative and exploratory notes—theological engagements with perceived cultural and religious "others" like the West, Christianity, atheism, and even pluralism.

Critics and Builders of Modernity: Louis Dupré

> Modernity is an *event* that has transformed the relation between the cosmos, its transcendent source, and its human interpreter. To explain this as the outcome of historical precedents is to ignore its most significant quality—namely, its success in rendering all rival views of the real obsolete. Its innovative power made modernity, which began as a local Western phenomenon, a universal project capable of forcing its theoretical and practical principles on all but the most isolated civilizations. "Modern" has become the predicate of a unified world culture.[18]
>
> Critics of modernity implicitly accept more of its assumptions than they are able to discard. Even those who globally reject its theoretical principles continue to build on them.
>
> —Louis Dupré[19]

Religious philosopher Louis Dupré, like Haight, stresses the global aspect of modernity. Modernity is so pervasive that even critics struggle to fully divest themselves of its principles. Are Turkish theologians primarily critics of Western religious tradition and modernity? Do they approve of or positively represent some of its assumptions? Do they hold themselves to intellectual criteria determined by modernity; and in doing so do they redefine such criteria? Can they not act as critics of modernity in its Western forms but also function as supporters and developers of the principles associated with modernity? I suggest that Turkish theological criticisms of modernity entail criticizing some aspects while actively building upon the principles of modernity which they positively value.

Among Turkish theologians, while there is literature devoted to the criticism of an unhealthy expression of Western Christianity and Western modernity, there is also a deep sense of identification and embroilment with this same heritage. Turkish theology was founded on an ideal of the academic and scientific study of religion—an ideal grounded in Ottoman and Turkish appropriation of sociology of religion. The physical faculties themselves reflect this admixture of traditional Islamic sciences and Western academic divisions, so much so that it is standard for a faculty to have, for instance, both a *tafsīr* department and instruction dedicated to psychology of religion under the roof of one larger edifice. Also, Turkish theology has a relatively strong international component—pressing many of its scholars to attend and host international conferences and to collaborate with scholars of other academes to increase both their visibility and the quality of their own research.[20] There is a globally minded element to much Turkish theology. Certainly, not all Turkish theologians are equally interested in this broader picture, but, as we have seen, many are interested, and their scholarly journeys and output reflect this. Turkish theology, as I have argued throughout, boasts a strongly dialogical component. Much of its output is done in conversation with or reference to Western voices, Christian figures and philosophers.

The cases of Recep Alpyağıl and Şaban Ali Düzgün present Turkish theologians who approve of certain aspects of both modernity and postmodernity, reconnecting both concepts to perceived past values and pointing to ways forward.[21] Turkish theologians—some having aligned more closely with the Ankara Paradigm than others—do not necessarily reject modernity when they criticize Christianity or Western ontotheology. Historically, and even today, many embrace and defend principles strongly associated with the Enlightenment, modernity, and postmodernity. And as we saw in chapter seven on Turkish discussions of other religions and religious pluralism, there exists simultaneously a robust emphasis on ontotheology and a strong confidence in its superiority to Western ontotheology.

On the subject of Western ontotheology, Dupré speaks of a "double breakup" clefting a rift between Creator and Cosmos and also between the human individual and the Cosmos; he identifies a Christian "ontotheological synthesis" between God, humanity, and world, whose rupture "guided Western thought to break down."[22] This rupture he uses to mark the dawn of modernity. Düzgün's work offered a modern Turkish interpretation of Māturīdī *kalām*, where in Māturīdī *kalām* the bonds between Creator and Cosmos maintain person- and life-affirming harmony. This is a harmony that Dupré judged Western ontotheology to have lost. In the case of Düzgün, the affirmation of Māturīdī thought over Ashʿarī thought (where Creator and Cosmos are arguably put more at odds in debates on divine agency and causality) is also an affirmation of Muslim ontotheology in the face of a perceived failure in Western ontotheology,[23] a failure which Düzgün cites Christian and Western thinkers in order to articulate and affirm. Düzgün's work points to a confidence in Muslim ontotheology to produce meaningful and effective answers to the challenges of modernity.

Turkish theological responses to modernity fall into a broader context of reengaging the past critically to move forward. This past is a mixed past—one that includes Islamic, Ottoman, and Western history. Moreover, Turkish theologians today are not the only generation to have encountered and responded to intellectual trends in the West. Ottoman and Turkish historian İsmail Kara says more generally in his work *Between Religion and Modernization*:

> The human being is a forward-looking being, his face, his eyes, and his feet have also been created to point forward. But [. . .] the future is a recollection, a chain of transmission, a perception, and built first upon a mental/theoretical foundation it can then be constructed practically. [. . .] The future should not be called an order of coincidences, but rather a construction operation.[24]

Kara uses the word construction to speak of the human (and by extension Turkish) relation to past and future. I have used the word constructive to describe theological projects examined here, Alpyağıl and Düzgün receiving especial attention. Construction stresses agency over the negative associations of criticism, and this positive agency prevails in a number of Turkish theological projects which engage the Western intellectual tradition. Turkish theologians like Düzgün and Alpyağıl do more than deconstruct and criticize, they integrate, re-narrate, and construct. Turkish theologians not only criticize but also positively use Western categories to break assumptions of intellectual dependence to those same categories.

To use an anecdote for an analogy, when scholar and British diplomat Arnold Toynbee saw how Turkey employed the Western principle of national sovereignty to assert itself against Western aggression and encroachment post-World War I, he remarked, "indeed, Mustafa Kemal was defending the most exalted principles of the West—against the West itself."[25] It may be safe to say that, even beyond the scope of Kemalism, Turkey has found other ways to defend principles of the West against Western bias and encroachment—in the case of Turkish theology faculties, scholars have defended Muslim identity along with religious freedom, individual authority, the importance of a scriptural hermeneutics not limited to one tradition's text, and even comparative philosophy of religion. While caricatures of Muslim identity stress irrationality, coercion, close-mindedness, and blind following of tradition, Turkish theological scholars engage Western theological resources and Western ideals to actively challenge such easy assumptions.

Dialogue, an Ongoing Conversation

> . . . we cannot deny that we have learned quite a lot about Islam from serious [non-Muslim] Western scholars. Certainly, the historical research they have done on Islam cannot count as a contribution to "normative Islam." Nevertheless, it is still a historical reality that their [contributions] have sped the increase of creative thought and commentaries regarding normative Islam.
>
> —M. S. Aydın[26]

These words come from the pen of Turkish theologian and respected philosopher of religion Mehmet S. Aydın. It is striking to note this positive recognition of non-Muslim scholars to the understanding of Islam and the enrichment of normative discussions of Islam amongst Turkish theologians. Turkish theologians not only learn from Christian theologians who speak about Christianity, they also learn from non-Muslim scholars who speak about Islam. Are there similarly ways in which Christian thinkers and theologians might recognize and respond to Turkish theology, which engages both Christian history and theology?²⁷ This final section turns to the question of further academic dialogue, drawing on the work of Oddbjørn Leirvik and his case for interreligious studies, with the suggestion that Turkish theologians are important colleagues and partners in the Euro-American academic trend towards an interreligious studies that increasingly blurs the distinction between believer and scholarly observer.

Oddbjørn Leirvik, a professor of interreligious studies at Oslo University, is a scholar of Christianity and Islam as well as an active proponent of interreligious studies. He lent academic attention to the practical sides of dialogue in his book *Interreligious Studies: A Relational Approach to Religious Activism and the Study of Religion* (2014). In this work, Leirvik speaks of a "relational approach" to studying religion as the defining trait of interreligious studies.²⁸ When Leirvik stresses the relational aspect of the study of religion, he advocates for an awareness of *intra* and *inter*.²⁹ That is, when it comes to the pressures and stresses of culture, faith, and politics, "the fields of tension are just as often to be found within the religions as between them."³⁰ This means that dividing and uniting factors cut across academic and confessional environments, not just between them. It is not advisable to assume that an individual of one faith (or academy) has necessarily more or less in common with those of the same or divergent confession.

Central to the present discussion, Leirvik argues that the new discipline of interreligious studies is best seen as "an academic endeavor—marked by relational perspectives both on dialogue and other forms of religious activism."³¹ Or, in other words, he advocates for relational, academic dialogue between faiths as a distinct endeavor:

> there is something essentially relational with interreligious studies that make them different from religious studies [. . .] and from confessional theology.³²

Leirvik stresses that "interreligious studies is something essentially relational."³³ Interreligious studies is relational in three ways: first, its object of study is interreligious; second, the subject carrying out the study does so in an interdisciplinary manner; and third, the discipline of interreligious studies is only meaningful in conversation with different "faith traditions."³⁴ As he notes, interreligious studies grew out of theology rather than religious studies.³⁵ Befitting of its theological origins, interreligious studies engages both instances of dialogue and is itself a space for dialogue.[36] Leirvik admits that it is hard to clearly differentiate between interfaith dialogue and interreligious studies, but he nonetheless stresses that it would be reductive to approach interreligious studies as the study of interfaith dialogue:

> the distinction between interreligious studies and interfaith dialogue is hard to make in practice, and also in the academic context. It would be simplistic to see interfaith dialogue solely as an object of study. Insights from dialogue may also affect the way in which religion is studied and taught in the academy.[37]

Bearing in mind the potential gains interreligious studies might bring to the wider study of religion, Leirvik affirms academic rigor but resists that such a relational discipline can or should boast scholarly neutrality:

> it is difficult to see how anyone [. . .] should be able to posit oneself outside of the cultural and religious encounters and explore them from a completely detached position. Such insights render the old distinction between a (theological) insider perspective and a (religious studies) outsider perspective not so meaningful . . .[38]

Leirvik thus challenges the insider–outsider distinction. All scholars must place themselves; everyone exists and moves within various formative contexts. Further, in maintaining an academic space for dialogue, Leirvik underscores that dialogue should not be understood in contradistinction to confrontation. Asking whether the dialogical motion is from confrontation to dialogue, or if it is simultaneously both, he ultimately argues for a both/and approach to confrontation and dialogue.[39] Leirvik affirms that sometimes stereotypes are true: "Both Christian and Muslim do, in fact . . . often struggle to 'Christianize' or 'Islamicize' their environments . . ."[40] With this in mind he urges those considering interreligious studies that scholars need to be "honest about the unpleasant" in order to move forward with dialogue.[41]

Turkish theologians routinely study and engage Christianity and other non-Muslim faiths and, accordingly, they potentially share challenges and aims with Anglophone and European theologians. As Leirvik remarks:

> social contractions do not always coincide with religious borders. If one looks more closely into the matter, one will find that social and ideological differences are generally more conspicuous *within* the religions than *between* them.[42]

In terms of doing academic theology in dialogue with other theological and intellectual traditions, I would argue that Turkish theologians share many aims and challenges with Christian theologians who wish to pursue interreligious dialogue at the academic level. Further, increased conversations between Turkish theologians and Christian theologians could lead to more precise formulations of shared aims and challenges.

Finally, Leirvik, who accepts, like some Turkish theologians, that the Qur'ān positively affirms the plurality of human belief and culture, also challenges Christian theologians, writing:

> But the question remains of how Christians will respond to the fundamental qur'anic acceptance of religious plurality as a divine *test* and a potential *blessing*.[43]

The question also remains as to how Christian theologians will respond to Turkish theologians' efforts to engage Christianity and its associated Western intellectual tradition. As with all continuing conversations, the fruits will continue to depend on the mutual efforts of both sides. Truly dialectical encounters are fundamentally ongoing conversations.

Notes

1. Mahmut Aydin, "Religious Pluralism: A Challenge for Muslims—A Theological Evaluation," *Journal of Ecumenical Studies* 38 (2001): p. 331.
2. When I visited Ankara, Prof. Mualla Selçuk graciously gave me the opportunity to share a Christian perspective on *tawḥīd* (influenced by Schleiermacher, Rahner, and contemporary comparative theology) and express how it affected my own understanding of religious pluralism in her graduate seminar (December 4, 2015). Unbeknownst to me, it happened to be a day already set aside for the discussion of *tawḥīd*, so my reflections were well received. Not only that, but my view that *tawḥīd* was an appropriate concept to bring into the discussion of religious pluralism also seemed to resonate. Then, as I looked deeper into the literature of theologians that engage Christianity and religious pluralism, I also found that *tawḥīd* was referenced, as I have noted in prior discussions here. Theologically speaking, it is a topic that still needs deeper investigation.
3. For a Christian philosophical perspective on this statement, see Schleiermacher's *Second Speech on Religion*. For a recent translation of the 1806 edition of this famous work, see F. D. E. Schleiermacher, *Christmas Dialogue, The Second Speech,*

and Other Selections, ed. and trans. Julia A. Lamm (New York and Mahwah, NJ: Paulist Press, 2014). Schleiermacher also elaborates on this theme and its implications for piety and consciousness of relationship with God in his monumental *The Christian Faith*, ed. H. R. Mackintosh and J. S. Stewart (London and New York: T. & T. Clark, 1999), pp. 5–26 (i.e., §3–§5, which discuss piety and consciousness of human agency) and pp. 131–41 (i.e., §32–§35, which discuss the feeling of absolute dependence in relation with relative dependence and agency in the world).

4. Roger Haight, *Ecclesial Existence*, vol. 3 of *Christian Community in History* (London: Bloomsbury, 2004; 2014), p. 245.
5. Şaban Ali Düzgün, "Pluralism and Christianity in a Postmodern Age: An Interview with Roger Haight," *Ankara Üniversitesi İlahiyat Fakültesi Dergisi* 47 (2006): pp. 43–66. I mention this interaction in chapter seven.
6. Haight, *Ecclesial Existence*, p. 245.
7. Haight, *Ecclesial Existence*, p. 247.
8. Haight, *Ecclesial Existence*, p. 247.
9. Haight, *Ecclesial Existence*, p. 249. This appeal to human freedom and values resonates strongly with the work of Düzgün.
10. For instance, see chapter six on Şaban Ali Düzgün.
11. In terms of valuing pluralism but criticizing the false pluralism of globalization, two authors come to mind: Fatma K. Barbarosoğlu and Düzgün. Both authors include criticism of globalism and modernity's negative impact on healthy diversity, stressing instead the value of local diversity (Barbarosoğlu) and divinely willed human diversity (Düzgün).
12. Shahab Ahmed, *What is Islam? The Importance of Being Islamic* (Princeton, NJ: Princeton University Press, 2016), p. 302.
13. Ahmed, *What is Islam?*, p. 303.
14. The question of the normative credibility of Turkish theology faculties, as a whole, is both fascinating and beyond the scope of this project.
15. This is Philip Dorroll's term. I did not use it in my treatments of theologians, but Şaban Ali Düzgün, for instance, exhibits many of the traits of the Ankara Paradigm.
16. On Karaman's criticism of the Ankara Paradigm, see Philip Dorroll, "The Turkish Understanding of Islam," *Journal of the American Academy of Religion* 82 (2014): 1059–60.
17. See, for example, Hayreddin Karaman, *Hayatımızdaki İslâm 1* [*Islam in our Life 1*] (Istanbul: İz Yayıncılık, 2002) or his *İslâm Hukuk Tarihi* [*A History of Islamic Law*] (Istanbul: İz Yayıncılık, 1999).

18. Louis Dupré, *Passage to Modernity: An Essay in the Hermeneutics of Nature and Culture* (New Haven and London: Yale University Press, 1993), p. 249.
19. Dupré, *Passage to Modernity*, p. 6.
20. For instance, in the 1990s Ekrem Sarikcioğlu, an influential proponent of the phenomenological study of religion in Turkish theology, pushed the study to adhere to international standards of study of religions. Sinasi Gunduz, "From Apology to Phenomenology: The Current State of the Studies of the History of Religions in Turkey," in Sinasi Gunduz and Cafer S. Yaran (eds), *Change and Essence* (Washington, DC: The Council for Research in Values and Philosophy, 2005), p. 40.
21. As yet another example, though his work does not feature here, Turkish theologian İlhami Güler, for example, recommended the author read Richard Kearney on the subject of religion and postmodernity, upon visiting the Ankara Theology Faculty (December 3, 2015). Güler is in fact responsible for introducing the author to Kearney's work.
22. Dupré, *Passage to Modernity*, p. 3.
23. For a short overview on agency and causality in Ashʿarī thought, see George F. Hourani, *Reason and Tradition in Islamic Ethics* (Cambridge: Cambridge University Press, 1985), pp. 118–23. See also Majid Fakhry, *A History of Islamic Philosophy*, 3rd edn (New York: Columbia University Press, 1970; 1983; 2004), pp. 209–39.
24. İsmail Kara, *Din ile Modernleşme Arasında: Çağdaş Türk Düşüncesinin Meseleleri* [*Between Religion and Modernization: Issues of Contemporary Turkish Thought*] (Istanbul: Dergâh Yayınları, 2003), p. 449. Turkish: "İnsanoğlu ileriye doğru seyreden bir varlıktır, yüzü, gözleri ve ayakları da öne doğru yaratılmıştır. Fakat [. . .] İstikbal ancak bir hafıza, bir silsile, bir idrak ve bir zemin üzerinde önce zihnî/nazarî olarak ardından da fiilî olarak inşa edilebilir. İstikbal bir tesadüfler manzumesi değil bir inşa ameliyesinin adı olmak gerekir."
25. Halil İnalcik, *Turkey and Europe in History* (Istanbul: Eren Yayıncılık, 2006), p. 83. Note that Toynbee in *The Murderous Tyranny of the Turks* (London, New York and Toronto: Hodder & Stoughton, 1917) praises nearly all non-Turkish peoples of the Ottoman Empire and portrays Turks as good at nothing but fighting—e.g., "The Arabs are still the most progressive race in the Islamic world; they are almost as numerous as the Turks in the population of the Ottoman Empire, and they are not divided from the Turks by differences of religion" (p. 9). Later in his career, Toynbee took up the study of Turkish in London—not without ruffling some feathers—but having at last made Turkish friends,

softened his attitude towards Turkish culture and society. See Arnold J. Toynbee, *Acquaintances* (London: Oxford University Press, 1967), pp. 249–51.
26. M. S. Aydın, "Fazlur Rahman ve İslâm Modernizmi," *İslâmi Araştırmlar* 4:4 (1990): p. 281. Turkish: "ciddi batılı alimlerden İslam hakkında çok şey öğrendiğimizi inkar edemeyiz. Onların tarihi İslam hakkında yaptıkları araştırmaları, elbetteki 'normatif İslâm'a bir katkı sayamayız. Fakat onların normatif İslam'la ilgili yaratıcı düşünce ve yorumları hızlandırdığı da tarihi bir gerçektir."
27. It has been argued that Christian theologians profited in a limited manner from earlier encounters with Ottoman Islam. Mark Sedgwick notes periods of intellectual transmission from Ottoman, Islamic culture into European culture in his *Western Sufism: From the Abbasids to the New Age* (Oxford: Oxford University Press, 2017).
28. Oddbjørn Leirvik, *Interreligious Studies: A Relational Approach to Religious Activism and the Study of Religion* (London and New York: Bloomsbury, 2014).
29. Leirvik, *Interreligious Studies*, p. 1.
30. Leirvik, *Interreligious Studies*, p. 8.
31. Leirvik, *Interreligious Studies*, p. 5. The term "interreligious studies," he remarks, was rarely used before the 1990s (p. 7).
32. Leirvik, *Interreligious Studies*, p. 10.
33. Leirvik, *Interreligious Studies*, p. 11.
34. Leirvik, *Interreligious Studies*, p. 10.
35. Leirvik, *Interreligious Studies*, p. 11.
36. Leirvik, *Interreligious Studies*, p. 12.
37. Leirvik, *Interreligious Studies*, p. 139.
38. Leirvik, *Interreligious Studies*, p. 144.
39. Leirvik, *Interreligious Studies*, p. 59.
40. Leirvik, *Interreligious Studies*, p. 64.
41. Leirvik, *Interreligious Studies*, p. 65.
42. Leirvik, *Interreligious Studies*, p. 81.
43. Leirvik, *Interreligious Studies*, p. 129.

Bibliography

900. *Vefat Yılında İmâm Gazzâlî: 7–9 Ekim 2011, İstanbul* [*On the 900th Anniversary of Ghazālī's Death: 7–9 October, 2011, Istanbul*] (Istanbul: Marmara Üniversitesi İlâhiyat Fakültesi Vakfı Yayınları, 2012).

Abbas, Tahir, *Contemporary Turkey in Conflict: Ethnicity, Islam and Politics* (Edinburgh: Edinburgh University Press, 2017).

Abdel Haleem, M. A. S., *The Qur'ān: A New Translation* (Oxford: Oxford World's Classics, 2008).

Abduh, Muhammad, *The Theology of Unity*, translated by Kenneth Cragg (Selangor: Islamic Book Trust, 2003).

Abu Zayd, Nasir Hamid, "Al-Ghazālī's Theory of Interpretation," *Journal of Osaka University of Foreign Studies* 72 (1986): pp. 1–24.

Açıköz, Mustafa, *Sextus Empirikus ve Şüphe* [*Sextus Empiricus and Doubt*] (Ankara: Elis Yayınları, 2006).

Açıköz, Mustafa, *Skeptikus Şüphe ve Bilgi* [*Skepticism, Doubt, and Knowledge*] (Ankara: Elis Yayınları, 2006).

Açıköz, Mustafa, *Tevhidi Kozmik Holizm, Şüphe ve Eski Uygarlıklar* [*Tawḥīdic Cosmic Holism, Doubt, and Ancient Civilizations*] (Ankara: Elis Yayınları, 2006).

Ahmed, Shahab, *What is Islam? The Importance of Being Islamic* (Princeton, NJ: Princeton University Press, 2016).

Akgün, Mehmet, *Materyalizmin Türkiye'ye Girişi* [*The Arrival of Materialism in Turkey*] (Ankara: Elis Yayınları, 2005. First printing 1988).

Aktay, Yasin, "The Historicist Dispute in Turkish-Islamic Theology," in Sinasi Gunduz and Cafer S. Yaran (eds), *Change and Essence: Dialectical Relations Between Change and Continuity in the Turkish Intellectual Tradition* (Washington, DC: The Council for Research and Values in Philosophy, 2005), pp. 65–85.

Al-Azmeh, Aziz, *Islams and Modernities*, 3rd edn (London: Verso, 2009).

Alper, Hülya, *İmam Mâtürîdî'de Akıl-Vahiy İlişkisi* [*The Relation of Reason and Revelation According to Imam Māturīdī*] (Istanbul: İz Yayıncılık, 2008).

Alper, Ömer Mahir, "The Conceptions of Islamic Philosophy in Turkey," in Sinasi Gunduz and Cafer S. Yaran (eds), *Change and Essence: Dialectical Relations Between Change and Continuity in Turkish Intellectual Tradition* (Washington, DC: The Council for Research in Values and Philosophy, 2005), pp. 123–44.

Alper, Ömer Mahir, *Varlık ve İnsan: Kemalpaşazâde Bağlamında Bir Tasavvurun Yeniden İnşası* [*Being and Humanity: The Recreation of an Idea in the Context of Kemalpaşazâde*] (Istanbul: Klasik, 2010; 2013).

Alpyağıl, Recep, "Derrida and Islamic Mysticism: An Undecidable Relationship," in Z. Direk and L. Lawlor (eds), *A Companion to Derrida* (Chichester: Wiley Blackwell, 2014), pp. 480–9.

Alpyağıl, Recep, *Derrida'dan Caputo'ya Dekonstrüksiyon ve Din* [*From Derrida to Caputo: Deconstruction and Religion*] (Istanbul: İz Yayınları: 2007; 2010).

Alpyağıl, Recep, *Din Felsefesi Açısından Mutezile Gelen-Ek-i: Klasik ve Çağdaş Metinler Seçkisi I* [*The Muʿtazilite Tradition from the Perspective of Philosophy of Religion: Classic and Contemporary Text Sections I*] (Istanbul: İz Yayınları, 2014).

Alpyağıl, Recep, *Din Felsefesi Açısından Mutezile Gelen-Ek-i: Klasik ve Çağdaş Metinler Seçkisi II* [*The Muʿtazlite Tradition from the Perspective of Philosophy of Religion: Classic and Contemporary Text Sections II*] (Istanbul: İz Yayınları, 2014).

Alpyağıl, Recep, *Fark ve Yorum: Kur'an'ı Anlama Yolunda Felsefi Denemeler II* [*Difference and Commentary: Philosophical Essays on Understanding the Qur'ān II*] (Istanbul: İz Yayıncılık, 2009; 2014).

Alpyağıl, Recep, *Gelen-Eksel ve Çağdaş Metinlerle Din Felsefesine Dair Okumalar I* [*Readings on Philosophy of Religion with Traditional and Modern Texts I*] (İstanbul: İz Yayınları, 2011).

Alpyağıl, Recep, *Gelen-Eksel ve Çağdaş Metinlerle Din Felsefesine Dair Okumalar II* [*Readings on Philosophy of Religion with Traditional and Modern Texts II*] (Istanbul: İz Yayınları, 2012).

Alpyağıl, Recep, *Kimin Tarihi, Hangi Hermenötik? Kur'an'ı Anlama Yolunda Felsefi Denemeler I* [*Whose History Which Hermeneutic? Philosophical Essays on Understanding the Qur'ān I*] (Istanbul: Ağaç Yayınları, 2003; 2013).

Alpyağıl, Recep, "Trying to Understand Whitehead in the Context of Ibn 'Arabi," in *Ishraq, Islamic Philosophy Yearbook No. 3* (Moscow: Vostochnaya Literatura Publishers, 2012), pp. 220–9.

Alpyağıl, Recep, *Türkiye'de Bir Felsefe Gelen-ek-i Kurmaya Çalışmak: Feylesof Simalardan Seçme Metinler I* [*Attempting to Found a Tradition of Philosophy in Turkey: Selected Texts from Philosophical Figures*] (Istanbul: İz Yayınları, 2010).

Alpyağıl, Recep, *Türkiye'de Bir Felsefe Gelen-ek-i Kurmaya Çalışmak: Feylesof Simalardan Seçme Metinler II* [*Attempting to Found a Tradition of Philosophy in Turkey: Selected Texts from Philosophical Figures*] (Istanbul: İz Yayınları, 2011).

Alpyağıl, Recep, *Türkiye'de Otantik Felsefe Yapabilmenin İmkanı ve Din Felsefesi: Paul Ricoeur örneği üzerinden bir soruşturma* [*The Possibility of Creating an Authentic Philosophy in Turkey and Philosophy of Religion: An Investigation into the Example of Paul Ricoeur*] (Istanbul: İz Yayınları: 2010).

Alpyağıl, Recep, *Wittgenstein ve Kierkegaard'dan Hareketle Din Felsefesi Yapmak* [*Doing Philosophy of Religion with Wittgenstein and Kierkegaard as Points of Departure*] (Istanbul: İz Yayıncılık, 2002; 2013).

Anawati, Georges C., "Polémique, apologie et dialogue islamo-chrétiens: Positions classiques médiévales et positions contemporaines," *Euntes Docete* 22 (1969): pp. 375–451.

Arat, Necla, Aziz Çalışlar, Arslan Kaynardağ, Uluğ Nutku, Tüten Anğ, and Selâhattin Hilâv, "Felsefe Forumu," *Felsefe Dergisi* 1 (1986): pp. 82–133.

Aristotle, *The Basic Works of Aristotle*, edited by Richard McKeon (New York: The Modern Library, 2001).

Asad, Muhammad, *Kur'an Mesajı: Meal-Tefsir*, translated by Cahit Koytak-Ahmet Ertürk (Istanbul: İşaret Yay., 1996).

Asad, Talal, *Anthropology and the Colonial Encounter* (London: Ithaca Press, 1973).

Asad, Talal, *Formations of the Secular: Christianity, Islam, Modernity* (Stanford: Stanford University Press, 2003).

Asad, Talal, *Genealogies of Religion: Discipline and Reasons of Power in Christianity and Islam* (Baltimore: The Johns Hopkins University Press, 1993).

Asad, Talal, *The Idea of an Anthropology of Islam* (Washington, DC: Center for Contemporary Arab Studies, 1986).

Aslan, Adnan, *Din Felsefesine Giriş* [*Introduction to Philosophy of Religion*] (Istanbul: Ufuk Yayınları, 2015).

Aslan, Adnan, *Dinî Çoğulculuk, Ateizm, ve Geleksel Ekol: Eleştirel Bir Yaklaşım* [*Religious Pluralism, Atheism, and the Perennial School: A Critical Approach*] (Istanbul: İSAM Yayınları, 2010).

Aslan, Adnan, *Religious Pluralism in Christian and Islamic Philosophy: The Thought of John Hick and Seyyed Hossein Nasr* (Abingdon: RoutledgeCurzon, 2004).

Avicenna, *The Metaphysics of The Healing: A Parallel English–Arabic Text*, translated by M. E. Marmura (Provo, UT: Brigham Young University Press, 2005).

Aydın, Hasan, *Gazzâlî: Felsefesi ve İslam Modernizmine Etkileri* [*Ghazali: His Philosophy and Influences on the Modernization of Islam*] (Istanbul: Bilim ve Gelecek Kitaplığı, 2012).

Aydın, Mahmut, "A Muslim Pluralist: Jalaluddin Rûmi," in Paul F. Knitter (ed.), *The Myth of Religious Superiority: A Multifaith Exploration* (New York: Orbis Books, 2005), pp. 220–36.

Aydın, Mahmut (ed.), *Hıristiyan, Yahudi ve Müslüman Perspektifinden Dinsel Çoğulculuk ve Mutlaklık İddiaları* [*Religious Pluralism and Absolute [Truth] Claims from Christian, Jewish, and Muslim Perspectives*] (Ankara: Ankara Okulu, 2005).

Aydın, Mahmut, *Monologdan Diyaloğa: Çağdaş Hıristiyan Düşüncesinde Hrıstiya-Müslüman Diyaloğu* [*From Monologue to Dialogue: Christian–Muslim Dialogue in Contemporary Christian Thought*] (Ankara: Ankara Okulu, 2001).

Aydın, Mahmut, "Religious Pluralism: A Challenge for Muslims—A Theological Evaluation," *Journal of Ecumenical Studies* 38 (2001): pp. 330–52.

Aydın, Mehmet S., *Din Felsefesi* [*Philosophy of Religion*] (Izmir: İzmir İlâhiyat Vakfı Yayınları, 2014).

Aydın, Mehmet S., "Fazlur Rahman ve İslâm Modernizmi" ["Fazlur Rahman and Islamic Modernism"], *İslâmi Araştırmlar* 4:4 (1990): pp. 273–84.

Aydın, Mehmet S., *İslam'ın Evrenselliği* [*The Universality of Islam*] (Istanbul: Ufuk Kitapları, 2006. First printing 2000).

Aydın, Ömer, "*Kalam* between Tradition and Change: The Emphasis on Understanding Classical Islamic Theology in Relation to Western Intellectual Effects," in Sinasi Gunduz and Cafer S. Yaran (eds), *Change and Essence: Dialectical Relations Between Change and Continuity in Turkish Intellectual Tradition* (Washington, DC: The Council for Research in Values and Philosophy, 2005), pp. 103–21.

Aydın, Ömer, *Türk Kelâm Bilginleri* [*Turkish Kalām Scholars*] (Istanbul: İnsan Yayıları, 2004).

Badiou, Alain, *Saint Paul: la foundation de l'universalisme* (Paris: Universitaires de France, 2002).

Barlas, Asma, *"Believing Women" in Islam: Unreading Patriarchal Interpretations of the Qur'an* (Austin: University of Texas Press, 2002).

Bauer, Thomas, *Die Kultur der Ambiguität: Eine andere Geschichte des Islams* [*Culture of Ambiguity: An Alternate History of Islam*] (Berlin: Verlag der Welt Religionen, 2011).

Bayrakdar, Mehmet, *İslâm'da Bilim ve Teknoloji Tarihi* [*History of Science and Technology in Islam*] (Ankara: TDVY, 2012).

Bayrakdar, Mehmet, *İslâm Düşüncesi Yazıları* [*Writings on Islamic Thought*] (Ankara: Elis Yayınları, 2004).

Bayrakdar, Mehmet, *Pascal Oyunu: Hz. Ali Gazzâlî ve Pascal'a Göre Âhirete Zar Atmak* [*Pascal's Wager: Betting on the Afterlife According to Ali, Ghazālī, and Pascal*] (Istanbul: İnsan Yayınları, 2013).

Beiser, Frederick C., *The Fate of Reason: German Philosophy from Kant to Fichte* (Cambridge, MA: Harvard University Press, 1987).

Berkes, Niyazi, *The Development of Secularism in Turkey* (New York: Routledge, 1998).

Black, Deborah L., "Psychology: Soul and Intellect," in P. Adamson and R. C. Taylor (eds), *The Cambridge Companion to Arabic Philosophy* (Cambridge: Cambridge University Press, 2005), pp. 308–26.

Blundell, Boyd, *Paul Ricoeur Between Theology and Philosophy* (Bloomington, IN: Indiana University Press, 2010).

Brown, Jonathan, "al-Dārimī," in *Encyclopaedia of Islam*, 3rd edn, edited by Kate Fleet, Gudrun Krämer, Denis Matringe, John Nawas, and Everett Rowson.

Bruckmayr, Philipp, "The Spread and Persistence of Māturīdī Kalām and Underlying Dynamics," *Iran and the Caucasus* 13 (2009): pp. 59–92.

Bumin, Tülin, *Tartışılan Modernlik: Descartes ve Spinoza* [*Disputed Modernity: Descartes and Spinoza*] (Istanbul: Yapı Kredi Yayınları, 1996; 2015).

Burak, Guy, *The Second Formation of Islamic Law: The Hanafi School in the Early Modern Ottoman Empire* (New York: Cambridge University Press, 2015).

Çapak, İbrahim, *Gazâlî'nin Mantık Anlayışı* [*Ghazālī's Understanding of Logic*] (Ankara: Elis Yayınları, 2011).

Caputo, John D., "In Praise of Ambiguity," in Craig J. N. de Paulo, Patrick Messina, and Marc Stier, *Ambiguity in the Western Mind* (New York: Peter Lang, 2005), pp. 15–34.

Casanova, José, *Public Religions in the Modern World* (Chicago: University of Chicago Press, 1994).

Çiftçi, Adil, *Fazlur Rahman ile İslam'ı Yeniden Düşünmek* [*Rethinking Islam with Fazlur Rahman*] (Ankara: Ankara Okulu, 2000).

Cragg, Kenneth, *The Event of the Qur'an: Islam and Its Scripture* (Oxford: One World, 1994).

Coşkun, İbrahim, *Ateizm ve İslam: Kelamî Açıdan Modern Çağ Ateizminin Eleştirisi* [*Atheism and Islam: A Kalām Critique of Atheism in the Modern Era*] (Ankara: Ankara Okulu, 2014).

Dalrymple, William, "The Truth about Muslims," *New York Review of Books* 51.17 (November 1, 2004): pp. 31–4.

Demir, Osman, "Vicdan," in *İslâm Ansiklopedisi* (Türkiye Diyanet Vakfı), <http://www.islamansiklopedisi.info/> (last accessed September 20, 2018).

Deringil, Selim, *The Well-Protected Domains: Ideology and the Legitimation of Power in the Ottoman Empire 1876–1909* (New York: I. B. Tauris, 1999; 2011). Depicts Ottoman state as part of a global move towards modernity.

Dorroll, Philip C., "Modern by Tradition: Abu Mansur al-Maturidi and the New Turkish Theology," doctoral dissertation, Emory University, 2013.

Dorroll, Philip C., "The Turkish Understanding of Religion: Rethinking Tradition and Modernity in Contemporary Turkish Islamic Thought," *Journal of the American Academy of Religion* 82:4 (2014): pp. 1033–69.

Dressler, Markus, "Rereading Ziya Gökalp: Secularism and the Reform of the Islamic State in the Late Young Turk Period," *International Journal of Middle East Studies* 47 (2015): pp. 511–31.

Dupré, Louis, *Passage to Modernity: An Essay in the Hermeneutics of Nature and Culture* (New Haven and London: Yale University Press, 1993).

Düzgün, Şaban Ali, *Allah, Tabiat ve Tarih: Teolijide Yöntem Sorunu ve Teolojinin Metaparadigmatik Temelleri* [*God, Nature, and History: The Question of Method in Theology and Theology's Metaparadigmatic Foundations*] (Ankara: Lotus Yayınevi, 2005; 2012).

Düzgün, Şaban Ali, *Çağdaş Dünyada Din ve Dindarlar* [*Religion and Religious [People] in the Contemporary World*] (Ankara: Lotus Yayınevi, 2012; 2014).

Düzgün, Şaban Ali, *Din, Birey ve Toplum* [*Religion, Individual, and Society*], 3rd edn (Ankara: Akçağ Yayınları, 2013; originally published 1997).

Düzgün, Şaban Ali, *Nesefî ve İslâm Filozoflarına Göre Allah-Alem İlişkisi* [*The God–World Relationship according to Nasafi and the Philosophers of Islam*] (Ankara: Akçağ Yayınları, 1998).

Düzgün, Şaban Ali, "Pluralism and Christianity in a Postmodern Age: An Interview with Roger Haight," *Ankara Üniversitesi İlahiyat Fakültesi Dergisi* 47 (2006): pp. 43–66.

Düzgün, Şaban Ali, *Sarp Yokuşun Eteğinde İnsan* [*Humans Surrounded by a Precipitous Slope*] (Ankara: Otto, 2016).

Düzgün, Şaban Ali, *Seyyid Ahmed Han ve Entellektüel Modernizmi* [*Sayyid Ahmed Khan and Intellectual Modernism*] (Ankara: Akçağ Yayınları, 1997).

Düzgün, Şaban Ali, *Sosyal Teoloji: İnsanın Yeryüzü Serüveni* [*Social Theology: Humanity's Worldly Adventure*], 3rd edn (Ankara: Lotus Yayınevi, 2012).

Düzgün, Şaban Ali, *Varlık ve Bilgi Aydınlanmanın Keşif Araçları* [*Being and Knowledge: The Ways of Revealing Enlightenment*] (Ankara: Beyaz Kule, 2008).

Düzgün, Şaban Ali (ed.), *Mâtürîdî'nin Düşünce Dünyası* [*Māturīdī's Intellectual World*] (Ankara: Filiz Matbaacılık, 2011; 2014).

El-Kayserî, Dâvûd, *Ledünnî İlim ve Hakiki Sevgi* [*Otherworldly Knowledge and Divine Love*], translated by Mehmet Bayrakdar (Istanbul: Kurtuba Kitap, 2011).

El-Rouayheb, Khaled, *Islamic Intellectual History in the Seventeenth Century: Scholarly Currents in the Ottoman Empire and the Maghreb* (New York: Cambridge University Press, 2015).

El-Rouayheb, Khaled, *Relational Syllogisms and the History of Arabic Logic, 900–1900* (Leiden and Boston: Brill, 2010).

El Shamsy, Ahmed, "The Social Construction of Orthodoxy," in Tim Winter (ed.), *The Cambridge Companion to Classical Islamic Theology* (Cambridge: Cambridge University Press, 2008), pp. 97–120.

Eren, Mustafa, *John Hick'te Dini Çoğulculuk* [*Religious Pluralism in John Hick*] (Istanbul: Otorite Kitab, 2016).

Esed, M., *Kur'an Mesajı: Meal-Tefsir* [*The Message of the Qur'an: A Translation and Interpretation*], translated by Cahit Koytak-Ahmet Ertürk (Istanbul: İşaret Yay., 1996).

Fakhry, Majid, *A History of Islamic Philosophy*, 3rd edn (New York: Columbia University Press, 2004).

Gadamer, Hans-Georg, *Truth and Method*, 2nd revised edn, translated by J. Weinsheimer and D. G. Marshall (New York: Crossroad, 1989).

Gazzali, Ebu Hamid, *Mişkatü'l-envar: (Nurlar Feneri)*, translated by Süleyman Ateş (Istanbul: Bedir Yayınevi, 1966).

al-Ghazālī, Abū Ḥāmid, *The Niche of Lights*, translated by David Buchman (Provo, UT: Brigham Young University Press, 1998).

Giddens, Anthony and Christopher Pierson, *Conversations with Anthony Giddens: Making Sense of Modernity* (Stanford, CA: Stanford University Press, 1998).

Goddard, Hugh, *Christians & Muslims: From Double Standards to Mutual Understanding* (Surrey: Curzon Press, 1995).

Gökalp, Ziya, "İttihad ve Terakki Kongresi," *İslam Mecmuası* 3 (1916): pp. 975–8.

Göle, Nilüfer, "The Civilizational, Spatial, and Sexual Powers of the Secular," in Michael Warner et al. (eds), *Varieties of Secularism in a Secular Age* (Cambridge, MA: Harvard University Press, 2010), pp. 243–64.

Griffel, Frank, *Al-Ghazali's Philosophical Theology* (Oxford: Oxford University Press, 2009).

Griffel, Frank, *Gazâlî'nin Felsefî Kelâmı* [*Al-Ghazālī's Philosophical Theology*], translated by İbrahim Halil Üçer, 2nd printing (Istanbul: Klasik Yayınları, 2015).

Güler, İlhami, *Dine Yeni Yaklaşımlar* [*New Approaches to Religion*] (Ankara: Ankara Okullu Basım, 2011; 2014).

Güler, İlhami, *Direniş Teolojisi* [*Theology of Resistance*] (Ankara: Ankara Okulu, 2010; 2011; 2015).

Güler, İlhami, *Sabit Din Dinamik Şeriat* [*Unchanging Religion, Dynamic Sharia*] (Ankara: Ankara Okulu Yayınları, 1999; 2002; 2012).

Güler, İlhami, *Vicdan Böyle Buyurdu* [*Thus Conscience Decreed*] (Ankara: Ankara Okulu Yayınları, 2015).

Günay, Mustafa, "21. Yüzyılda Türkiye'de Felsefe Yapmak" ["Doing Philosophy in Turkey in the Twenty-first Century"], in B. Çotuksöken and S. İyi (eds), *Kimin İçin Felsefe* (Istanbul: Heyamola Yayınları, 2006), pp. 77–89.

Gündüz, Şinasi, "From Apology to Phenomenology: The Current State of the Studies of the History of Religions in Turkey," in Sinasi Gunduz and Cafer S. Yaran (eds), *Change and Essence: Dialectical Relations Between Change and Continuity in the Turkish Intellectual Tradition* (Washington, DC: The Council for Research in Values and Philosophy, 2005), pp. 25–43.

Gündüz, Şinasi, *Küresel Sorunlar ve Din* (Ankara: Ankara Okulu Yayınları, 2005; 2010).

Gündüz, Şinasi, *Pavlus Hıristiyanlığı Mimarı* [*Paul the Architect of Christianity*] (Ankara: Ankara Okulu, 2001; 2004; 2011; 2014).

Habermas, Jürgen et al., *An Awareness of What is Missing: Faith and Reason in a Post-Secular Age* (Cambridge and Malden, MA: Polity Press, 2010).

Hahn, Lewis E. (ed.), *The Philosophy of Paul Ricoeur* (Chicago: Open Court, 1995).

Haight, Roger, *Ecclesial Existence*, vol. 3 of *Christian Community in History* (London: Bloomsbury, 2004).

Halefullah, Muhammed Ahmed, *Kur'an'da Anlatım Sanatı*, translated by Şaban Karataş (Ankara: Ankara Okulu Yayınları, 2002).

Hallaq, Wael B., *Sharīʿa: Theory, Practice, Transformations* (Cambridge: Cambridge University Press: 2009).

Hanioğlu, M. Şükrü, "Blueprints for a Future Society: Late Ottoman Materialists on Science, Religion, and Art," in Elisabeth Özdalga (ed.), *Late Ottoman Society* (Abingdon: RoutledgeCurzon, 2005), pp. 28–116.

Hanıoğlu, İsmail, *Fahruddîn er-Râzî'de Felsefî Teolojik Antropoloji* [*Theological Anthropology in the Philosophy of Fakhr al-Dīn al-Rāzī*] (Ankara: Araştırma Yayınları, 2014).

Harputi, Abdullatif, *Kelâm Tarihi* [*A History of Kalām*], edited by Muammer Esen (Ankara: Ankara Okulu Yayınları, 2014).

Heck, Paul L., "Conscience across Cultures: The Case of Islam," *The Journal of Religion* 94:3 (2014): pp. 292–324.

Heck, Paul L., "Jihad Revisited," *Journal of Religious Ethics* 32 (2004): pp. 95–128.

Heck, Paul L., "Sufism—What Is It Exactly?", *Religion Compass* 1 (2007): pp. 148–64.

Hick, John, *Problems of Religious Pluralism* (New York: St. Martin's Press, 1985).

Hilmi, Şehbenderzade Filibeli Ahmet, *İslam Tarihi* [*History of Islam*] (Istanbul: Huzur Yayınevi, 2011).

Hourani, George F., *Reason and Tradition in Islamic Ethics* (Cambridge: Cambridge University Press, 1985).

Ibn Ḥazm, *al-Fiṣal fī al-Milal wa-al-Ahwā' wa-al-Niḥal* (Beirut: Dar al-Jil, 1985).

İnalcik, Halil, *The Ottoman Empire: The Classical Age 1300–1600* (London: Weidenfeld & Nicolson, 1973).

İnalcik, Halil, *Turkey and Europe in History* (Istanbul: Eren Yayıncılık, 2006; 2008).

Irzik, Gürol, "Hans Reichenbach in Istanbul," *Synthese* 181 (2011): pp. 157–80.

Işık, Harun, *Maturidi'de İnsan Özgürlüğü* [*Human Freedom According to Māturīdī*] (Ankara: Araştırma Yayınları, 2013).

Işık, Hidayet, *Âmirî'ye Göre İslâm ve Öteki Dinler* [*Islam and Other Religions according to al-Āmirī*] (Istanbul: İz Yayıncılık, 2006).

İslamiyet-Hıristiyanlık Kavramları Sözlüğü [*A Conceptual Dictionary of Islam and Christianity*], vols 1 and 2, edited by Mualla Selçuk, Halis Albayrak, Peter Antes, Richard Heinzmann, and Martin Thurner (Ankara: Ankara Üniversitesi Yayınevi, 2013).

Izutsu, Toshihiko, *Ethico Religious Concepts in the Qur'ān* (Montreal and Kingston: McGill-Queen's University Press, 2002).

Jabré, Farid, *Essai sur le lexique de Ghazali* (Beirut: Lebanese University Publications, 1970).

John of Damascus, *Saint John of Damascus Writings: The Fount of Knowledge—The Philosophical Chapters, on Heresies, the Orthodox Faith* (*The Fathers of the Church, Vol. 37*) (South Bend, IN: Ex Fontibus, 2015).

Jungkeit, Steven R., *Spaces of Modern Theology: Geography and Power in Schleiermacher's World* (New York: Palgrave Macmillan, 2012).

Kalın, İbrahim, "Hocazade (Muslihiddin Mustafa)," in Oliver Leaman (ed.), *The Biographical Encyclopedia of Islamic Philosophy* (London: Bloomsbury, 2006; 2015), pp. 151–2.

Kaplan, David M. (ed.), *Reading Ricoeur* (Albany: State University of New York Press, 2008).

Kara, İsmail, *Din ile Modernleşme Arasında: Çağdaş Türk Düşüncesinin Meseleleri* [*Between Religion and Modernization: Issues of Contemporary Turkish Thought*] (Istanbul: Dergâh Yayınları, 2003).

Karaman, Hayreddin, *Hayatımızdaki İslâm 1* [*Islam in our Life 1*] (Istanbul: İz Yayıncılık, 2002).

Karaman, Hayreddin, *İslâm Hukuk Tarihi* [*A History of Islamic Law*] (Istanbul: İz Yayıncılık, 1999).

Karamustafa, Ahmet T., "Kaygusuz Abdal: A Medieval Turkish Saint and the Formation of Vernacular Islam in Anatolia," in Orkhan Mir-Kasimov (ed.), *Unity in Diversity: Mysticism, Messianism and the Construction of Religious Authority in Islam* (Leiden and Boston: Brill, 2014), pp. 329–42.

Kaya, M. Cüneyt (ed.), *Gazzâlî Konuşmaları* [*Ghazālī Talks*] (Istanbul: Küre Yayınları, 2012; 2013).

Kemerli, Pınar, "Religious Militarism and Conscientious Objection in Turkey," *International Journal of Middle East Studies* 47 (2015): pp. 281–301.

Kierkegaard, Søren, *Fear and Trembling/Repetition: Kierkegaard's Writings, Vol. 6.*, edited and translated by Howard V. Hong and Edna H. Hong (Princeton: Princeton University Press, 1983).

Kırbaşoğlu, M. Hayri, *İslam Düşüncesinde Sünnet: Eleştirel Bir Yaklaşım* [*The Sunna in Islamic Thought: A Critical Approach*], 15th printing (Ankara: Ankara Okulu Yayınları, 2015).

Korlaelçi, Murtaza, *Pozitivizmin Türkiye'ye Girişi* [*The Arrival of Positivism in Turkey*] (Ankara: Kadim Yayınları, 2014).

Körner, Felix, *Alter Text - neuer Kontext: Koranhermeneutik in der Türkei heute. Ausgewählte Texte, übersetzt und kommentiert von Felix Körner SJ. Freiburg, Basil* (Wien: Herder, 2006).

Körner, Felix, *Revisionist Koran Hermeneutics in Contemporary Turkish University Theology: Rethinking Islam* (Würzburg: Ergon Press, 2005).

Körner, Felix, "Turkish Theology Meets European Philosophy: Emilio Betti, Hans-Georg Gadamer and Paul Ricœur in Muslim Thinking," *Revista Portuguesa Filosofía* 62 (2006): pp. 805–9.

Köylü, Mustafa, *Dinler Arası Diyalog* [*Dialogue between Religions*] (Istanbul: İnsan Yayınları, 2001; 2007).

Köylü, Mustafa, "Religious Education in Modern Turkey," in Sinasi Gunduz and Cafer S. Yaran (eds), *Change and Essence: Dialectical Relations Between Change and Continuity in the Turkish Intellectual Tradition* (Washington, DC: The Council for Research in Values and Philosophy, 2005), pp. 45–64.

Kutlu, Sönmez, *Çağdaş İslamî Akımlar ve Sorunları* [*Contemporary Islamic Trends and Questions*] (Ankara: Fecr Yayınları, 2016).

Kutlu, Sönmez (ed.), *İmam Mâturîdî ve Maturidilik* [*Imam Māturīdī and Māturīdism*], 3rd expanded edn (Ankara: Otto Yayınları, 2011; originally published 2003).

Kutluer, İlhan, *İbn Sina Ontolojisinde Zorunlu Varlık* [*Necessary Being in the Ontology of Ibn Sīnā*] (Istanbul: İz Yayınları, 2013).

Lamptey, Jerusha Tanner, *Never Wholly Other: A Muslima Theology of Religious Pluralism* (Oxford: Oxford University Press, 2014).

Leirvik, Oddbjørn, *Human Conscience and Muslim–Christian Relations: Modern Egyptian Thinkers on al-Ḍamīr* (London and New York: Routledge, 2006).

Leirvik, Oddbjørn, *Interreligious Studies: A Relational Approach to Religious Activism and the Study of Religion* (London: Bloomsbury, 2014).

Ljamai, Abdelilah, *Ibn Ḥazm et la polémique islamo-chrétienne dans l'histoire de l'islam* (Leiden and Boston: Brill, 2003).

Ludington, Nicholas S., "Turkish Islam and the Secular State," *The Muslim World Today* (1984).

MacCulloch, Diarmaid, *Christianity: The First Three Thousand Years* (New York: Penguin Books, 2010).

MacIntyre, Alasdair, *After Virtue: A Study in Moral Theory*, 2nd edn (Notre Dame, IN: University of Notre Dame Press, 1984).

MacIntyre, Alasdair and Paul Ricoeur (eds), *The Religious Significance of Atheism* (New York and London: Columbia University Press 1969; 1970).

Madelung, Wilfred, "al-Māturīdī," in P. Bearman, Th. Bianquis, C. E. Bosworth, E. van Donzel, and W. P. Heinrichs (eds), *Encyclopedia of Islam*, 2nd edn.

Madelung, Wilfred, "Māturīdiyya," in P. Bearman, Th. Bianquis, C. E. Bosworth, E. van Donzel, and W. P. Heinrichs (eds), *Encyclopedia of Islam*, 2nd edn.

Madigan, Daniel A., "Sacred Text: Koran," in Maryanne Cline Horowitz (ed.), *New Dictionary of the History of Ideas Vol. 5* (Detroit: Charles Scribner's Sons, 2005), pp. 2164–7.

Madigan, Daniel A., *The Qur'an's Self-Image* (Princeton: Princeton University Press, 2000).

Mahmood, Saba, *Politics of Piety: The Islamic Revival and the Feminist Subject* (Princeton, NJ: Princeton University Press, 2005).

Makdisi, George, *Ibn 'Aqil: Religion and Culture in Classical Islam* (Edinburgh: Edinburgh University Press, 1997).

Mannion, Gerard, "Constructive Comparative Ecclesiology: The Pioneering Work of Roger Haight," *Ecclesiology* 5 (2009): pp. 161–91.

Marshall, David, "Muhammad in Contemporary Christian Theological Reflection," *Islam and Christian–Muslim Relations* 24:2 (2013): pp. 161–72.

Masuzawa, Tomoko, *The Invention of World Religions, or, How European Universalism was Preserved in the Language of Pluralism* (Chicago: University of Chicago Press, 2005).

al-Māturīdī, Abū Manṣūr, *Ta'wīlāt al-Qur'ān*, edited by Ahmet Vanlıoğlu and Bekir Topaoğlu (Istanbul: Mizan Yayınevi, 2005).

Mir-Kasimov, Orkhan (ed.), *Unity in Diversity: Mysticism, Messianism and the Construction of Religious Authority in Islam* (Leiden and Boston: Brill, 2014).

Moore, Matthew J., "Pluralism, Relativism, and Liberalism," *Political Research Quarterly* 62:2 (2009): pp. 244–56.

Moosa, Ebrahim, *Ghazālī & the Poetics of Imagination* (Chapel Hill, NC and London: University of North Carolina Press, 2005).

Mufti, Malik, "The AK Party's Islamic Realist Political Vision: Theory and Practice," *Politics and Governance* 2 (2014): pp. 28–42.

Nasr, Seyyed Hossein, *The Heart of Islam: Enduring Values for Humanity* (New York: HarperCollins, 2004).

Ocak, Ahmet Yaşar, *Osmanlı Toplumunda Zındıklar ve Mülhidler 15–17. Yüzyıllar* [*Atheists and Heretics in Ottoman Society of the 15th to 17th Centuries*] (Istanbul: Tarih Vakfı Yurt Yayınları, 1998).

Olgun, Hasan, *Protestanlık: Sekülerliğin Teolojik Kurgusu* [*Protestantism: The Theological Foundation of Secularism*] (Istanbul: İz Yayıncılık, 2006).

Öncü, Ayşe, "Becoming 'Secular Muslims': Yaşar Nuri Öztürk as a Super-Subject on Turkish Television," in Birgit Meyer and Annelies Moors (eds), *Religion, Media, and the Public Sphere* (Bloomington, IN: Indiana University Press, 2006), pp. 227–50.

Özcan, Hanifi, *Mâtüridî'de Dînî Çoğulculuk* [*Religious Pluralism in Māturīdī*], 3rd printing (Istanbul: Marmara Üniversitesi İlâhiyat Fakültesi Vakfı Yayınları, 1999; 2013).

Özcan, Hanifi, *Mâtüridî'de Bilgi Problemi* [*The Problem of Knowledge in Māturīdī*] (Istanbul: Marmara Üniversitesi İlâhiyat Fakültesi Vakfı Yayınları, 1993).

Özcan, Hanifi, "Modern Çagda Dinin Birey ve Toplum için Anlamı" ["The Meaning of Religion for Society and Individual in the Modern Age"], *Akademik Araştırmalar Dergisi* 32 (2007).

Özcan, Zeki, *Teolojik Hermenötik* [*Theological Hermeneutics*] (Istanbul: ALFA Yayınları, 1998; 2000).

Özdalga, Elisabeth, introduction to *Late Ottoman Society*, edited by Elisabeth Özdagla (Abingdon: RoutledgeCurzon, 2005), pp. 1–13.

Özdalga, Elisabeth (ed.), *Late Ottoman Society: The Intellectual Legacy* (Abingdon: RoutledgeCurzon, 2005).

Özdemir, Sema, *Dâvûd Kayserî'de Varlık Bilgi ve İnsan* [*Being, Knowledge, and Humanity in Davūd al-Qayṣarī*] (Istanbul: Nefes Yayınları, 2014).

Özden, H. Ömer, *İbn Sînâ-Descartes Metafiziği* [*The Metaphysics of Ibn Sīnā and Descartes*] (Istanbul: Dergâh Yayınları, 1996; 2015).

Öztürk, Yaşar Nuri, *Deizm: Tanrı, Akıl ve Ahlaktan Başka Kutsal Tanımayan İnanç* [*Deism: Belief that Recognizes Nothing Sacred except God, Reason, and Morals*] (Istanbul: Yeni Boyut, 2015).

Öztürk, Yaşar Nuri, *Kur'an Verileri Açısından Laiklik* [*Laicism from the Perspective of Quranic Data*] (Istanbul: Yeni Boyut, 2003).

Paçacı, Mehmet, *Kur'an'a Giriş* [*Introduction to the Qur'an*] (Istanbul: İSAM Yayınları, 2006 and 2007).

Paçacı, Mehmet and Yasin Aktay, "75 Years of Higher Religious Education in Modern Turkey," in Ibrahim Abu-Rabi' (ed.), *The Blackwell Companion to Contemporary Islamic Thought* (Oxford: Blackwell, 2006), pp. 122–44.

Paçacı, Mehmet and Yasin Aktay, "75 Years of Higher Religious Education in Modern Turkey," *Muslim World* 89:3–4 (1999): pp. 389–413.

Pattabanoğlu, Fatma Zehra, *İbn Kemmûne ve Felsefesi* [*Ibn Kammūna and His Philosophy*] (Ankara: Elis Yayınlar, 2014).

Pulcini, Theodore, *Exegesis as Polemical Discourse: Ibn Ḥazm on Jewish and Christian Scriptures* (Atlanta, GA: Scholars Press, 1998).

Rahman, Fazlur, *Ana Konularıyla Kur'an* [*Major Themes of the Qur'ān*], translated by Alparslan Açıkgenç (Ankara: Ankara Okulu, 1996).

Rahman, Fazlur, *İslam* [*Islam*], translated by Mehmet Aydın and Mehmet Dağ (Ankara: Ankara Okulu, n.d.).

Rahman, Fazlur, *Islam and Modernity: Transformation of an Intellectual Tradition* (Chicago: University of Chicago Press, 1984).

Rahman, Fazlur, *İslam'da İhya ve Reform* [*Revival and Reform in Islam*], translated by Fehrullah Terkan (Ankara: Ankara Okulu Yayınları, 2006).

Rahman, Fazlur, *İslam ve Çağdaşlık* [*Islam and Modernity*], translated by M. Hayri Kırbaşoğlu (Ankara: Ankara Okulu, n.d.).

Rahman, Fazlur, *Major Themes of the Qur'an*, 2nd edn (Chicago and London: University of Chicago Press, 2009).

Rahman, Fazlur, *Tarih Boyunca İslami Metodoloji Sorunu* [*Islamic Methodology in History*], translated by Salih Akdemir (Ankara: Ankara Okulu Yayınları, 1997).

Rahner, Karl, *Foundations of Christian Faith: An Introduction to the Idea of Christianity*, translated by William V. Dych (New York: Crossroads, 1993; original German published 1976).

Rahner, Karl, *Hearer of the Word: Laying the Foundation for a Philosophy of Religion*, translated by Joseph Donceel (New York: Continuum, 1994).

Reed, Howard, "The Faculty of Divinity at Ankara I," *Muslim World* 46 (1956): pp. 295–312.

Reed, Howard, "The Faculty of Divinity at Ankara II," *Muslim World* 47 (1957): pp. 22–35.

Reynhout, Kenneth A., "Ricoeur and Interdisciplinarity," *Literature and Theology* 27 (2013): pp. 147–56.

Ricoeur, Paul, *Başkası olarak Kendisi* [*Oneself as Another*, trans. Kathleen Blamey (1992)], translated by Hakkı Hünler (Ankara and Istanbul: Doğubatı Yayınları, 2010).

Ricoeur, Paul, *Çeviri Üzerine* [*On Translation*, trans. Eileen Brennan (2006)], translated by Sündüz Ö. Kasar (Istanbul: YKY, 2008).

Ricoeur, Paul, *Être, essence et substance chez Platon et Aristote: Cours professé à l'université de Strasbourg en 1953–1954* (Paris: Seuil, 2011).

Ricoeur, Paul, *Histoire et verité* (Paris: Seuil, 1964).

Ricoeur, Paul, *Main Trends in Philosophy* (New York: Holmes & Meier Publishers, 1979).

Ricoeur, Paul, "The Creativity of Language," in Mario J. Valdés (ed.), *A Ricoeur Reader: Reflection and Imagination* (Toronto: University of Toronto Press, 1991), pp. 463–81.

Ricoeur, Paul, *The Rule of Metaphor: Multi-disciplinary Studies of the Creation of Meaning in Language* translated by Robert Czerny, Kathleen McLaughlin, and John Costello (Toronto: University of Toronto Press, 1977).

Ricoeur, Paul, "Toward a Hermeneutic of the Idea of Revelation," *The Harvard Theological Review* 70 (1977): pp. 1–37.

Ricoeur, Paul, "Toward a Hermeneutic of the Idea of Revelation," in Lewis S. Mudge (ed.), *Essays on Biblical Interpretation* (Philadelphia: Fortress Press, 1980), pp. 73–118.

Ricoeur, Paul, *Yoruma Dair: Freud ve Felsefe* [*Freud and Philosophy: An Essay on Interpretation* (1970)], translated by Necmiye Alpay (Istanbul: Metis Yayınları, 2006).

Ricoeur, Paul, *Yorumların Çatışması I* [*The Conflict of Interpretations, Vol. I*], translated by Hüsamettin Arslan (Istanbul: Paradigma Yayıncılık, 2007).

Ricoeur, Paul, *Yorumların Çatışması: Hermenoytik Üzerine Denemler I* [*The Conflict of Interpretations* (1974)], translated by Hüsamettin Arslan (Istanbul: Paradigma Yayıncılık, 2009).

Ricoeur, Paul, *Yorumların Çatışması II* [*The Conflict of Interpretations, Vol. II*], translated by Hüsamettin Arslan (Istanbul: Paradigma Yayıncılık, 2009).

Ricoeur, Paul, *Yorum Teorisi: Söylem ve Artı Anlam* [*Interpretation Theory: Discourse and the Surplus of Meaning* (1976)], translated by Gökhan Yavuz Demir (Istanbul: Paradigma Yay., 2007).

Ricoeur, Paul, *Zaman ve Anlatı: 1* [*Time and Narrative, Vol. I* (1984)], translated by Mehmet Rifat and Sema Rifat (Istanbul: YKY, 2007).

Ricoeur, Paul, *Zaman ve Anlatı: 2* [*Time and Narrative, Vol. II* (1984)], translated by Mehmet Rifat (Istanbul: YKY, 2009).

Rifâî, Ken'ân, *İlâhiyât-ı Kenan* (Istanbul: Eğitim, Kültür ve Sağlık Vakfı Neşriyat, 2013).

Rubin, Uri, *The Eye of the Beholder: The Life of Muhammad as Viewed by the Early Muslims* (Princeton: The Darwin Press Inc, 1995).

Sacks, Oliver, *Karısını Şapka Sanan Adam* [*The Man Who Mistook His Wife for a Hat*], translated by Çiğden Çalkılıç (Istanbul: Yapı Kredi Yayınları, 1997).

Saffari, Siavash, *Beyond Shariati: Modernity, Cosmopolitanism, and Islam in Iranian Political Thought* (Cambridge: Cambridge University Press, 2017).

Saktanber, Ayşe, *Living Islam: Women, Religion & the Politicization of Culture in Turkey* (New York and London: I. B. Tauris, 2002).

Saleh, Walid A., *The Formation of the Classical Tafsīr Tradition: The Qurʾān Commentary of Al-Thaʿlabī (d. 427/1035)* (Leiden: Brill, 2004).

Sands, Justin, "Passing through Customs: Merold Westphal, Richard Kearney, and the Methodological Boundaries between Philosophy of Religion and Theology," *Religions* 7 (2016): 83, doi:10.3390/rel7070083.

Saritoprak, Zeki and Sydney Griffith, "Fethullah Gülen and the People of the Book: A Voice from Turkey for Interfaith Dialogue," *Muslim World* 95 (2005): pp. 447–67.

Schleiermacher, F. D. E., *Christmas Dialogue, The Second Speech, and Other Selections*, edited, translated, and with an introduction by Julia A. Lamm (New York and Mahwah, NJ: Paulist Press, 2014).

Schleiermacher, F. D. E., *The Christian Faith*, edited by H. R. Mackintosh and J. S. Stewart (London and New York: T. & T. Clark, 1999).

Sedgwick, Mark, *Western Sufism: From the Abbasids to the New Age* (New York: Oxford University Press, 2017).

Sevgi, Ahmed H., "İlâhiyât Fakültesi," in *İslâm Ansiklopedisi* (Türkiye Diyanet Vakfı), <http://www.islamansiklopedisi.info/> (last accessed February 20, 2017).

Shah-Kazemi, Reza, *The Other in the Light of the One: The Universality of the Qur'ān and Interfaith Dialogue* (Cambridge: Islamic Texts Society, 2006).

Shields, Christopher, "Aristotle," in Edward N. Zalta (ed.), *The Stanford Encyclopedia of Philosophy*, Winter 2016 Edition, <https://plato.stanford.edu/archives/win2016/entries/aristotle/> (last accessed March 27, 2018).

Silverstein, Brian, *Islam and Modernity in Turkey* (New York: Palgrave Macmillan, 2011).

Skinner, Quentin, "Modernity and Disenchantment: Some Historical Reflections," in James Tully (ed.), *Philosophy in an Age of Pluralism: The Philosophy of Charles Taylor in Question* (Cambridge: Cambridge University Press, 1994), pp. 37–48.

Stroumsa, Sarah, *Freethinkers of Medieval Islam: Ibn al-Rawandi, Abu Bakr al-Razi, and their Impact on Islamic Thought* (Leiden and Boston: Brill, 1999).

Şentürk, Recep, "Islamic Reformist Discourses and Intellectuals in Turkey: Permanent Religion with Dynamic Law," in Shireen T. Hunter (ed.), *Reformist Voices of Islam: Mediating Islam and Modernity* (Armonk, NY: M. E. Sharpe, 2009), pp. 227–46.

al-Suyūṭī, Jālal al-Dīn, *El İtkan fi Ulumi'l-Kur'an* [*The Perfect Guide to the Sciences of the Qur'an*], vol. 1 (Damascus: Darub-u Kesir, 1987).

Taglia, Stefano, *Intellectuals and Reform in the Ottoman Empire: The Young Turks on the Challenges of Modernity* (New York: Routledge, 2015).

Taslaman, Caner, *Modern Bilim Felsefe ve Tanrı* [*Modern Science, Philosophy, and God*] (Istanbul: İstanbul Yayınevi, 2015).

Taşpınar, İsmail, *Hacı Abdullah Petricî'nin Hıristiyanlık Eleştirisi* [*Haji Abdullah Petriji's Critique of Christianity*], 3rd edn (Istanbul: Marmara Üniversitesi İlâhiyat Fakültesi Vakfı Yayınları, 2014).

Tatar, Burhanettin, *Felsefî Hermenötik ve Yazarın Niyeti: Gadamer versus Hirsch* [*Philosophical Hermeneutics and Authorial Intention: Gadamer vs. Hirsch*] (Istanbul: Vadi Yayınları, 1999).

Tatar, Burhanettin, "The Hermeneutical Turn in Recent Turkish Intellectual Thought," in Sinasi Gunduz and Cafer S. Yaran (eds), *Change and Essence: Dialectical Relations Between Change and Continuity in the Turkish Intellectual Tradition* (Washington, DC: The Council for Research in Values and Philosophy, 2005), pp. 145–58.

Taylor, Charles, *A Secular Age* (Cambridge, MA: Belknap Press of Harvard University Press, 2007).
Taylor, Charles, *Benliğin Kaynakları: Modern Kimliğin İnşası* [*Sources of the Self*], translated by Bilal Baş and Selma Aygül Baş (Istanbul: Küre Yayınları, 2012).
Taylor, Charles, *Sources of the Self: The Making of the Modern Identity* (Cambridge, MA: Harvard University Press, 1989; 1992).
Terkan, Fehrullah, *Çatışmanın Dinamikleri: Din ve Felsefe Uzlaşmazlığı Üzerine* [*Opposing Dynamics: On the Incompatibility of Religion and Philosophy*] (Ankara: Elis Yayınları, 2007).
Theobald, Werner, "Spuren des Mythos in der Aristotelischen Theorie der Erkenntnis: 'Hypolepsis' bei Aristoteles, *De anima* und *Anal. post*," *Archiv für Begriffsgeschichte* 44 (2002): pp. 25–37.
Toynbee, Arnold J., *Acquaintances* (London: Oxford University Press, 1967).
Toynbee, Arnold J., *The Murderous Tyranny of the Turks* (London, New York and Toronto: Hodder & Stoughton, 1917).
Tunç, Mustsafa Şekip, *Bir Din Felsefesine Doğru* [*Towards a Philosophy of Religion*] (Istanbul: Türkiye Yayınevi, 1959).
Tunç, Mustsafa Şekip, *Felsefe-i Din* [*Philosophy of Religion*] (Istanbul, 1927).
Türkçe Sözlük, compiled by Şükrü Halûk Akalın (Ankara: Türk Dil Kurumu Yayınları, 2011).
Türker, Ömer, *İbn Sînâ Felsefesinde Metafizik Bilginin İmkânı Sorunu* [*The Question of the Possibility of Metaphysical Knowledge in the Philosophy of Ibn Sīnā*] (Istanbul: İSAM Yayınları, 2010).
Türker, Sadık, *Aristoteles, Gazzâlî ile Leibniz'de Yargı Mantığı* [*The Logic of Judgment in Aristotle, Ghazālī and Leibniz*] (Ankara: Dergâh Yayınları, 2002).
Türkmen, Yaşar (ed.), *Gazâlî ve Nedensellik* [*Ghazālī and Causality*] (Ankara: Elis Yayınları, 2012).
Turner, Colin and Hasan Horkuc, *Said Nursi* (London and New York: I. B. Tauris, 2009).
Uluç, Tahir, *Sühreverdî'nin ibn Sînâ Eleştirisi* [*Suhrawardī's Critique of Ibn Sīnā*] (Istanbul: İnsan Yayınları, 2012).
Uludağ, Süleyman, "Keşf," in *İslâm Ansiklopedisi*, vol. 25 (Türkiye Diyanet Vakfı, 2002), <http://www.islamansiklopedisi.info> (last accessed September 19, 2016).
Uyanık, Mevlüt, "Türkiyedeki İlahiyat Fakülteleri" ["Theology Faculties in Turkey"] on Eilahiyat.com, <http://eilahiyat.com/index.php/arsiv1/kategoriler/ilahiyatci-yazarlar/191-mevlut-uyanik/2839-turkiyedeki-ilahiyat-fakulteleri> (last accessed November 3, 2016).

Vahide, Şükran, "A Chronology of Said Nursi's Life," in *On the Life and Thought of Bediuzzaman Said Nursi*, edited by Ibrahim Abu-Rabi' (Albany: State University of New York Press, 2003), pp. xvii–xxiv.

Vahide, Şükran, *The Author of the Risale-i Nur: Bediuzzaman Said Nursi* (Istanbul: Sözler Publications, 1992).

Valkenberg, Pim, *Renewing Islam by Service: A Christian View of Fethullah Gülen and the Hizmet Movement* (Washington, DC: The Catholic University of America Press, 2015).

Vanhoozer, Kevin J., *Is There a Meaning in This Text? The Bible, The Reader, and the Morality of Literary Knowledge* (Grand Rapids, MI: Zondervan, 1998).

Vural, Mehmet, *Gazzâlî Felsefesinde Bilgi ve Yöntem* [*Knowledge and Method in the Philosophy of Ghazālī*] (Ankara: Ankara Okulu Yayınları, 2004; 2011).

Walton, Jeremy F., *Muslim Civil Society and the Politics of Religious Freedom in Turkey* (Oxford: Oxford University Press, 2017).

White, Hayden, "The Historical Text as Literary Artifact," in B. Fay and P. Pomper (eds), *History and Theory: Contemporary Readings* (Oxford: Blackwell, 1998), pp. 15–33.

Wilkinson, Taraneh, "On Drawing and Being Drawn: On Applying Friendship to Comparative Theology," *Journal of Ecumenical Studies* 48 (2013): pp. 307–16.

Wilkinson, Taraneh, "Moderation and al-Ghazali in Turkey: Responses to Skepticism, Modernity and Pluralism," *The American Journal of Islamic Social Sciences* 32:3 (2015): pp. 29–43.

Yaran, Cafer S., *Bilgelik Peşinde: Din Felsefesi Yazıları* [*In Pursuit of Wisdom: Essays on Philosophy of Religion*] (Istanbul: Ensar Neşriyat, 2011).

Yaran, Cafer S., "Non-exclusivist Attitudes towards Other Religions," in Sinasi Gunduz and Cafer S. Yaran (eds), *Change and Essence: Dialectical Relations Between Change and Continuity in the Turkish Intellectual Tradition* (Washington, DC: The Council for Research in Values and Philosophy, 2005), pp. 7–23.

Yaran, Cafer S., *Understanding Islam* (Edinburgh: Dunedin Academic Press, 2007).

Yasa, Metin, *Ibn Arabî ve Spinoza'da Varlık* [*Being in Ibn 'Arabī and Spinoza*] (Istanbul: Elis Yayınları, 2003; 2014).

Yavuz, M. Hakan, *Toward an Islamic Enlightenment: The Gülen Movement* (Oxford: Oxford University Press, 2013).

Yavuz, Yusuf Şefki, "Kelâm," in *İslâm Ansiklopedisi* (Türkiye Diyanet Vakfı), <https://islamansiklopedi.org.tr/kelam ilim> (last accessed October 1, 2018).

Yavuz, Yusuf Şefki, "Usûl-i Selâse," in *İslâm Ansiklopedisi* (Türkiye Diyanet Vakfı), <http://www.islamansiklopedisi.info/> (last accessed September 20, 2018).

Yazçiçek, Ramazan, *Anonim Din Arayışı ve Dinsel Çoğulculuk* [*The Search for Anonymous Religion and Religious Pluralism*] (Istanbul: Ekin Yayınları, 2008; 2014).

Yazıcı, Muhammet, *Gazzâli Sonrası Ehl-i Sünnet Kelâmı'nda Varlık Anlayışı* [*The Understanding of Being in the Sunni Kalām after Ghazālī*] (Erzurum: Salkımsöğüt Yayınevi, 2010).

Yazoğlu, Ruhattin, *Dinî Çoğulculuk Sorunu: John Hick Üzerine Bir Araştırma* [*The Problem of Religious Pluralism: A Study of John Hick*] (Istanbul: İz Yayıncılık, 2007).

Yörükân, Yusuf Ziya, *Müslümanlik ve Kur'an-ı Kerim'den Âyetlerle İslâm Esasları* [*Muslim-ness and the Foundations of Islam with Verses from the Holy Qur'ān*], edited by Turhan Yörükân (Istanbul: Ötüken Neşriyat, 2006).

Zürcher, Erik-Jan, "Ottoman Sources of Kemalist Thought," in Elisabeth Özdalga (ed.), *Late Ottoman Society* (Abingdon: RoutledgeCurzon, 2005), pp. 14–27.

Index

Abduh, Mohammad, 207–8
Abraham (prophet), 200–1
Abu Zayd, Nasr Hamid, 97, 101, 197
Açıköz, Mustafa, 188, 190–1, 203, 213n, 221n
agency, 19, 31, 34, 36, 39, 71, 76, 108, 111, 127, 129, 132, 137, 139–40, 162–77, 193
Ahmed, Aziz, 106
Ahmed, Shahab, 231, 233–6
AK Party, 8–9, 23n, 230
Akbāriyya, 38–9
Aktay, Yasin, 6, 9–10, 31, 65, 83n, 119n, 120n
Alper, Ömer Mahir, 5, 39, 189
Alpyağıl, Recep, 18–21, 38, 47, 65–123, 127, 138–9, 143, 145, 154n, 159n, 196–7, 199–203, 211, 220n, 221n, 228–30, 233, 235, 237–9
Ankara Okulu *see* Ankara School
Ankara Paradigm, 4, 17–18, 27–61, 236, 237, 243n
Ankara School, 31–2, 50n, 116n
Arat, Necla, 96
Ash'arī theology, 36, 38–9, 56–7n, 143–4, 157n, 238, 244n
Aslan, Adnan, 20, 205–11, 212, 223n, 224n, 230

atheism, 19–20, 39–42, 43, 187–95, 203, 205, 207–8, 211–12, 215n, 230, 235–6
authenticity, 18–19, 30, 33–5, 65–7, 69–82, 93–9, 110–13, 127, 135, 141, 155n, 163, 165, 169, 177n, 179n, 190, 194, 228–9, 232, 233–6
Avicenna *see* Ibn Sīnā
Aydın, Mahmut, 204–5, 209, 210, 212, 222n, 227, 230
Aydın, Mehmet S., 36, 51n, 52n, 188, 213n, 239
al-Azmeh, Aziz, 72–3

Bauer, Thomas, 44–7, 233–6
Bayrakdar, Mehmet, 20, 56n, 196–9, 220n

canon, 18, 35, 65–92, 93–108, 110–13, 127, 198, 228, 229, 233
Casanova, José, 45
Cevdet, Abdullah, 41, 58n
common sense (*sağduyu*), 105, 129, 130, 132, 135, 140, 144, 145, 150n, 159n, 168, 175, 229
conscience (*vicdan*), 129, 130, 131, 132, 135, 136, 140, 141–2, 144–5, 152n, 156n, 158n, 163, 165, 175–6, 183n, 184n, 190, 193–4, 229

Çoşkun, İbrahim, 190–1, 199, 211, 214n, 215n, 255–6n

Darülfünun, 10, 133
deism, 163, 177–8n, 188–95, 230, 235
dependency theory, 133, 151n, 152n
Directorate of Religious Affairs *see Diyanet*
Diyanet, 7, 8, 23n
Dorroll, Philip C., 4, 16, 17–18, 27–8, 29–30, 32–8, 50n, 51n, 52n, 150n, 243n
Dupré, Louis, 216n, 217n, 236–9
Düzgün, Şaban Ali, 19–21, 37–8, 68, 84–5n, 125–84, 190–3, 197, 210–12, 214–15n, 217n, 228–9, 232, 235, 237–9, 243n

Eren, Mustafa, 208, 209–10
Eurocentricism, 70, 79, 90–1n, 94–5
exclusivism, 164, 177n, 203, 206

al-Fārābī, 96, 112, 189
fideism, 69, 121n, 199–202, 208
fiṭra, 19, 129, 130, 135, 139–49, 150n, 156n, 157n, 159n, 165–7, 171, 175, 192

Gadamer, Hans-Georg 4, 31, 36, 46, 53n, 99, 105, 106, 108, 119n, 137–8, 145, 153–4n
  Gadamer's fusion of horizons, 137, 153–4n
al-Ghazālī, 36, 38–9, 54n, 80–1, 89n, 97, 115n, 140, 151n, 189, 197–9, 202, 206–8
Güler, İlhami, 47, 51n, 61, 107, 120n, 244n

Haight, Roger, 210–12, 222n, 231–3, 236
Ḥanafī jurisprudence, 33, 35–6, 37–8, 53n, 54n, 143, 144, 156–7n, 176, 229
hermeneutics, 17, 18, 30–2, 36, 67–8, 74–82, 85–6n, 88n, 91n, 92n, 103–8, 112, 114n, 115n, 116n, 118n, 136–8, 154n, 197, 218n, 239
Hick, John, 203, 205–6, 208–10, 221n, 224–5n
historicity, 4, 31–2, 36, 46, 50n, 68–9, 71–4, 80, 83n, 89n, 99–108, 119n, 120n, 137, 153–4n, 165, 170, 210
humanism 33, 35–6, 37–8, 87–8n, 169
hypoleptic continuity, 18, 108–13

Ibn 'Arabī, 38–9, 55–6n, 115n
Ibn Sīnā, 13–14, 38–9, 54–5n, 95–8, 115n
ilahiyat, 13–14, 25n
  ilahiyatçı, 14
  ilahiyat faculty, 3, 6–14
inclusivism, 163, 177n 178n, 203, 206, 210, 212, 226n, 230, 235
İSAM, 8, 23n

al-Jabri, Muhammed Abed, 97–9

kalām, 6, 13, 37, 192, 211, 225n, 238
Kara, İsmail, 238
Karaman, Hayreddin, 236, 243n
kashf, 136–7, 171
Kemalism, 8, 16, 32, 33, 193, 195, 230, 239
Khalafallah, Muhammad Ahmad, 100–2, 116n
khalīfa, 168–9, 175
Kierkegaard, Søren, 177n, 199–200, 202, 220n
Körner, Felix, 4, 9–10, 16, 17–18, 23n, 25n, 27–32, 36, 50n, 52n
Köylü, Mustafa, 22n, 24n, 209, 224n

Leirvik, Oddbjørn, 156n, 240–2
logos, 136–7

MacFarlane, Charles, 41
MacIntyre, Alasdair, 110, 118n, 128
materialism, 39–42, 135, 169, 188, 193, 196, 212n
Māturīdī theology, 33, 35–6, 37–9, 53n, 56–7n, 129, 143, 157–8n, 175, 210, 229, 238

narrative, 99–103, 108, 110–12, 197
Nasr, Seyyed Hossein, 140, 172, 182n, 208
nous, 136–7

Olgun, Hakan, 197
ontotheology, 188–91, 211, 237–8
Özcan, Hanifi, 35–6, 37, 52n, 209, 210
Özcan, Zeki, 80, 85n, 90n, 91n, 197, 218n
Özsoy, Ömer, 107, 120n
Öztürk, Yaşar Nuri, 47, 163, 178n, 193–5, 211, 217n, 218n, 230, 235

Paçacı, Mehmet, 6, 9–10
Pascal, Blaise, 128, 197–9
Perennialist School, 203, 206, 208
Phillips, D. Z., 201–2
pluralism, 19–20, 80, 133, 138–9, 171–5, 187–8, 197, 203–12, 230, 235–6
postmodernity, 45–6, 59n, 60n, 68, 123n, 128, 130, 132, 134–5, 202, 210, 237

Rahman, Fazlur, 4, 31–2, 36, 46, 52–3n, 105–7, 113, 114n, 119n, 120n, 129, 159–60n
Rahner, Karl, 157–8n, 180n, 206–7, 208, 217n, 223–4n
relativism (*görecilik*), 138, 182n, 214n, 235
Ricoeur, Paul, 18, 66, 69, 74–82, 86n, 87n, 88n, 90–1n, 92n, 94n, 118n, 128, 188, 197, 203

Sacks, Oliver, 111
skepticism, 39–42, 106, 187–226, 230, 235
spiral, 18, 94–5, 110, 114n

Tanzimat, 6, 40, 76, 88n, 133
Taşpınar, İsmail, 12, 196
Tatar, Burhanettin, 47, 109, 115n, 121n
tawḥīd (divine unity), 19, 35–6, 52n, 150n, 162–84, 188–93, 194, 196, 211–12, 213n, 226n, 230, 242n
Taylor, Charles, 43–4, 150n
Toynbee, Arnold, 239, 244–5n
truth monopoly, 134, 152n
Tunç, Mustafa Şekip, 69

Vanhoozer, Kevin J., 137, 154n
vicdan see conscience

Wittgenstein, Ludwig, 97, 100, 118n, 192, 199, 201

Yaran, Cafer Sadık, 83n, 202, 209, 216n, 221n
Yazoğlu, Ruhattin, 208–9
Yörükân, Yusuf Ziya, 37, 183n

EU representative:
Easy Access System Europe
Mustamäe tee 50, 10621 Tallinn, Estonia
Gpsr.requests@easproject.com

www.ingramcontent.com/pod-product-compliance
Lightning Source LLC
Chambersburg PA
CBHW050212240426
43671CB00013B/2310